The
Podcast
Pantheon

THE PODCAST PANTHEON

101 Podcasts That Changed How We Listen

FROM *WTF* TO *SERIAL*

Sean Malin

Foreword by
Jon Hamm

CHRONICLE BOOKS
SAN FRANCISCO

For my parents, the best listeners in the world

Foreword

I don't get asked to write a lot of forewords. Although I consider myself to be a fairly avid reader and a lover of the form, for whatever reason I'm just not considered. Which, honestly, is mostly fine with me. I usually skip them unless they're written by the author, and if that's the case, why not just make it part of the book, y'know?

But when Sean asked me, I knew I had to take part in this one.

Even before I saw the list of who was being considered for this "pantheon" of all-time greats in the sector, I knew I would most likely have a history with all or most of them.

Of the one hundred or so podcasts in this book, I have probably been a guest on or contributor to at least ten, and have been a listener/fan of anywhere from a third to half of them. Long story short, I am a fan of the form.

But more importantly, I was an *early adopter* of the form. I was on *Comedy Bang! Bang!* when it was called *Comedy Death-Ray*—and broadcast on terrestrial radio. I was on the first "season" of *Never Not Funny*. Ditto with early appearances on *WTF, Dead Eyes, Thrilling Adventure Hour,* and the list goes on and on.

The point of all this (besides the obvious humblebrag) is that I understood the tremendous potential of this new and exciting way to communicate, create, share, and entertain. Podcasts were the explosive result of the combination of a groundbreaking new technology (direct-download content players, specifically the iPod) and the ubiquity of an affordable, convenient broadband connection. Suddenly bespoke content became a possibility not just for the elite and the wealthy, but for *everybody*. The cost of admittance was a relatively quiet room, a microphone, an idea, and a way to upload it.

Thus it began: a revolution in how we as a culture consume entertainment, paralleled on the visual side by the streaming wars but with a significantly more democratic price point (for the most part *free*) and with, essentially, no rules. Comics, storytellers, advice columnists, sports guys, movie fans, comic book people, anyone (and, by now, it seems *everyone*) could start a podcast. And they did.

Eventually, as happens with all new things, the novelty coalesced into the great American search for profit and monetization. And, boy, has it. As interview podcasts supplant (and most likely overtake) late-night television, and comedy podcasts launch careers, these little engines that could are now part of vast media holdings and are acquired to the tune of eight- and nine-figure paydays. Such is the value of content in the early twenty-first century.

But to read this book is to magically teleport back to a simpler time. When it was all potential. A potential that has been realized as what now looks like a "Golden Age" of podcasting. With a past this rich, the future looks exciting and bright indeed. Enjoy.

Jon Hamm

Introduction

"I do this podcast out of my garage that has had over twenty million downloads in less than two years. It is critically acclaimed. I have interviewed over two hundred comics; created live shows; I'm writing a book. I have a loyal, borderline-obsessive fan base who bring me baked goods and artwork. I have evolved as a person and a performer. I am at the top of my game and no one can tell me what to do. I built it myself. I work for myself. I have full creative freedom. I am the future of show business. Not your show business—my show business."
—Marc Maron, Just for Laughs Keynote Address, 2011

In 2009, comedian Marc Maron was at the end of his rope. His internet talk show *Break Room Live* had just been canceled; his touring schedule as a veteran stand-up had dried up after more than twenty years on the road; he was middle-aged, unemployed, and suicidal. Fresh from a second divorce, Maron was desperate for someone—anyone—to talk to. So he and Brendan McDonald, his producer at *Break Room*, used key cards their former employers forgot to destroy to record a secret pilot in Air America's studios, then quietly published it online.

Fifteen years later, the DIY talk show Maron and McDonald stumbled into, *WTF with Marc Maron*, has become *the* template for success in the world of podcasting. Since its ignominious founding, when JustCoffee .Coop was the main sponsor and half the guests had bones to pick with him, *WTF* has seen Maron interview many of the most famous people in history, including Jane Goodall, Bruce Springsteen, and President Barack Obama. He even had one of his episodes (number 67, with Robin Williams) inducted into the Library of Congress. But Maron's new empire, which today encapsulates hundreds of millions of downloads a year, half a dozen comedy specials, multiple bestselling books, and acclaimed acting roles in award-winning films, is far from an anomaly. On the contrary, in the time it took *WTF* to become a cultural phenomenon, a whole generation of fellow podcasts, podcasters, and podcast aficionados was emerging right alongside it.

The term "podcast" itself is barely older than Maron's show. In 2004, journalist Ben Hammersley offhandedly used it to describe a then-recent rise in online radio production he attributed to the advent of Apple's iPod and other MP3 players. At the time, well-known internet blogging pioneers like Dave Winer, Christopher Lydon, Doug Kaye, and Adam Curry were discovering that the lack of a pricey budget or recording studio was no longer the barrier to entry it had once been when it came to finding one's audience. By uploading downloadable audio files directly onto the web—a practice stretching back to the late 1980s but made popular by Napster—one could suddenly say anything one wanted to say without the interference of regulators or corporations. "With no publisher to appease, no editor to report to, and an abundance of cheap tools," Hammersley wrote in *The Guardian*, "anyone can be a broadcaster." iPod. Broadcaster. Et voilà!

Within a year, as Engadget's Thomas Ricker reported, Apple had built its first "podcast" directory into iTunes, thus taking independent broadcasters out of the realm of self-distribution once and for all and putting them permanently into the ears of the world's listeners. The field expanded quickly and ferociously in response. Within months, celebrities (Ricky Gervais), politicians (George W. Bush), and corporations (PBS) had all launched shows in direct competition for spots on the iTunes Top 100 podcasts list, alongside those early ~~amateur~~ self-produced programs (more on those below). In December, the editors of the *New Oxford American Dictionary* declared "podcast" the Word of the Year. Writing for *Slate*, Andy Bowers took things one step further, proclaiming 2005 "The Year of the Podcast."

Bowers and the dictionary people, however, may have been a touch hasty. Twenty years since those bold declarations, we are just *now* entering what by any metric must be considered the Golden Age of Podcasting. In January 2023, *Forbes* estimated that there were already more than five million active podcasts produced around the globe, with downloads in the United States alone accounting for more than ninety million listens per week (equal to around 31 percent of all Americans). Podcast revenue solely from advertisers is projected to exceed $4 billion in 2025, according to an IAB *US Podcast Advertising Revenue Study*, up from $708 million only five years previous—and that doesn't even account for merchandising, live tours, or the more than six million subscribers who support podcasts directly on self-publishing platforms like Patreon, Libsyn, RedCircle, and Podbean. Seemingly every day, new podcasts are adapted into blockbuster films, event television, and bestselling books; their hosts are immortalized in Halloween costumes, tattoos, and murals; people even name their animals after characters from their favorite shows. At this point, everybody either makes podcasts, listens to them, or gets FOMO from hearing everyone else talk about them.

That is why the establishment of a critical canon representing the true GOATs in this massively popular medium feels so desperately overdue. That such a collection has not already been entered into the annals of entertainment history is understandable primarily as a matter of glut: In a landscape this expansive, keeping up can be a Sisyphean task, no matter how much free time you have. And there is a generational aspect at play too. Certain technological changes—such as Apple's removal of the headphone jack from iPhones in 2017, or the mass migration away from MP3 downloading toward audio streaming apps like Spotify, Amazon Music, and Deezer—simply occur too fast for some of us to keep up with what's new.

But at the scale with which podcasts are now (and, even more pressingly, will be) consumed, the ramifications of this lack are too significant to ignore any longer. Never mind the documented dangers of trusting the internet alone to maintain our media histories. Instead, consider the potential exploitation of vulnerable listeners. In a world without an established pantheon for podcasts, how are those with no experience as listeners to keep from wasting their short, precious lives trying to find something they like without hearing thousands upon thousands of hours of trash first? How can anyone avoid the influence of corporate marketing, algorithms, or AI-generated listicles about what is truly worth one's time when the internet is our primary collective resource? And for that matter, what are the standards that differentiate a legitimately worthwhile podcast from an overhyped flash in the pan in the first place?

The Podcast Pantheon was created to answer these questions. Whether you are a dedicated, omnivorous listener with decades of fandom, a casual downloader looking to expand your horizons, an audio skeptic convinced that no show could match your particular wants and needs, or a late-to-the-game newcomer concerned that dipping even the tiniest toe into the podcasting world will overwhelm you, this book wants to help guide you through the labyrinth that is downloadable audio to a place of safety and warmth.

The 101 podcasts profiled here represent the most groundbreaking, beautiful, compelling, experimental, touching, human, artful, and funny works the medium has yet offered, each distinct from the next in its accomplishments. In some cases, podcasts were selected because their creators are indisputable pioneers in the field. In others, the podcasts themselves influenced history, reshaped popular culture, or impacted the minds and hearts of their listeners in discernable ways, sometimes with just one masterful episode. There are also shows in this book known only to small or niche audiences and deserve something more—hidden gems with the potential to change listeners' lives for the better but obscured by the more widely known, well-moneyed, and influential players in the industry. And then there are those rare one-of-a-kind podcasts nominated to the pantheon because they do things with audio that no other program has yet or could ever do.

No matter the podcast, each profile features never-before-heard commentary from the teams involved, including creators, hosts, producers, writers, and even subjects. Many share stories from behind the scenes of their shows, while others graciously offer insights into how their personal lives have shaped the work. It is only through their extraordinary candor, I believe, that the public can truly understand how the sausage gets made.

What this book cannot and does not attempt to do is speak for everyone who loves, hates, or makes podcasts. For one thing, while I've spent far, far more time than the average listener enjoying, consulting for, guesting on, and writing about podcasts as a working cultural critic since 2007, I am still limited by my monolingualism to those first produced in English. Yet podcasts are a global art form, and this book recognizes that there are worlds upon worlds of multilingual audio outside the United States that it does not explore.

Additionally, the pantheon that I propose here intentionally excludes any podcasts that do more harm than good to the world, whether as mouthpieces for hate speech or for the literal or tacit espousal of political or physical violence against others. Undeniably, many such programs carry immense influence in our society and deserve to be recognized for that influence, however insidious, by scholars in this field. As the adage goes, those who ignore history are doomed to repeat it. But I am a podcast critic, not a historian, and *The Podcast Pantheon* is not a history book. So fuck 'em.

Of course, it is impossible to guess how the tides of culture will turn, and how what now seems righteous or revolutionary might someday come to seem dumb or dangerous (or vice versa). Today, it is hard to imagine a world in which *WTF*—one of the most iconic success stories in audio history—would not be welcomed into the hall of immortal podcasts. But like literature, cinema, and television, podcasting is an ever-evolving art form, with new shows challenging Maron and McDonald for their spots on Mount Olympod (Podlympus?) faster than I can type this sentence.

The Podcast Pantheon is meant to accommodate such fluidity. My greatest pleasure would be for this book to serve as a template for reconsidered, alternative, or even completely contrapuntal canons to draw from or debate. And should the opportunity to revise the pantheon for a new edition someday arise, it would naturally require substantial updates to reflect all the ground that has since been broken in this still-young medium. For me, that is the real magic of podcasts: They never stop getting better.

Savage Lovecast

"If you're stuck in a relationship quandary or if you're looking for sexual harmony, well, there's nothing you can't ask on the *Savage Lovecast*" goes the jingle. But ask the *Savage Lovecast*'s namesake, Dan Savage, how he turned his sex and relationship advice show into the classic of the genre it is today and he'll demur: "The podcast was Nancy Hartunian's idea, and it's her baby—we've been working on the show together the entire time, and Nancy has final say about the questions we run and my intros."

Hartunian and Savage have produced *Savage Lovecast* together since 2006, making it one of the oldest and most trusted advice podcasts in history. Savage was already well known at the time for his unbridled sex column, Savage Love, and the books its syndication spawned, but he was still an unknown quantity in the world of broadcasting. At first, "I saw the podcast as a sideline to—or an extension of—the column, which had been in print for fifteen years by the time we started the *Lovecast*," he explains when we correspond. Hartunian pushed him to record his responses to readers who wrote or phoned in seeking help with issues ranging from how to use cock cages safely to where to find phthalate-free dildos, and then to have a team of "tech-savvy at-risk youth" release those recordings for download.

Hindsight being what it is, she was clearly prescient. Despite concerns that he "sucked" at hosting—concerns listeners sometimes preyed on by writing in to correct or challenge him—Savage found himself baffled to learn that some of the people thanking him for his wisdom and assistance every week had never read his column. Even when the It Gets Better Project, a suicide prevention nonprofit for LGBTQIA+ youth he founded with his husband, Terry Miller, went viral four years into the show, it still surprised him that audiences had learned en masse about it from an episode. Only after a frantic encounter with a longtime listener in a Starbucks line did the reality of this newfangled podcaster fame truly sink in. "It wasn't really a conversation," he says. "They just wanted me to look at them and say things. So I told them what I had for breakfast and what I was planning to have for lunch. They said, 'No,

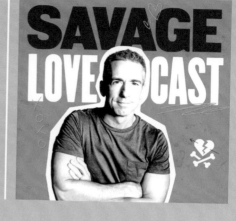

HOSTED BY
Dan Savage

GENRE
Advice

FIRST EPISODE
"Savage Love Episode 1"
(October 26, 2006)

INFLUENCES
Ann Landers, Xaviera Hollander,
Judith Savage

WHERE TO LISTEN
Savage.Love

SEAN'S PICK
"Savage Love Episode 271"
(December 27, 2011)

tell me a sex thing.' So I told them about how the ancient Greeks used to treat anal warts (crushing them between stones)."

Facts like these are a dime a dozen for Savage, as are the bawdy, poetic phrasings he has pioneered to help normalize all manner of sexual engagement. "Pegging," "dickful thinking," "monogamish"—terms now firmly enmeshed in the popular lexicon—are among his best-known Savagisms. Here he is in episode #907, "Help! My Wife Is Dating Her Tattoo Artist!," attempting in his typically blue way to calm prudish listeners' discomfort with anal sex and cunnilingus during menses: "It's a butt, you're fucking a butt, shit happens. It's a pussy, you're fucking a pussy, blood happens."

Though he has at times courted controversy with such glib commentary (indeed, many episodes end with Savage apologizing for offering clumsy or inefficient advice the previous week), as of May 2024, six hundred thousand listeners downloaded the show every month. Twenty thousand of those identify as "Magnum Subs," superfans desperate for the personal assistance of live question-and-answer sessions with Savage, as well as interviews with expert guests like sex therapist Claire Perelman, evolutionary biologist Matilda Brindle, and writer Manuel Betancourt, author of *The Male Gazed*. It is important to reiterate here that there is no shame in wanting to join them, as sex between consenting adults can be a socially complex and challenging endeavor for many. Just remember that when you do ultimately succeed in landing someone "good, giving, and game," or GGG, you owe Hartunian and Savage a word of thanks.

Why Won't You Date Me?

"Oh boy, let me tell you about the roller coaster that's been *WWYDM*." This is host Nicole Byer's immediate response to a question about how her show *Why Won't You Date Me?* has changed since it premiered on the Headgum network at the end of 2017. In the pilot, "Tinder Troubles," Byer explains that she has embarked on a quest to understand why she remains perpetually single despite the fact that she has a fat ass (her words) and a libido to match. At first, that meant ambushing men she'd already hooked up with, like Will Hines, Dan Lippert, and Nick Snow, with the titular question, only to learn that it wasn't really personal: They just didn't fully click, energy-wise. In later episodes, she also seeks advice from trusted friends in more successful relationships, like married couple Madeline Walter and Ben Greene, artist Lisa Hanawalt, and Sasheer Zamata, her co-host on Earwolf's *Best Friends* podcast.

This all changed with an innocent little prank. In what she calls "a moment of pure mischief (and maybe a lot of alcohol)" in early 2023, Byer reposted an Instagram picture featuring her kissing comedian Dan Black during an improv scene, along with the caption "2022 is when I met my boyfriend. I love this guy @danblackattack." The post sparked a frenzy. Loyal *WWYDM* fans, who had followed the show from network to network and invested completely in the twists and turns of its host's love life, wrote by the dozens to congratulate Byer for finally locking a man down. Newspapers and tabloids picked the story up too, giving widespread coverage to the *Nailed It!* star's well-meaning joke and sending some unwanted flack Black's way.

That incident, Byer explains, permanently changed how she and her producer, Marissa "Mars" Melnyk, "steered the ship"—for the better: "Instead of just focusing on my own dating life, we started diving into all things love, sex, and relationships." In its evolved form, the podcast has blossomed into a more expansive, less myopic weekly space to discourse on dating in a post-pandemic society. Whereas the old *WWYDM*

Advice

18

often finds Byer rehashing stories about the fuckboy who smelt like a dishrag or the Irish "chucklefucker" she took home after a gig, the new-and-improved version more often finds her educating herself and her guests on subjects like racism, the rights of sex workers, and support for the LGBTQIA+ community. (As Byer puts it in a Valentine's Day episode with guest Laurie Kilmartin, "Straight men are *not* my demographic.") Not that it's some "stiff lecture," Byer clarifies: "My listeners can engage with these tough topics *and* we can all have a nice teeheehee while sorting out life's messy parts."

As drastically as *Why Won't You Date Me?* has changed, its champions are no less dogged. Byer proudly cites the listener who staged their marriage proposal at her live show in Chicago, as well as the guest who lost his virginity after talking about the hardships of dating in your thirties. *WWYDM*'s host also gleefully notes that Mars "didn't just get new co-workers" from producing the show: She met her partner when the show joined Team Coco in 2021. "So while I'm over here piecing together why I'm single, the podcast is out there writing these love stories for other people," Byer jokes. "How ironic is that?"

HOSTED BY
Nicole Byer

GENRE
Advice

FIRST EPISODE
"Tinder Troubles (w/ Will Hines)"
(December 1, 2017)

INFLUENCES
"Jon Gabrus, the idea
of exploring love" (Byer)

WHERE TO LISTEN
Spotify

SEAN'S PICK
"Nicole's Pussy Pic That Went
Too Far (w/ Sasheer Zamata)"
(December 15, 2017)

WHY WON'T YOU
DATE ME?
WITH **NICOLE BYER**

Love + Radio

In podcasting, as in much of the world's media, an imaginative avant-garde has borne some of the format's most delicious fruit. Inevitably, when it comes time for this expansive, thriving sector of audio to be properly historicized and canonized on its own terms, many scholars will begin with the loopy, dark, and exuberantly strange *Love + Radio*. Over more than twenty years, this ethereal curiosity has grown into something of a bizarro *This American Life*, complete with a visionary creator-director-host that feeds on—and twists into shapes unseen anywhere else—real human experience. "The number one question I get is 'where do you find all these wild stories?'" Nick van der Kolk, the aforementioned factotum, tells me in the summer of 2024. His answer? Serendipity: "Despite the Google Street Viewification of the world, there are still many dark spots of the psychogeographic map, and you only find them by getting offline and getting out of your comfort zone."

Van der Kolk brought *Love + Radio* into the world in 2005 with an episode about guns. Only it isn't really about weapons, or killing, or industry, exactly; it is about closing the empathy gap between those raised in a culture of war tools and those to whom such a culture is foreign. At least, that is how I interpret its fractured, cubistic sound design: as an invitation into experiences abstract from one's own, like the auditory equivalent of seeing a film by Chick Strand or an exhibit of Magritte paintings. Five more equally distinctive episodes followed on an irregular schedule, earning the show its first home with alt.NPR, a repository for independently minded, not-so-public-radio-friendly podcasting.

Experimental

So began van der Kolk's slow, ongoing push into public recognition among the vanguard of audio's most adventurous auteurs. In 2011 and 2013 came awards from the Third Coast International Audio Festival (perhaps the most prestigious of its kind in North America and a subject overdue for its own book-length history, in my opinion), followed in 2014 by a move to a more standard, season-by-season release schedule through the Radiotopia network. Actually, that was the only thing standard about the endeavor. Over the next decade (which featured jumps first to Luminary, and later to Patreon), van der Kolk and a rotating crew of teammates including Nick Williams, Julia DeWitt, Phil Dmochowski, and Brendan Baker (see *Marvel's Wolverine: The Long Night*, p. 194) continued to strive toward an untamed aesthetic diversity in their work.

In an episode like "The Magical World of Eva Julia Christiie," from season four,[*] they might soak the true story of a Norwegian magician and her tigers hiding out in Moldova in the wake of conflict in Ukraine through with techno, making the narrator sound like a world-weary DJ leading a poetry reading. Another, like season six's "Photochemical," might be diced into so many tiny moments that the tale of an objectophiliac's obsession with photo booths starts to take on the disparate logic of a wet dream. Sound beds, music, narration, frequencies, tempos—all were treated as fair game for experimentation, provided that they did not fully obscure the beating emotional heart at each episode's center. "*Love + Radio* is a labor of love . . . and radio," goes van der Kolk's sign-off.

This approach has turned the show into a particular favorite among fellow podcasters and earned its creator a reputation as a true podcaster's podcaster. But van der Kolk stresses that the podcast only reflects the talent of his collaborators, as it is only through them that such "wild stories" can still fall into his lap, even after all these years. "Serendipity is dead," he declares. "Long live serendipity!"

HOSTED BY
Nick van der Kolk

GENRE
Experimental

FIRST EPISODE
"With a Bullet" (October 18, 2005)

INFLUENCES
Errol Morris, Ira Glass, António Damásio, Benjamen Walker

WHERE TO LISTEN
Patreon

SEAN'S PICK
"Photochemical" (October 13, 2017)

[*] Van der Kolk notes that such an episode "only came about because some friends of mine had moved to Moldova for work, and wanted to explore the Chișinău State Circus. They'd just had a baby, and had her strapped in a carrier while we stepped through broken windows to marvel at the brutalist architecture and crumbling circus sculptures."

Mystery Show

In 2013, I took a job as an assistant at the Perry-Castañeda Library to pay my way through graduate school at the University of Texas at Austin. My primary tasks were scanning microfiche, sorting the periodicals, and, on quiet days, reshelving books. One day, I had to return an old leather-bound manuscript to an unusually faraway shelf on floor five, outside my normal runs between floors two and four. When I got to the manuscript's home, though, I noticed another tome—an early printing of Helen Hunt Jackson's *Ramona*—poking inappropriately out into the aisle. As soon as I made contact, it split open like a coconut, revealing an ancient, discolored Polaroid of a smiling family. There were no notes on the back, no names visible, and when I brought it to lost and found, I was instructed to toss it, as it would be a fool's errand to attempt to locate its rightful owner. Instead, I kept it for almost a decade, wondering if someone, someday, might be able to help me to reunite the portrait with its family.

If only I had met Starlee Kine before I eventually, inevitably lost it. For six glorious, irreplaceable episodes, the writer and regular NPR contributor solved riddles of a similarly personal and mundane nature on her half-hour Gimlet podcast *Mystery Show*. Working as a sort of citizen detective, Kine captured the pride of using sheer grit and the kindness of strangers to answer the kinds of questions that won't stop itching at the back of your brain: Why would someone get a license plate that reads "I♥911"? What happened to that one video store? How tall is Jake Gyllenhaal, actually? It was probably the most ticklish and spritely "thriller" ever produced, and certainly the most wondrous. I constantly pine for more of it.

Getting Kine—who, after announcing in 2016 that season one would be the one and only, went on to a career as an esteemed television writer—to speak to me for this book was not unlike a typical episode. Following the 2023 Writers Guild of America strike, I reached out through official channels and then tried her on Twitter (now X) before ultimately sending emails to two separate addresses. I was stymied again and again until, after a few months, she apologetically touched back.

When we speak, she admits that it makes her "quite sad" to be reminded that nine years had passed since *Mystery Show* ended, "Like my dreams have been unsettled since reading that sentence." She reminds me that she started working on *Mystery Show* in January 2015, while the last episode came out in early August 2015. "Seven months to make those six episodes," Kine says wistfully. "Creating stuff is hard. It's magic when it's going well. That's how putting together that entire season was. I was locked in, as they say. Everything kept clicking." She also adds that it was not her idea to stop her investigations, which seems particularly true in light of the fact that the show "was an instant hit." Four writers for *The Guardian* dubbed it "a profound, life-affirming joy"; *Vulture*'s Margaret Lyons described it as "your next podcast obsession"; it was given prize after prize. Kine even made global news when she got Gyllenhaal to admit in "Case #5 Source Code" that he was exactly five feet, eleven and one-half inches tall.

Regardless, she remained at odds with the network, "stemming from what I now realize were opposing goals," she says. "I thought we were there to make shows we loved. I now understand that for

HOSTED BY
Starlee Kine

GENRE
Experimental

FIRST EPISODE
"Case #1 Video Store" (May 21, 2015)

INFLUENCES
"*Columbo*, the scenic texture of *Raising Arizona*, the Mike scene in *Fargo*, the montage sequence in *Footloose*, friendship" (Kine)

WHERE TO LISTEN
Gimlet

SEAN'S PICK
"Case #3 Belt Buckle" (June 5, 2015)

Gimlet"—which Spotify purchased for $230 million in 2019—"the goal was to be acquired." As a result, listeners may never get another season so perfectly constructed again. Thankfully, that hasn't stopped people discovering the show, like a six-year-old girl Kine was told about who played it "every day on the way to school for something like a whole year" and a young boy with a mom-based mystery who whispered, "If anyone can solve it, Starlee Kine can." Kine says she thinks about that boy, and the faith he had in her, often. "I think art at its best can make you the best, most fully realized version of yourself. That might be what I miss most."

Nocturne

Vincent van Gogh once said, "It often seems to me that the night is much more alive and richly colored than the day." Yeah, man. Spot on.

There is nothing else like Vanessa Lowe and Kent Sparling's *Nocturne* in audio, and there likely never will be. Here is a podcast woven with the utmost care, a paean to personal art making tethered to that most universal of all phenomena: darkness. Hosted and produced by Lowe, a musician and storyteller from California's Bay Area, the series can be enjoyed much like an encounter with Pierre Soulages's outrenoir paintings, in which layers of black upon black reveal not a darker, dimmer world, but a brighter one. It is an almost sacred experience.

Every episode is a tone poem about the spectrum of experiences humans share with the night: the awe of stumbling upon a coyote killing its prey; sadness at the sight of the starry sky being swallowed by the brightness of urbanity; the spine-bending chill that greets the unzipping of a camping tent. Though these installments are often experimental in form and structure, virtually all open with an unforgettable six-note melody composed by Sparling and layered with sounds so eerily evocative of the nightscape outside my own childhood bedroom on the edge of the Angeles National Forest that the first time I heard them, I jumped.

Since launching independently in 2014 (the show was distributed by KCRW between 2018 and 2020 but has since joined the monetization platform Patreon), *Nocturne* has become the program of choice for night dwellers. "Like many people, I appreciate the night for its quiet," Lowe reveals, "but a big part of why I love it is because I'm so scared of the dark! I have an incredibly vivid imagination, and can go to fear pretty easily." This, I would theorize, is something all her devoted listeners, including me, share. Recently, the host stayed "at a tiny cabin in an isolated dark wood," only to hear the unmistakable sounds of a stranger stalking the grounds in the all-consuming blackness outside. Lowe's partner offered to stay on the phone with her while she sprinted to an outhouse to pee, but as she unlocked the door, the call dropped, leaving her alone with a full bladder and scary thoughts. Inevitably, this will make its way into *Nocturne*.

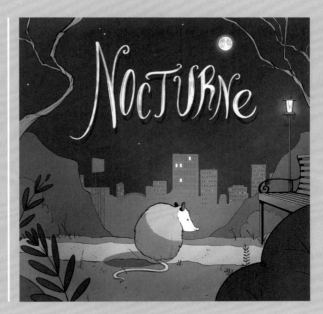

HOSTED BY
Vanessa Lowe

GENRE
Experimental

FIRST EPISODE
"Night Owls"
(November 17, 2014)

INFLUENCES
"Film sound, Kent Sparling's
ambient music, and
the delicious fear and
excitement of standing in a
dark wood" (Lowe)

WHERE TO LISTEN
NocturnePodcast.org

SEAN'S PICK
"What the Baker Saw"
(January 22, 2015)

As *The New Yorker*'s Sarah Larson reported, it was Sparling who suggested that Lowe turn her nyctophobia into a podcast of her own. "I wrote like three pages of ideas to make sure that I'd have enough episodes to go for a while," Lowe recalls. "I made a commitment to myself to make the show for three years, and then evaluate how it was going and if I wanted to continue." At the time of this writing, *Nocturne* is celebrating its tenth year in production, with new essay-sodes of about half an hour apiece still being released once a month. "Bit by bit, as I've explored stories of darkness, this hidden landscape has become even more rich, textured, and beautiful to me," Lowe says. She has "no plans to ever stop."

Bad with Money

When Gabe Dunn founded his podcast *Bad with Money* in 2016, he was struggling to balance a $32,000 debt load while attempting to break into Hollywood as a writer, producer, and director. His goal, he explains, was "to supersede the financial podcasts that make people feel stupid and small," and in the process move away from a lifetime of silly money mistakes.

Early expert guests, like a student loan agent and a therapist specializing in financial stress, did their best to help Dunn sort through long-standing issues with saving, earning, and investing; others, like Dunn's parents and his longtime comedy partner, Allison Raskin, seemed more concerned about his own growth. Their fears were (in the long run, at least) unfounded. After ten years of broadcasting, *Bad with Money* remains among the most beloved business shows on the podcast charts, and Dunn one of a select few hosts considered a true guru in the field.

With his highly personal, empathy-driven approach, Dunn has spent over a dozen seasons resolving serious problems for hundreds of thousands of listeners without ever coming across as a know-it-all or con man. He simply wants to help, a fact evidenced by *BWM*'s massive success, which includes a bestselling 2019 spin-off book and a production deal with Universal TV.

As his show has grown in popularity, so too have its host's ambitions. Dunn, a longtime LGBTQIA+ advocate, has released several episodes interrogating abuses in the financial sector against people in the queer community, as well as others looking at the many inequities in wealth distribution in societies around the world. One such investigation even led to an unusual conversation with one of the world's most renowned financial advisors. As Dunn recalls now for the first time, "Suze Orman made me answer a big Q&A about my own finances via email before she would agree to come on the show." But Orman (who, Dunn reminds, "lives on a private island") did not stop there: "If I skipped a question, she'd write back and admonish me for missing one. Then, at one point, she sent me a bunch of photos of her catching massive fish on her boat."

That trademark combination of idiosyncratic humor and the landing of an expert guest helped turn Dunn's Orman interview into a pivotal episode. But it is his stalwart commitment to financial justice that keeps *Bad with Money*'s global fan base feeling comfortable writing in for his advice, week after week, and pushing the podcast to the top of the business charts. "I hope *Bad with Money* can eliminate the shame and elitism from money conversations," Dunn confides. Well, Gabe, mission accomplished.

HOSTED BY
Gabe Dunn

GENRE
Business and Finance

FIRST EPISODE
"Jagged Little Bills"
(August 23, 2016)

INFLUENCES
"Not Dave Ramsey, unpaid internships, and universal basic income" (Dunn)

WHERE TO LISTEN
Patreon

SEAN'S PICK
"Earning That Private Island
(w/ Suze Orman)"
(April 24, 2019)

Freakonomics Radio

"It's hard to express how grateful I am that I stumbled into making this podcast long ago, and 'stumble' is the right word," Stephen J. Dubner says. It was 2010, and Dubner and co-author Steven Levitt had just turned in the manuscript for *SuperFreakonomics*, their follow-up to the barnstorming *New York Times* bestselling book *Freakonomics*. To promote it, they made countless TV and radio appearances, "providing content for other shows," as Dubner puts it nearly fifteen years later. Even with Levitt on hand, the experience was a "lonely" and "unsatisfying" one. So for his next project, Dubner decided he needed to try something more "fun" and "collaborative." "I mean, I'm a writer, and like most writers, I have an ego and I want *my* voice to be heard," he tells me, "but it struck me that it would be better to use my voice primarily to set up and frame a story rather than dominate it."

These instincts led Dubner to create *Freakonomics Radio*, a podcast at the intersection of economics, education, and culture. Primarily, it serves as a vehicle for Dubner—who hosts and also produces through Dubner Productions—to "surround" a given topic, exploring it from every conceivable angle with a "mash-up" of expert interviews, the original music of Luis Guerra, research materials, and prewritten narration. Public drunkenness, the meat industry, divorce rates, professional whale-hunting, Canadian immigration, finding dead rats in your lunch—all have come under Dubner's penetrating purview over the years.

Though each episode takes his staff months to produce, they rarely reach concrete conclusions about their subjects (Dubner likens himself more to a "proxy for the listener" than a "presenter"); instead, they illuminate wider social consequences of particular phenomena better than any one voice could articulate alone. The host sees this as "something of a corrective" to how modern reporters typically approach these subjects: "The whole point of seeking out smart, interesting, sometimes-weird people is to hear from *them*, not to tell you what I think about them," Dubner says. "It used to be that journalists would ask questions in order to inform readers about a particular issue. Today, a lot of journalism is more intent on telling people how to think about an issue."

As it turns out, the public was increasingly hungry for journalism in this mode—and Dubner had stumbled into a gold mine. Following the podcast's premiere, the Freakonomics empire expanded to include two more Levitt and Dubner books, a feature-length documentary, and eventually, their own Freakonomics Radio Network, which produces four additional podcasts. In 2023, the network partnered with YouTube to reach a generation of consumers ever more accustomed to watching their audio as they listen.

Despite such widespread recognizability, Dubner still seems shocked to have fallen face-first into the vanguard of economics podcasters, particularly given that he was intent on starting a career "as a rock star" in his younger days (if you see him, ask him about signing to a major label as a college freshman). "I don't know if my ear is better than anyone else's," he says. "What I do know is that I never get bored listening and hearing."

HOSTED BY
Stephen J. Dubner

GENRE
Business and Finance

FIRST EPISODE
"The Dangers of Safety"
(February 5, 2010)

INFLUENCES
Charles Mingus, Larry David, Elaine May and Mike Nichols, Chopin, *Exile on Main St.*, WNYC, NPR

WHERE TO LISTEN
Freakonomics.com

SEAN'S PICK
"Mouse in the Salad" (July 21, 2011)

Holly Randall
Unfiltered

Holly Randall Unfiltered **is an apt name** for a podcast that challenges you to "forget everything you think you know about porn." Indeed, as advertised, it presents an unvarnished, unromantic, and uncritical look at the most American business there is in hour-long chunks each week. At the same time, it also serves as an intimate audio diary of life in and around sex entertainment from one of the industry's most enduring and popular artists.

Ironically, Randall only found time to launch the namesake venture because she was in between gigs. She began her producing career in 2000 for Suze.net, the website founded by her mother (renowned erotic photographer Suze Randall) and her father (filmmaker and author Humphry Knipe). By 2008, Randall had formed her own (again eponymous) production company, demonstrating lifelong affinities for self-governance and business development. She was quickly heralded as a next-generation auteur by both performers and glamour companies like *Twistys*, *Club*, and *High Society* for her authentically sensuous, cinematic aesthetics. In 2013, she was announced as host and director of Playboy TV's *Adult Film School*, and that same year, AVN named her one of the industry's most influential "power players."

Still, when she felt new opportunities beginning to dry up toward the end of the decade, she already knew exactly how to pivot. "I always felt that the porn industry—and, more specifically, the people in it—were misunderstood," Randall writes by email. "I thought, *If only people knew these porn stars as I know them—funny, intelligent, creative, ambitious, free-spirited, independent—they might think differently*." At the time, there were already a few podcasts claiming "to interview porn stars as 'people,'" she remembers, but none from the perspective of a seasoned producer-director-photographer in the field. So working with producer Ernesto Hurtado, she conceived of a ten-episode test season for a show that was "about more than funny orgy stories and questioning if squirting is real."

HOSTED BY
Holly Randall

GENRE
Business and Finance

FIRST EPISODE
"Meet My Parents"
(July 19, 2017)

INFLUENCES
You're Wrong About,
This American Life

WHERE TO LISTEN
Pleasure Podcasts

SEAN'S PICK
"August Ames"
(September 13, 2017)

Unfiltered released its premiere episode, a conversation between the host and her parents, on July 19, 2017. That hour remains an object of quiet beauty—frank and funny and warm, without a hint of the hacky, tacky exposé stylings Randall so strenuously wished to avoid. Though intensely personal, it is also far from a trauma dump: At the end of the episode, Knipe and the Randalls cry with joy about getting to share life together. Although it didn't receive the same attention as the series' viral ninth episode, which features late starlet August Ames in one of her final interviews before her death (some of which can be read about in another entry in the pantheon, *The Last Days of August*; see p. 144).

The podcast once and for all affirmed Randall's bona fides as a revolutionary creative and one of adult entertainment's most vocal mascots. It also continues to reshape ideas about what constitutes mainstream podcasting today. In 2024, the show crossed 270,000 weekly subscribers on YouTube, with tens of millions of listens and views across its now-vast back catalog, putting it in very rarefied air. Randall was also inducted into the AVN Hall of Fame that year, with her advocacy on behalf of sex workers cited among her achievements.

Through all the accolades, Randall's goal remains simply to deepen listeners' understandings of the human experience. "The fact that adult performers trust me with these stories is really precious to me, because this is not the way most people see them," she says. "That is part of the entire reason I started this show."

How I Built This

Guy Raz can't seem to stop hosting podcasts. *The Great Creators*, *Wisdom From The Top*, *Wow in the World*, *The Rewind*, *TED Radio Hour*—each has helped Raz level up from onetime radio journalist to what *The New York Times* called "one of the most popular podcasters in history." The most significant factor in his rise—besides his David Cross-y, echinacea-soothed and Throat Coat–protected chirp (complimentary!)—is *How I Built This*, which Raz has hosted since 2016, originally for NPR and more recently for Amazon Music and Wondery. The program, in which Raz speaks with entrepreneurs behind the world's best-known companies—Instagram, Warby Parker, Etsy, Hinge—seems to attract two key groups of listeners: those who wish to learn from stories of financial success, and those who love to hate the financially successful. At least, that's how I imagined it before Raz and I wrote to each other.

"I would argue that, if you were to look at it from a global perspective, most people today, particularly people in developing and emerging markets, hold net positive views of modern innovators—even technology innovators—and find them tremendously inspiring," he corrects when I suggest that we've grown out of our onetime respect for the da Vincis and Rockefellers of the world. For instance, Steve Jobs—who, had he lived longer, would have made for the paradigmatic *HIBT* guest—"is seen as somebody who changed the world, and at least globally, most people think he has changed it for the better." That Raz himself is inspired by innovation is no secret: He is prone to stunned exclamations (like "Wow!" or "Oh yeah!" or "How did that *feel*?") and to the narrative beauty of a happy ending. Normally, the podcast functions as an extension of this connection to narrative, beginning with its guests' upbringings, then leading into the discovery of their big ideas and, ultimately, their breakthroughs to the highest echelons of achievement—all over the course of an episode.

Sometimes, though, Raz must play more flexibly with linearity. Many of the conversations on the podcast touch on moments in which an entrepreneur's ideas or decisions failed, or at least threatened to. Bar none, these are its juiciest and most beautifully human segments. In a classic early episode featuring Gary Erickson, the founder of Clif Bar & Company, Erickson reveals how his company faced multiple stumbling blocks on its path to ubiquity, including the preventable collapse of a $60 million deal with Quaker Oats and a handshake deal with a former colleague that went damagingly south. But rather than rescue Erickson from the doldrums, Raz pushes him to excavate what it felt like on the brink of disaster. "Did you ever think, *Maybe they're right. Maybe I'm crazy. What am I doing?*" he asks Erickson as pulse-pounding music plays in the background. Suddenly, a podcast about success in business sounds more like a corporate thriller.

Raz's willingness to "go there" with multimillionaires and billionaires more accustomed to being insulated from scrutiny or drama by teams of yes-men has landed him in a class by himself. His goal is for "every listener to feel like I am talking to them and with them. I also want them to feel like, at the end, they're glad that they gave me the gift of their time." In this, he is inarguably victorious: In addition to garnering tens of millions of downloads for his media empire, *How I Built This* is an annual fixture in the podcast awards race, with a Webby win for Best Business Podcast in 2023. That Raz nearly fumbled such a bag early in his broadcasting career by attempting to deepen his iconic voice to something in the Bob Edwards or Robert Siegel range now seems like the cherry on top of his career. "I ultimately concluded I just needed to be myself," he says, "and as is usually the case, that was the right choice."

HOSTED BY
Guy Raz

GENRE
Business and Finance

FIRST EPISODE
"Spanx: Sara Blakely"
(September 12, 2016)

INFLUENCES
Inside the Actors Studio, Dick Cavett, bad business school case studies

WHERE TO LISTEN
Wondery

SEAN'S PICK
"Radio One: Cathy Hughes"
(September 26, 2016)

Planet Money

There is an egolessness to _Planet Money_ that has made it among the most trusted financial podcasts on offer. Owing to its alternating hosts and regular reporting partnerships with other NPR podcasts, the show's only true star is knowledge. Further, that knowledge is communicated in terms both clean and concise; ideas as complex as universal basic income, global antitrust policy, and racism in business are synthesized into bite-size twenty-minute-or-so episodes every Wednesday and Friday. Here's executive producer Alex Goldmark on that model: "The purpose and goal of our work is to explain, to understand, to learn, and that is a generally positive, even joyful experience. We believe more people will listen and learn and come to feel confident in the face of confusing economic forces if they can enjoy the journey of understanding [them]."

Not that the podcast avoids stressful or heavy subject matter; poverty, inflation, corruption, and economic disasters have all been recurrent concerns from the very first episode, in which Adam Davidson and Brad Setser dissect China's stranglehold over American mortgage-backed securities. In fact, _Planet Money_'s staffers earned NPR a Peabody Award in 2016 for their reporting on Wells Fargo's treatment of whistleblowers during its cross-selling scandal. More accurately, Goldmark (one of the recipients of that Peabody) notes that each segment is custom-tailored to meet the specific topic at hand: "We cover our share of sad stories, and when we do, we moderate the tone to match."

On the few occasions when delivering information appropriately has proved an insurmountable challenge, episodes have been held back from air. Goldmark shares the example of an episode dedicated to how the Federal Reserve "creates money out of thin air, like magic." To produce it, a veteran reporter booked a former Fed staffer to crack wise about the "like magic" aspect with Usidore the Blue, a wizard from fellow pantheon member _Hello from the Magic Tavern_ (see p. 72). Ultimately, that now-lost conversation "didn't really end up explaining monetary policy enough or make us laugh enough" to meet the show's established benchmarks (Goldmark: "But we tried!").

Such instances are, in the executive producer's words, "very rare." This is a fact, not corporate spin. Longtime fans of *Planet Money* have come to count on its unshakable consistency, reliability, and seeming omnipotence. Its gargantuan, three-decade-spanning catalog touches on every conceivable sector of finance with NPR's signature precision and stateliness. Seasoned economists and casual investors alike have hailed it for increasing their understanding of the dollar without decreasing their personal joy. Where other money-minded podcasts promote urgency and catastrophic thinking as motivators to keep listening, *Planet Money* leans into the belief that one deserves to enjoy every penny while it lasts. "Delight," Goldmark stresses, "is a core value."

HOSTED BY
Various

GENRE
Business and Finance

FIRST EPISODE
"Brad Setser Explains the China
Thing" (September 8, 2008)

INFLUENCES
2007–2008 global financial crisis,
This American Life

WHERE TO LISTEN
NPR

SEAN'S PICK
"Maria Bamford Gets Personal (about)
Finance" (October 13, 2023)

Comedy Bang! Bang!

EARWOLF
SCOTT AUKERMAN'S
COMEDY
BANG!
BANG!

The cast of kooky characters introduced on Scott Aukerman's trendsetting podcast *Comedy Bang! Bang!* is large enough to fill its own book (literally, thanks to Abrams). In each episode since its debut as *Comedy Death-Ray* in 2009, Aukerman has invited a rotating crew of the world's best improvisers (Lauren Lapkus, Jessica St. Clair, others) onto each episode to perform as louts, weirdos, and creeps, all while seated beside a real famous person tasked typically only with keeping a straight face.

"In the early days, Hollywood celebs, used to bone-dry press requests, could be confused about the format," Aukerman reveals when we Zoom in 2024. Some, like Paul F. Tompkins's posh Lord Andrew Lloyd Webber or Mike Hanford as the revived corpse of John Lennon, became recurring guests after a few star-making appearances. Others like Neptuna (Andy Daly), an incomprehensible humanoid sea creature, or HP-DP-69B (John Gemberling), an inappropriately horny sex robot, came and went more abruptly. And in a few rare cases, an improviser's performance was so convincing that it disrupted the episode entirely, the host says: "One guest [on the show] to promote their latest film got into a screaming match with the comedian playing a character during the break. They stormed out of the studio, finally only convinced to return after being promised the offending comedy would be edited out of the program."

Through them all, "Scottie Auks" has remained *CBB*'s North Star, masquerading as what he calls the "incredulous straight man" in room after room of eccentrics. It's proven to be a very winning strategy: With more than 850 episodes, a litany of spin-off podcasts, a bestselling book, and even a five-season TV version of his own creation, Aukerman has established himself as one of podcasting's most revered Svengalis. In fact, the comedian's empire has grown so massive—encompassing not one but two podcast networks, Earwolf and Comedy Bang! Bang! World—that it has caught the attention of real-life strangers even more peculiar than his guests. Brett Morris, the co-founder and executive producer of Comedy Bang! Bang! World, tells me that he even received "a cold email from someone who proudly said they just got out of jail for robbing a bank and wanted to come on *CBB* to talk about it." Nonetheless, Morris says that neither he nor Aukerman see any reason to stop humanity's (and the animal kingdom's) podcast anytime soon. That is, of course, unless you've got a juicy acting role in mind for Scott, who once appeared back-first as the younger version of Austin Powers's dad in *Goldmember*. Just remember: He's offer only.

HOSTED BY
Scott Aukerman

GENRE
Comedy

FIRST EPISODE
"Welcome to Comedy Bang Bang"
(May 1, 2009)

INFLUENCES
Late Night with David Letterman,
Carl Reiner and Mel Brooks's
The 2000 Year Old Man

WHERE TO LISTEN
Comedy Bang! Bang! World

SEAN'S PICK
"Return to Suicide House"
(October 29, 2012)

Conan O'Brien Needs a Friend

When legendary late-night host Conan O'Brien announced his new career as a podcaster in the winter of 2018, the press was strongly divided. "O'Brien never planned on becoming the darling of the podcast world," wrote *Variety*'s Brent Lang and Todd Spangler adoringly, while in *The Guardian*, Fiona Sturges asked, "Are celebrities ruining podcasting?" Other questions arose as well: Was O'Brien equipped to chat with guests for hours, rather than for the six-to-eight-minute segments he was accustomed to? Would his particularly physical brand of absurdist comedy translate to audio? Would the Masturbating Bear be there? After all, wrote Sturges, "being a successful actor, or comic, or even a royal escapee does not automatically make someone a good interviewer—and interviews are the dominant format in the realms of star-studded pods."

Sturges need not have worried. Not only did O'Brien fast find his footing as the co-host of *Conan O'Brien Needs a Friend*, but the show became a ratings juggernaut with an average of nine million downloads a month—earthshaking numbers, even for such an established icon. It turned out that the flame-haired clown fans had come to know for more than three decades on television was a far more adept and serious interviewer than he'd let on.

Though his trademark self-deprecation remained, the conversations O'Brien conducted on the pod thrummed with unexpected warmth and wit, regardless of whether they were with real-life friends like Dana Carvey, mentors like *Saturday Night Live* writer Jim Downey, or creatives he admired, like former First Lady Michelle Obama. In its first fifty episodes or so, *CONAF* was premised on its namesake securing commitments of actual friendship from such guests by any means necessary. Yet as the show entered, then weathered, the pandemic, a new dynamic emerged between O'Brien; his devoted assistant, Sona Movsesian; and producer Matt Gourley: that of

Comedy

two perpetually put-upon parents corralling their antic child. Each frames that change in starkly different terms.

"Prior to the podcast I worked on controlling my rage, but lately Conan has been nudging this bear, and I find myself flying off the handle more than usual. It's more of a reversal in maturity," Movsesian says.

"What none of us probably foresaw was the sibling rivalry that would develop between [us] . . . I had to learn to be scrappy," Gourley says.

"*CONAF* feels suspiciously like a long-con sting operation, in which Matt and Sona are getting me relaxed enough to eventually admit that, yes, I tried to have Fidel Castro kidnapped in 1979. Once that it's said, just after an interview with Will Forte, I will be arrested and immediately detained in an undisclosed location," O'Brien says.

This three-headed comedy hydra catapulted *CONAF* into the highest echelon of podcasting, distinguishing it from other interview-based programs it once resembled and setting the stage for what would become its groundbreaking success. In 2022, SiriusXM acquired O'Brien's digital media production company, Team Coco, for an astounding $150 million, turning the comedian and his unsuspecting co-hosts into the new faces of audio. If the first wave of podcasting circa 2004 belonged to progenitors of the field like Adam Curry and Dave Winer, and the second wave heralded the rise of podcast-grown superstars like Sarah Koenig, Phoebe Judge, and regular O'Brien guest Marc Maron, then the third wave begins with O'Brien, Movsesian, and Gourley blowing through podcasting's financial glass ceiling.

So what is it like to be a true podcasting pioneer? Their responses are, gently put, humble.

"It makes me feel like I picked a good horse to hitch my wagon on to," Movsesian says.

"If ever there was a medium that has room for everyone, it's podcasting," Gourley says.

"I think the only person who reads the trades in our office is our producer, Adam Sachs, and he is not allowed to speak. So the rest of us are blissfully ignorant of the business side of our podcast. Matt asks to be paid in farm-fresh eggs, and Sona is still under the impression that she is an intern. I honestly don't know how a podcast works, when it drops, or how it is consumed, and I haven't read a comment section online since Nicolas Cage released *The Wicker Man*," O'Brien says.

HOSTED BY
Conan O'Brien, Matt Gourley, and Sona Movsesian

GENRE
Comedy

FIRST EPISODE
"Will Ferrell" (November 19, 2018)

INFLUENCES
"Warner Bros. cartoons of the 1940s and '50s, *Pee-wee's Playhouse*, *The French Chef with Julia Child*, the complete works of William Shakespeare (except for *Hamlet* . . . nobody likes that Hamlet)" (O'Brien); "Conan's own, unique voice" (Gourley); "Andy Richter" (Movsesian)

WHERE TO LISTEN
Team Coco

SEAN'S PICK
"Jim Downey" (September 25, 2023)

Hey, We're Back!

There exist in every generation certain comedic personalities so defined that they become planets unto themselves. In the mid-1990s, Jonathan Katz emerged as one such celestial body, drawing protégés, acolytes, and imitators into his orbit primarily as guests on his Peabody-winning series *Dr. Katz, Professional Therapist*. So masterfully did Katz, a stand-up comedian and writer for films and television, deploy his signature deadpan on the sitcom that he has been dogged ever since by the false belief that he is, in real life, a doctor.

In actuality, Katz has spent the better part of two decades practicing a much more important vocation: podcast hosting. An avid audiophile since his childhood, he and producer Dana Friedman began broadcasting *Hey, We're Back!* on www.wkatz.com in October 2007, when podcasts were still in their infancy. "In the Early Days, it was just me and Dana. One of the things that distinguished [our show] from other podcasts was my desire to record anything that struck me as funny that day," Katz says in a note after calling me to test my mettle first (Me: "I'm such a fan of *Dr. Katz* and *House of Games*!"; Katz: "Hm. And what about *Daddy Day Care*?"). That meant episodes could be short, between eight and ten minutes, and could publish at random intervals, sometimes week to week and sometimes with gaps of a year or more.

Katz and Friedman's masterstroke was bringing back members of the *Dr. Katz* repertory company, like Tom Snyder, H. Jon Benjamin, Laura Silverman, and Wendy Liebman, to recapture the TV show's era-defining chemistry. So bone-dry were their bits, however, that anyone stumbling on the podcast without knowing Katz's previous work might be furious to discover that Bob Dylan, Barry White, and Aretha Franklin were not actual guests on his show, as once advertised on Blogspot. Friedman says they quickly decided to call it an "internet radio show" to help clarify that they were making satire. Here's a telling exchange from an early sketch made to sound like a real talk radio interview between Katz and his old Hebrew school friend, "Al Schwarz," voiced by Benjamin:

Comedy

Katz: "It's just such an unusual choice to make for a sport."

Schwarz: "It was something that a lot of the other kids were not doing, basically."

Katz: "I'm sure that was part of the appeal for you."

Schwarz: "There wasn't a lot of log-rolling where I grew up, in New York City."

Katz: "Al, I've got to ask you: What inspired you to do this particular sport?"

Schwarz: "Trees."

Eventually, Katz and Friedman retooled the podcast to its current, more familiar long-form format, and brought Silverman on full-time as co-host/foil. "At first it was all interviews," Friedman notes, but recent episodes have also incorporated "sketches from earlier episodes that new fans might have missed." Between this medley of materials and its hosts' razor-sharp timing, the revitalized version has retained its position at the creative pinnacle of audio comedy, even for those who have trouble keeping up with its deadpan humor. If that includes you, don't worry: You're not alone, Katz says. "I don't get it myself."

HOSTED BY
Jonathan Katz

GENRE
Comedy

FIRST EPISODE
"Hey We're Back
(Premiere)"
(August 3, 2007)

INFLUENCES
Lenny Bruce, Burns and Schreiber, Ronnie Shakes,
Dom Irrera, H. Jon Benjamin, Rita Rudner, Woody Allen

WHERE TO LISTEN
JonathanKatz.com

SEAN'S PICK
"Telephone Support, with Jane Brucker"
(September 27, 2007)

Hollywood Handbook

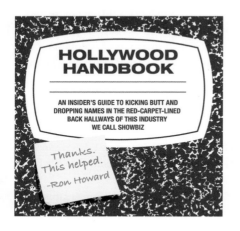

HOLLYWOOD HANDBOOK

AN INSIDER'S GUIDE TO KICKING BUTT AND
DROPPING NAMES IN THE RED-CARPET-LINED
BACK HALLWAYS OF THIS INDUSTRY
WE CALL SHOWBIZ

*Thanks.
This helped.
-Ron Howard*

Considering the immensity of labor and talent needed to remain in character for more than a decade, the longevity of *Hollywood Handbook* seems nothing short of a miracle.

Since 2013, the show has been hosted by Hayes Davenport and Sean Clements, two tall, handsome, blond comedians so adept at portraying bullying, self-absorbed LA insiders that, according to Davenport, their guests' most common question after recording is "Was that okay?" *Handbook* advertises itself as an advice podcast for Hollywood upstarts when it is in fact just the opposite: a satire of *Inside the Actors Studio*–type interview programming predicated on the understanding that anyone claiming to know the secret to success in show business is either a scam artist, a nepo baby, or an insufferable hack. "A lot of people come on the show without ever having heard it, and we do our best to explain in advance that our characters are awful and it's a bit," Davenport says by email. "But sometimes the show starts and the guest is just so visibly and instantly not feeling it, and we don't know what to do except helplessly make it worse for an hour as someone we really admire develops a lifelong negative association with our names and faces."

In reality, "the Boys" are accomplished comedy writers who met while staffing on a network television series. Davenport, a former editor of the *Harvard Lampoon*, left comedy to work as an activist on behalf of the unhoused. Clements, a veteran improviser at the Upright Citizens Brigade, acts and produces for beloved series like *Workaholics*, *Love*, and *Unstable*. On mic, however, "the Hayes man" is a droll, impatient control freak forced to wrangle "the Clemdog's" more mischievous, mocking tendencies. They regularly embarrass and undercut their guests, as in the landmark five hundredth episode when they pushed Ben Stiller for the actor Adam Scott's contact info instead of complimenting Stiller's own work. Inside jokes—which at first consisted mainly of mispronouncing simple terms ("Frankingstein," "*The Mimby Project*") and eventually morphed into the constant haranguing of producer and honorary Third Boy, "Chef" Kevin Bartelt—are invoked for guests who have no clue what they're hearing.

Even the show's financial partners sometimes wind up getting unwittingly wounded. Clements notes that they were dropped "by at least four different advertisers because of the elaborate 'comedy' we used when talking about their products." In response, loyal listeners made compilations highlighting their most outrageous commercials, like a multi-episode saga for a shaving company starring Santa Claus as an action hero battling Sherlock Holmes's nemesis, Moriarty . . . who is also Claus's stepdad. "Now our fans send each other the audio files and transcripts for the ads that got us in trouble like they're bootleg Dead show tapes or something," Clements says.

This two-pronged approach certainly calls to mind other iconic duos: Andy Kaufman and Bob Zmuda, Vladimir and Estragon, Tim & Eric. But over more than a decade together, Davenport and Clements have honed their podcast personae to a razor-sharpness completely their own, earning them a shared reputation as contenders for the funniest broadcasters working today. In addition to Stiller, high-wattage guests like Jon Hamm, Tony Hawk, and recurring fan favorite Ayo Edebiri continue to eagerly subject themselves to the Boys' absurd little games.

For his part, Bartelt recognizes that unfamiliar listeners might find it challenging to jump into the fifth installment of long-established bits like "Cowboy TV," a Western about two guys staring at a campfire, or the Clea DuVall saga centered on Osama Big Laden. The only solution, it seems, is to start at the beginning. "For better and for worse," Bartelt says, "there's no show like *Hollywood Handbook*. The bug is also the feature."

HOSTED BY
Sean Clements and
Hayes Davenport

GENRE
Comedy

FIRST EPISODE
"Jake Johnson, Our Close
Friend" (October 8, 2013)

INFLUENCES
Tom Scharpling

WHERE TO LISTEN
Patreon

SEAN'S PICK
"The Masked Engineer,
Our Masked Friend"
(January 21, 2019)

How Was Your Week?

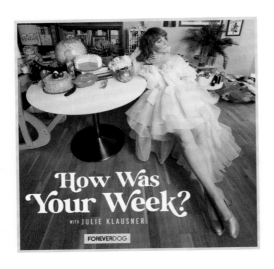

Late-night TV hosts and aspiring Shakespeareans alike could stand to learn a thing or two from Julie Klausner, podcasting's ranking monologist. On *How Was Your Week?*, which she founded in 2011, Klausner regales listeners with streams of consciousness so intellectually and comically nimble that it can be disorienting. *Wait*, you think as she slaloms through a fifteen-minute comparative analysis of the lyrics of Salt-N-Pepa and Billy Joel, *I thought we were talking about platypus poison?*

More often, though, getting carried away by her re-reading of *Rosemary's Baby* or live thoughts in the seconds just before jury duty feels deeply intimate. So familiar have her particular grievances (Andrew Lloyd Webber's attempts at lyricism) and predilections (the male co-stars of *Smash*) become to listeners that when Klausner eventually got to create, write, and star in a show with Billy Eichner for Hulu, many flocked to see them manifested visually. "The monologues were a form of journaling and when I got my show, *Difficult People*, I was able to draw from those ramblings," Klausner explains. "I was also live-broadcasting my life in a way, so when I DID meet fans of the show, they'd say things like 'I couldn't believe it when you broke up with [Klausner's ex-boyfriend] Jack' or 'I'm sorry [Klausner's beloved cat] Smiley Muffin passed.'"

She has also attracted a number of "marvelous" guests throughout her decade-plus run, bookending them with recordings made while she is "on the floor looking up at the ceiling wondering out loud what I could

Comedy

44

share that would make people laugh and enjoy my company," Klausner says. "In terms of memories, I will always cherish interviewing Joan Rivers in her living room while she was still in the big white sneakers she was wearing from her morning treadmill walk, and I remember passing the microphone back and forth to Sally Kellerman (one mic was busted and I was winging it) in her ranch in California as she told me about choosing the songs for her new album."

That Klausner never appears to break a sweat with these or any other big names (including Andrew McCarthy, Sandra Bernhard, and Kurt Loder, among others) has made *HWYW* an early and prominent model for what true creative independence looks like in comedy podcasting. Here is a show that switches formats often, lets its host be strange and hyperspecific, and still never loses its fastball. Equally remarkably, Klausner has to this day never diminished its legacy by making anything less than stellar. *Double Threat*, a culture-analyzing podcast she tag-teams with Tom Scharpling, is always savagely funny (and, frankly, a little slept on), while *Ask Julie*, another of Klausner's collaborations with the Forever Dog network, is as reliable a fount of wisdom as bonus content gets. Still, nothing can compete with the sheer ballsiness required to trust that someone somewhere might want to hear a comedian wax rhapsodic about the *American Psycho* musical for an hour straight.

HOSTED BY
Julie Klausner

GENRE
Comedy

FIRST EPISODE
"Natasha Vargas-Cooper, Julie's Parents, 'Oscar Madison Won't Let You Pack Your Bags'" (March 8, 2011)

INFLUENCES
"I was inspired by the structure of *WTF* and Tom Scharpling's broadcasting style from *The Best Show*, but ultimately my biggest inspirations are Fran Lebowitz and John Waters. I'm also a great admirer of Joan Rivers's interviewing style from when she hosted *The Tonight Show*. She was the greatest and we did not deserve her." (Klausner)

WHERE TO LISTEN
Forever Dog

SEAN'S PICK
"Chaotic Tumescence" (June 28, 2018)

Keith and the Girl

"Give a fuck! Care! Don't put out bullshit!" This, Keith Malley reminds us, is the guiding principle behind *Keith and the Girl*, the foul-mouthed, Howard Stern–inspired talk show he and Chemda Khalili began hosting in March 2005. Barely a year after the term "podcast" was first coined to describe downloadable audio, Malley and Khalili, his real-life ex-girlfriend, started publishing their conversations about sex, comedy, and stupid news online and for free nearly every day. "We literally recorded [episode one] an hour after we broke up," Malley says almost twenty years later. "No one knew the word 'podcasts.' It wasn't even a category on iTunes!"

KATG, as its fans quickly abbreviated it, was instantly revolutionary, broadcasting bawdily into the distant corners of a patch of the internet that even preceded YouTube. But being the first in this new field also meant that there was no clear model for making money or finding an audience for the show. It was actually "scary as fuck" at the time, Malley remembers: "We had to quit regular jobs to make it work. I remember going to Guitar Center and trying to buy the right mixer. Me: 'I'm looking for an interface from a mic to my computer.' Guitar Center: 'For music?' Me: 'No. Just for talking, but nice audio.' Guitar Center: 'We don't have that.' Me: 'Then yes, for music.'"

Thankfully, as more podcasts emerged and coalesced into their own true art form over the next few months and years, this brazen little comedy program evolved into a deepening look at divorce, open-heart surgery, career changes, and more, pushing *KATG*, slowly but surely, into the rarified air of true cult status. Today, Malley and Khalili's devoted followers consider them podcasting's Nichols and May, digital pioneers whose willingness to take their international audience through utterly personal experiences without ever abandoning their creative or fiscal independence has paved the way for millions of fellow broadcasters.

With what is believed to be more published episodes than any other comedy podcast ("Are we the most prolific? Sure. Stop it! No, YOU hang up!" Malley jokes) and dozens of spin-off podcasts, *Keith and the Girl*

Keith and The Girl

FREE COMEDY TALK SHOW

HOSTED BY
Chemda Khalili
and Keith Malley

GENRE
Comedy

FIRST EPISODE
"KEITH AND THE GIRL!"
(March 7, 2005)

INFLUENCES
Wendy Williams,
Howard Stern

WHERE TO LISTEN
Spotify

SEAN'S PICK
"Show #2,000"
(June 23, 2014)

has become the audio world's ultimate long-distance marathon, leaving behind many an exhausted former competitor and setting the gold standard for podcasts of every genre without ever accepting a dime of corporate cash. It has also, according to Khalili—who ceded her hosting duties in the spring of 2024—given them each a deeper personal purpose: "Podcasting helped me find myself," she says. "I feel less embarrassed in general from years of being open and vulnerable on mic."

As for those who have never heard of *KATG*, its founders have hidden a message for you in their theme song: "Hey, all you assholes, come and listen to us—it's the *Keith and the Girl* show!"

Never Not Funny

THE JIMMY PARDO PODCAST

NEVER NOT FUNNY

"It's funny to think folks that made fun of me for doing 'my little dining radio show' all have podcasts now!" says Jimmy Pardo, the host and co-creator of *Never Not Funny*. When Pardo and producer Matt Belknap recorded the first episode in early 2006, the medium was still in its creative infancy. Pardo had spent the previous eighteen years as a working stand-up, with gigs as Conan O'Brien's longtime warm-up guy and the host of *National Lampoon's Funny Money* under his belt. After seeing his Upright Citizens Brigade stage show, *Running Your Trap*, Belknap invited Pardo to an interview for A Special Thing, an essential forum for fans of alternative comedy. Their chemistry on mic was explosive. Soon, Pardo and Belknap announced they would launch a comedy talk show that could be downloaded from the internet. Podcasting itself was barely two years old at the time, and the prospect of supporting oneself with it was virtually untested. No wonder some were a little baffled.

Nonetheless, Pardo and Belknap began releasing hour-long riff sessions (first with co-host Mike Schmidt, and later with recurring guests like Pat Francis and Graham Elwood) every Wednesday. They talked about everything and nothing: music, baseball, marriage, old Hollywood, perfect joke structure. It was silly and speedy, and it sparkled. Strangers began tuning in. Within months, Belknap and Ryan McManemin had launched an independent comedy label, Aspecialthing Records, to help produce more shows; by 2008, *Never Not Funny* was popular enough to sustain a paid subscription model. Suddenly, Pardo was being hailed as an emissary for podcasters everywhere when he went out on tour. "I never even knew what a podcast was until Jimmy Pardo started making his show available

Comedy

through that medium," comedian Howie Nave confessed in the *Tahoe Daily Tribune*.

In the nearly two decades since, this has all become part of *Never Not Funny* lore. There was also the "Earwolf Era," a five-year period without the subscription paywall, as well as the more recent era under the leadership of Pardo and Belknap's Misfit Toys Podcast Co-op, an independent comedy curation and incubation service run through ART19. But even after many thousands of episodes and several spin-off shows (including a personal favorite, *Jimmy's Records and Tapes*), the podcast still sounds like an artifact of a bygone era in media production. Pardo refers to it as "a loose show" for its rambling, bells-and-whistles-free format. Guests come and go from episode to episode, but amid it all, the hosts just keep talking about this, that, and the other.

Today, *NNF* is consumed as much for the entertainment value inherent in Pardo's distinctive, booming motormouth as for its larger historical import. Though they were not the first to put their conversations on the internet, he and Belknap are often described as "pioneers," "forefathers," and "godfathers" of podcasting for having turned the two-headed comedy venture into a sustainable, artist-run business known around the world.

HOSTED BY
Jimmy Pardo

GENRE
Comedy

FIRST EPISODE
"Pardcast—Episode One" (April 4, 2006)

INFLUENCES
Johnny Carson, Don Rickles, Robert Klein

WHERE TO LISTEN
Spotify

SEAN'S PICK
"721—Jon Hamm" (October 26, 2010)

In fact, it is still not fully understood just how widespread the influence of *Never Not Funny* is on comedy podcasting writ large. Among the publications that regularly cite it in academic histories of comedy are *Studies in American Humor*, the *ARSC Journal*, and the *Journal of Broadcasting & Electronic Media*. Similarly, fellow hit podcasters like Marc Maron, Scott Aukerman, and Paul Gilmartin have all referred to it as one of the shows that made theirs possible. Rather than let me assign credit for the rise of the most popular podcasting genre in the world to him, however, Pardo shrugs it off. "I started this show as an outlet for people to enjoy my nonsense," he says. "What I didn't expect was to touch as many hearts as we have with the show. Good heavens, that sounds like a voice-over for an animated animal movie!"

Normal Gossip

"Gossip is what no one claims to like, but everybody enjoys," wrote Joseph Conrad in *The End of the Tether*, and the immense popularity of Defector's flagship podcast on the subject proves just how correct Conrad was. Kelsey McKinney and Alex Sujong Laughlin, Defector's co-owners, launched *Normal Gossip* in early 2022 at a pivotal moment for podcasts: The COVID-19 vaccine rollout was ongoing, and people around the world were seeking time fillers anew for their commutes and returns to public spaces. And a frothy comedy show in which McKinney talked shit about jagoffs and troublemakers wreaking havoc on their friends and neighbors? It fit the bill beautifully.

McKinney, the author of *God Spare the Girls*, and Laughlin, a veteran audio producer, knew they'd hit a gold mine even before the first episode came out. "I had worked almost a decade in audio and had only ever felt these kinds of prelaunch tingles once: before the launch of *Thirst Aid Kit* at BuzzFeed in 2018," Laughlin says by email. "Still, we weren't prepared for the specific fascinations the audience had with the 'truth' of the stories."

Across ten episodes a season, McKinney regales guests like Samantha Irby, Samin Nosrat, and Youngmi Mayer with tales of hot goss submitted to the Defector inbox. The tea is intentionally low stakes, the oft-provincial kind of tittle-tattle that makes for big arguments on small-town Facebook groups: Did someone hijack an animal mayoral race? Did a girl really poop into a Ziploc bag during a date? *Normal Gossip*'s host—a fellow writer, who, prior to taking the gig, "had listened to podcasts, been a guest on some, and made zero"—is a bubbly, pithy storyteller, quick with a zippy one-liner and more than slightly judgmental. Yet she is never cruel, castigating only the characters she's been told are hurting others for their naughty behavior.

Also key, Laughlin points out, is the anonymization process: By telling modern urban legends that could have come from anyone, anywhere, *Normal Gossip* emerged as a virtual space that people from everywhere could feel a part of. The podcast has been named to a slew of yearly best-of lists and birthed two hot-ticket live tours precisely because to listen to

Comedy

HOSTED BY
Kelsey McKinney

GENRE
Comedy

FIRST EPISODE
"Gossiptonin with Virgie Tovar"
(January 5, 2022)

INFLUENCES
Another Round, Tuca & Bertie,
Pen15, Scam Goddess,
"those 'bevragino' meme
women" (Laughlin)

WHERE TO LISTEN
Defector

SEAN'S PICK
"Righteous Lesbian Energy
with Samantha Irby"
(September 7, 2022)

McKinney and Laughlin throw down is to bond with other listeners at a time when more manifest avenues for person-to-person connection have disappeared. "Our goal has always been to tell a fun story, to give people a break from the horrors of the world," Laughlin says. "Gossip isn't a universal good by any means, but in its best form, that is what it does for people."

This Is Branchburg

According to the United States Census Bureau, as of July 1, 2022, Branchburg Township in Somerset County, New Jersey, has a total population of 14,835. Incorporated in 1845, Branchburg is known as the home of Olympic equestrian Frank Chapot and as the site of a historic one-room schoolhouse off Route 22. It is also where the comedians Brendan O'Hare and Cory Snearowski met playing Little League, not knowing that in the next decade, they would form the comedy team Brendan and Cory and create one of the funniest and strangest audio programs known to humankind.

O'Hare and Snearowski broke out on Twitter, delivering slow-motion one-liners with pops of surrealist imagery (O'Hare, in 2012: "DATE TIP: Hold doors. Pull the chair out for your date. Burp your date. Change your date oh god you are on a date with a baby ok stay cool"). That soon gave way to a flurry of viral videos, including the Difficulty Man series and the modern YouTube classic "I Just Got a New Computer, Real Nice One Too," in which Snearowski's kooky alter ego devolves into a tech-induced panic attack.

In 2019, after stints writing for ClickHole and *The New Yorker*, the duo partnered to create their magnum opus, *This Is Branchburg*. Produced by Adult Swim and Abso Lutely Productions, the sketch podcast features O'Hare and Snearowski as a bevy of left-of-center characters of the kind they encountered in childhood: a milkman defiant in his journey to deliver milk on foot, a grape farmer forcing his crop down ShopRite shoppers' throats, a power-mad school principal with a vainglorious motorcade. Part Alan Partridge, part *A Prairie Home Companion*, it is indescribably and ineffably itself.

In O'Hare's opinion, that idiosyncratic tone is a direct reflection of his and Snearowski's rigorous production process. During the show's development, they drafted scripts for entire episodes that went unproduced because they were not yet up to par. "We would rewrite and reshape things endlessly; there are Google Docs full of bits hundreds of pages long that we scrapped because they didn't meet our standard," he tells me. Both seasons were also recorded in the bedroom of sound engineer Alex Gilson, a fellow Branchburg native whom Snearowski met in Boy Scouts, to fully capture the township's local flavor. "The Gilson family was so kind to let us cause a ruckus in their house for almost two years," Snearowski shares gratefully. "Each time a sketch involved screaming, we had to walk into the kitchen to warn his parents about how loud it was going to be."

For those aware of the show's sui generis genius, the possibility of hearing a potential season three is painfully low, as both founders are in high demand as comedy writer-performers ("We had a blast making *This Is Branchburg* from start to finish" is all Snearowski will offer on the matter). But should the opportunity someday arise, the duo clearly has more hometown stories to tell. O'Hare highlights one untold story about the Branchburg Country Fair in which a low-achieving fifth grader is to be dropped into a dunk tank and a man will learn that there is no heaviest pig contest in which to enroll his 500-pound pig. It sounds hilarious, but for now, that particular piece still remains a work in progress, O'Hare says wistfully. "Maybe one day we'll figure it out."

HOSTED BY
Brendan O'Hare and
Cory Snearowski

GENRE
Comedy

FIRST EPISODE
"Welcome to Branchburg"
(May 8, 2019)

INFLUENCES
"The Chris Morris radio show
Blue Jam was our biggest
inspiration, along with the
two-person comedy of Peter
Cook and Dudley Moore"
(O'Hare/Snearowski)

WHERE TO LISTEN
Adult Swim

SEAN'S PICK
"The Branchburg Goblin
(feat. Gary Richardson)"
(October 29, 2020)

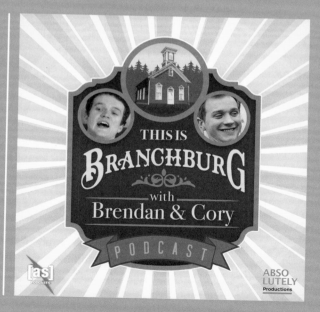

THIS IS
BRANCHBURG
with
Brendan & Cory
PODCAST

[as]

ABSO
LUTELY
Productions

Criminal

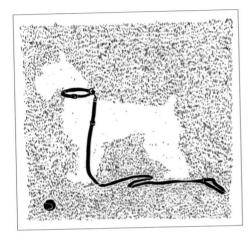

Phoebe Judge and Lauren Spohrer first met while working on a public radio show that got canceled. "We needed to find new jobs," Spohrer explains. "At the time, Phoebe lived in a garage apartment on a retired biologist's small farm. There was a donkey named Patches, three cows, one pig, and guinea fowl running around everywhere." Kibitzing over cigarettes one night in 2013, they discovered that they shared a dream of a show programmed exclusively to their personal interests, free from story notes and the exhausting bureaucracies of corporate audio. "It didn't matter to us if no one listened," Spohrer remembers thinking.

They needn't have worried about that. The following year, along with producer Eric Mennel, Spohrer and Judge created *Criminal*, a podcast about "people who've done wrong, been wronged, or gotten caught somewhere in the middle." Hosted by Judge in otherworldly, mesmeric tones, the series rejected narrative tropes then in vogue in so-called true-crime films and television. Early episodes, like one that profiles a woman lured into counterfeiting money by a devious boyfriend and another that examines a dangerous black market for Venus flytraps, were conspicuously antisensationalist, eliding gory or otherwise grotesque imagery in favor of sociological details that help to paint holistic pictures of crimes. Even on occasions when Judge and Spohrer do dip into famous cases, like the trials of Michael Peterson and John Wayne Gacy, their reporting prizes fascination and empathy over scandalization and horror, bemusement and humor over false, manipulative intensity. By the end of 2014, *The Huffington Post* (now *HuffPost*) declared theirs "the best new radio show in America."

HOSTED BY
Phoebe Judge

GENRE
Crime

FIRST EPISODE
"Animal Instincts"
(January 30, 2014)

INFLUENCES
Diet Coke, American Spirits

WHERE TO LISTEN
Vox Media

SEAN'S PICK
"Masterpiece"
(February 9, 2018)

CRIMINAL

VOXMEDIA

More than a decade later, the number of hit podcasts to follow in *Criminal*'s wake is now inestimable. While many are quick to credit the rise of true-crime podcasting to the earthshaking successes of *My Favorite Murder* and *Serial*, which premiered nine months after *Criminal*, the series still prides itself on being "the first of its kind." More recent installments—like deep dives into the consequences of the Triangle Shirtwaist Factory fire and the kidnapping of a high-society count's prized poodle—are no less humanistically investigated, or beautifully narrated, than before. And though both their creative team and their personal slates have expanded drastically (including with Criminal Plus, a subscription-only behind-the-scenes look at the series, as well as access to the vastly different *This Is Love* podcast), Spohrer and Judge still record the show at WUNC in Chapel Hill, North Carolina, perhaps in an effort to keep hold of the magic they first captured on that biologist's porch all those years back.

"We worked on *Criminal* before work, after work, and on the weekends. Our friends thought it was a mistake to spend that much time on such a small thing," Spohrer says wryly. "A lot has changed. Patches the donkey is still there."

Dr. Death

For a podcast that does not advertise itself as horror, *Dr. Death* is as haunting as audio gets. Since 2018, the Wondery production has homed in on the true crimes of disgraced doctors Christopher Duntsch, Farid Fata, Paolo Macchiarini, and Serhat Gumrukcu. While each committed historically unique atrocities against patients—a point made clearly in the first season—together they represent the terrifying capacity for abuse enabled by a private equity–strangled, Big Pharma–entrenched medical system. Thus, *Dr. Death* allocates six episodes apiece to their stories—not to give each crook more airtime but to make righteous arguments for the necessity of reform in an increasingly dangerous and corrupt health-care environment.

Medical journalist Laura Beil hosts every season; she also reported and wrote season one (subsequent seasons were reported by Heather Schroering, Nikka Singh, and Benjamin Gray). Outside her estimable expertise, Beil is a shrewd and natural tragedian given to pronouncements of extreme gravity, provided they are (1) entirely factual, and (2) respectful of more squeamish listeners. "I've always been cognizant of the fact that as journalists, we ask people to talk about the worst thing that has ever happened to them," she tells me. "We have a responsibility to respect those stories and do our best not to retraumatize people."

Though she favors "Spineless," her first installment to publicly excoriate the American medical infrastructure, Beil cites the gut-wrenching series premiere, "Three Days in Dallas," as particularly "difficult to hear" for most people. Throughout the episode, Beil describes several botched spinal surgeries in hardcore Cronenbergian fashion, conjuring images of loose vertebral fragments and screws stupidly embedded directly into flesh. Her attention to these details is as admirable as it is nauseating; Beil only included them because "they were necessary to understanding Christopher Duntsch's incompetence, making it all the more shocking that he was allowed to continue operating," she says.

Even so, hypochondriacs should reconsider before engaging with *Dr. Death*, despite its creative accomplishment. After years of receiving honors for Beil's and the Wondery production team's fearless reporting, the podcast was adapted into a medical television anthology in 2021. That series, a handsome melodrama starring Joshua Jackson, Alec Baldwin, and Mandy Moore, emerged as one of the streaming service Peacock's most captivating originals, significantly elevating its name recognition among the wider public. To ignore the podcast entirely now would mean missing out on a global cultural phenomenon. On the other hand, ask yourself: *Do I have the stomach for this one?*

HOSTED BY
Laura Beil

GENRE
Crime

FIRST EPISODE
"Three Days in Dallas"
(September 4, 2018)

INFLUENCES
"My dad, Bill Moyers, Lois Norder, Tom Siegfried, Peter Moore, Bill Bryson, Annie Dillard, Anne Lamott, Tracy Kidder, Mary Roach, Atul Gawande, Lawrence Wright" (Beil)

WHERE TO LISTEN
Wondery

SEAN'S PICK
"Chris and Jerry"
(September 3, 2018)

My Favorite Murder

Even if you are among the millions of people already abjectly addicted to Georgia Hardstark and Karen Kilgariff's true-crime behemoth *My Favorite Murder*, it may shock you to learn that this disturbing, delicious podcast owes its very existence to Brené Brown. Hardstark and Kilgariff were already established entertainers—the latter as a comedian and writer for the Academy Awards and *Portlandia*, the former as a travel and food series host—when they got to talking at a Halloween party in 2014. Discovering they shared a secret zeal for true crime, they decided to take a Brownian leap of faith: They became new adult friends. Had they not both been reading *Daring Greatly*, the self-help guru's bestselling guide to acting with authenticity and courage in the face of internalized shame, at the time, "I truly don't think the podcast would exist, and all the good things that have come from it wouldn't have happened," Hardstark muses. "This whole experience, in fact, is a testament to Brené's philosophy of vulnerability."

When the duo launched *MFM* in January 2016 with two devastating deep dives into JonBenét Ramsey and the Golden State Killer, they had "zero pretenses about anyone actually listening." But if you listen today, it makes perfect sense why the show almost immediately exploded. Already present in that first episode were the bold dark humor and ribaldry that have become distinguishing hallmarks of the series' best investigations, as well as the still-tentative but palpable intellectual chemistry between the hosts. Additionally, it lacked the distant, almost academic polish often applied to more journalistic crime shows of the era; instead, the stories in it and in successive episodes were told with an explicit awareness that bordered on excitement at the darkness of it all. It was, as *The Atlantic* would later describe it, as much a support group for those living with some shame over their dark tastes as it was a podcast meant to satisfy them.

Indeed, Hardstark theorizes that it was "our openness about discussing our own mental health struggles with our audience without any shame or reservations, as well as our sharing the many (MANY) life lessons we'd learned the hard way," that ultimately "took us from just

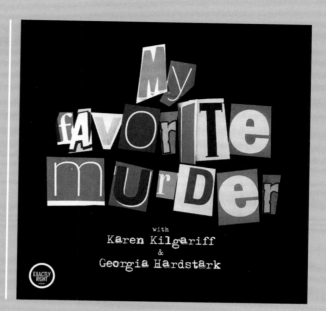

HOSTED BY
Georgia Hardstark
and Karen Kilgariff

GENRE
Crime

FIRST EPISODE
"My Firstest Murder"
(January 13, 2016)

INFLUENCES
Forensic Files

WHERE TO LISTEN
Exactly Right

SEAN'S PICK
"Namaste Sexy"
(August 25, 2016)

a true-crime podcast to a movement led by our listeners themselves." Of course, it may also have had something to do with the uncensored freedom to describe the depraved acts of Japanese cannibal-slash-necrophiliac Issei Sagawa or the psychopathic Tender Loving Care cult that podcasting offered them. Whatever the cause, less than ten months into production, the show broke into iTunes' Top 10, with each episode raking in nearly half a million downloads, according to *The San Diego Union-Tribune* (those numbers are significantly higher now). Then, after stays at two previous networks, Hardstark and Kilgariff announced the formation of their own, Exactly Right, in 2018. The following year, Forbes ranked them as the second-highest-earning podcasters on Earth.

In the years since, Exactly Right has become a launching pad for several other stellar high-concept shows, including Bridger Winegar's *I Said No Gifts!* (one of my mainstays), *Ghosted! by Roz Hernandez*, and *Bananas*, a wonderfully odd newscast from comedians Kurt Braunohler and Scotty Landes. Rightfully, however, *My Favorite Murder* remains Exactly Right's flagship, with loyal Murderinos around the globe continuing to find community through its various social media pages and live tours. If, like them, you have also managed to stay sexy and not get murdered, be sure to thank Brené Brown.

Small Town Murder

Get you a business partner who laughs at your jokes like Jimmie Whisman laughs at James Pietragallo's and you'll die happy. On *Small Town Murder*, their oft-indelicate foray into society's shadow realm, Whisman can barely hold it together whenever his co-host gets to mouthing off about the killers, rapists, and sociopaths among us. The concept for the show, a peerlessly caustic peg on the true-crime podcasting wheel, originated from the idea "that people have always thought they were safe in their small town—snugly tucked into their warm beds, while some kind of horrible fate waits to take them," Pietragallo and Whisman reveal in a joint statement. To both hosts, this seemed an extension of arrogance, as evidenced by the domination of similar "terrible stories" in media: Most people think they are "about a reality that some 'someone else' actually [had] to suffer through," they say.

Such widespread cognitive dissonance required a wake-up call: "Once we began to delve into the actual murders, we found out that it's just regular people coming to some of the worst ends imaginable—true tragedy, and pain." Listeners have come to expect to hear about those ends in microscopic detail. Once he and Whisman finish imitating anyone who impatiently demands that they "shut up and give me murder," Pietragallo blows them off by delving into the demographics, incomes, and histories of small American towns like Sarah, Mississippi (average home cost: $65,000), Hensley, West Virginia (population: 142), and Sequim, Washington (of the annual Sequim Lavender Festival). From there, he zeroes in on the locals' perspectives, reading reviews like some kind of murder Yelper. By the time "the murder train has begun pulling away from the station," Whisman is often already wheezing in the corner at Pietragallo's take-no-prisoners color commentary.

This pair succeeds where others in their category fail through an admixture of horror and humor. When it wants to be, *STM* is both the scariest comedy and the funniest thriller. Pietragallo and Whisman's telling of a triple

Crime

homicide in a Foster, Rhode Island, body shop (episode 395) treads this line masterfully. "This is a comedy show. We are comedians. But people will die in terrible ways and there's gonna be dead bodies," Pietragallo disclaims up top. But, he clarifies, they will not make fun of the victims or their families because "we're assholes, not scumbags."

Instead, he describes with a sociologist's precision how an unusually high average local income (around $80,000 a year) and rural boredom fomented violence between Foster police officer Robert Sabetta and teenagers Charles and Frank Sherman. Later, he describes Sabetta's shooting of the Shermans and their mechanic friends like a scene out of a Hitchcock film, the camera following the murderous cop out of the garage, onto the road, and into the river, where he ultimately throws his .357 Magnum. It all threatens to become too nerve-shredding until Sabetta, on the verge of conviction, moans that he might lose his badge. Whisman pounces. "You don't understand! He's gonna lose his job, guys!" he cries. "Do you know how hard it is to find another job right now?!" Pietragallo giggles back.

Admittedly, this approach to violence won't suit everyone. "If you think true crime and comedy should never go together," *STM*'s hosts warn, "this might not be the show for you." The podcast *is* for anyone who agrees that "comedy is the only way we are equipped to handle this brand of horror" as human beings. "After all," Pietragallo and Whisman ask, "if you can't make fun of a murderer... who can you make fun of?"

HOSTED BY
James Pietragallo and Jimmie Whisman

GENRE
Crime

FIRST EPISODE
"A Quadruple Murder in Mississippi"
(January 18, 2017)

INFLUENCES
George Carlin, Eddie Murphy, Hunter S. Thompson (Pietragallo); Howard Stern, Bill Burr, Doug Stanhope (Whisman)

WHERE TO LISTEN
Wondery

SEAN'S PICK
"Not Answering the Call of Duty—Foster, Rhode Island" (June 14, 2023)

Twenty
Thousand Hertz

When it comes to working in media, "sound people have a burning desire to contribute creatively and have so many great ideas," says veteran sound designer Dallas Taylor. But whenever Taylor brought up one of his own ideas with the people in charge of the films, television shows, or commercials for which he was hired, the response was always the same: "That's adorable, sound person. Now scoot along and let us visual people work out how the story goes."

So in 2016, fed up with years of second-class treatment and hungry to be taken more seriously as a creative, Taylor and his company, Defacto Sound, launched *Twenty Thousand Hertz*, a first-of-its-kind exploration of the world of sound. It was, in Taylor's words, a "mash-up" of *This American Life*, *Radiolab*, and *99% Invisible*, if each episode revolved around how and what we hear. From the pilot episode—a tantalizingly brief and curious look at Apple's digital assistant, Siri—Taylor and team infused the show with equal parts studied expertise and joie de vivre in an effort to reinvigorate the public's respect for audio art. It was a smashing gambit: Soon, the show was addressing distinct subjects ranging from the acoustics of human umbilical cords to the environmental impacts of noise pollution to the rare condition of misophonia for a global audience of more than 125,000 biweekly listeners.

Few of those, however, knew just what an immense labor of love the podcast was for Taylor. "I went into some pretty big debt and gut churn to make the show," he admits, a process he believes was necessary to keep the show independent from creative interference at a larger network. He also logged massive amounts of personal time in service to its production: "Generally speaking, every episode we make takes about 250 hours, and that's pushed up to 300, 400-plus hours for very short shows," he notes. That includes multiple pitch sessions and outlines, the hiring of external producers, and then sourcing interview subjects to discuss the episode's topic on air. From there, Defacto Sound begins its work designing the soundscapes, each of which is distinct from the next (no small feat across more than 175 episodes). "We work on razor-thin margins," Taylor says, "and we just keep going until it's right."

Resultantly, *Twenty Thousand Hertz* has received a number of industry accolades for its masterful production, including multiple Webby, Ambie, and Adweek awards. But Taylor remains dedicated to reaching audiences far outside the sometimes-insular audiophile community. "Too many people have been like, 'I just don't know about sound.' I'm like, 'Yes, you do!' You don't need to be a chef in order to appreciate or make great food. Sound is not culturally exclusive. It's a human experience."

HOSTED BY
Dallas Taylor

GENRE
Design

FIRST EPISODE
"Voice of Siri"
(October 31, 2016)

INFLUENCES
"This American Life × *Radiolab* ×
99% Invisible × Kid Friendly =
Twenty Thousand Hertz" (Taylor)

WHERE TO LISTEN
Spotify

SEAN'S PICK
"Silence" (January 14, 2019)

Moonface

The first things you hear in _Moonface_, James Kim's unforgettable fiction series, are the footsteps of a man entering a gay sex club. When Kim, a former public radio producer, originally pitched the pilot, it merely ended with its main character, Paul, getting laid. But Spotify, who expressed interest in producing the podcast, wanted Kim to cut the scene entirely. Instead, he doubled down. "Showing gay sex in a positive way was an important part of the show," Kim declares. "I didn't want to back down on that." Ultimately, he made it so that Paul got laid at both the beginning _and_ at the end of episode one, "Moaning." Needless to say, Spotify passed.

A better fate could not have befallen _Moonface_. In the years since Kim took out a $10,000 loan from his hometown bank, Downey Federal Credit Union, to complete it independently, the series has circulated among fellow podcast creators and fans on a whisper network of shared reverence. "I made friends with the loan officer, who didn't really listen to podcasts. I remember when I visited the bank to finalize my last loan payment, the officer said someone told her about the podcast, but she still didn't listen because it wasn't her thing," Kim recalls. Exactly. _Moonface_ is indeed the type of "thing" people hesitate to talk too much about—not because they dislike it but because they are afraid of their precious personal secret becoming someone else's.

Over six short, impressionistic episodes, the podcast tells the story of Paul (soulfully played by Joel Kim Booster), a twentysomething Korean American reckoning with creative and financial stagnation while living with his mom, Gina, a first-generation immigrant voiced with heartrending warmth by Esther Moon. Though his mother speaks only Korean, Paul speaks only English, which has kept him from revealing to her both that he is gay and that he is desperately bored of their Downey, California, home. Instead, he fritters away most evenings at the club with his friends Danny (Remy Ortiz) and Shayla (Mildred Marie Langford) before drifting out for anonymous hookups.

Part drama, part biography (Kim, a queer man, also grew up in Downey with immigrant parents), each episode of _Moonface_ boasts evocative

CREATED BY
James Kim

GENRE
Drama

FIRST EPISODE
"Moaning" (October 9, 2019)

INFLUENCES
Mike Mills, *Firewatch*,
Frank Ocean's *Blonde*

WHERE TO LISTEN
Pandora

SEAN'S PICK
"Breathing" (October 9, 2019)

sound design by Artin Aroutounians and a lush original score by Andrew Eapen of the band Oyster Kids before closing with a contemporary song close to its creator's heart. Kim, who wrote the show with a team of five others, directs it with a piquant melancholy informed by such disparate sources as the films of Mike Mills and the video game *Firewatch*. Given its closeness to his life, he obsessed over every detail. "Artin and I would spend late nights going back and forth on edits for *Moonface*," he says. "I wanted the ruffling of clothes or how someone sat down on a chair to add to the personality of a character."

Such intense commitment to authenticity remains a hallmark of Kim's productions, including his wonderful 2023 follow-up podcast, *You Feeling This?* But as more and more listeners learn of him, they may never again be able to achieve the sense of beguilement that comes with hearing Kim's work cold, unexplained, simply experienced. "I feel like public radio and podcasting don't really take risks," Paul declares in episode three, "Eating." It's the one lie in all of *Moonface*.

Lecture Hall

Getting schooled has rarely been so fun as on *Lecture Hall*, the upside-down history podcast hosted by comedy writer Broti Gupta and actor Dylan Gelula. Each episode takes an absurdist approach to sharing tales of the past, with one host introducing a cultural figure or event—say, the invention of PB&J sandwiches, the architecture of William Faulkner's Rowan Oak, or the life and death of Typhoid Mary—only for the other to lob ridiculous, momentum-ending jokes about it for forty-five minutes. Imagine AP American History as taught by the panel from *Ridiculousness* and you're partly there.

Recorded over Zoom during the COVID-19 lockdown in September 2020, the podcast at first functioned purely as a balm for its intellectually curious yet forcibly sequestered hosts. Though Gupta and Gelula ostensibly research their subjects in advance, both quickly made clear that relaying factual information about their chosen subjects was far less important to them than getting off a few good zingers. As a result, despite their evident reluctance to market the program or distribute it on any service besides their shared Patreon (for a fifteen-dollar monthly subscription, the hosts promise that "one of us will incept your dreams and kiss you on the lips"), *Lecture Hall* quickly emerged as one of the pandemic's most dependable weekly joys.

Then, according to Gupta and Gelula, something unusual happened: "Our listeners straight up became the bosses of our podcast. Instead of having merch we control in any way, our listeners put together a site on our behalf featuring souvenirs they designed with arbitrary quotes from us that don't seem to reflect any sort of fundamental theme of the show (which is . . . learning? We think?)."

The fans, they now confess, became virtually rabid, unpacking every guest appearance and historical detail scattered throughout one-hundred-plus episodes like conspiracy-mongers unpacking the Zapruder film. Lectureheads made sweatshirts emblazoned with "Like a House of Cards: Lecture Hall," a reference to a non sequitur from an early conversation. "Sometimes we take messages from one listener to another listener on air," they say, nearly trembling. "The fans correct our mistakes; mock up images of Jesus chasing Pontius Pilate with a big net for us; create theme music for us that we don't know how to incorporate into the show. We live in fear of what they are capable of."

To appease their wild, growing fan base, Gupta and Gelula have had to get imaginative with their subscription tiers. Anyone willing to give $1,000 a month to support the show's continued existence has their permission to do whatever they want, the hosts boast. "Go nuts. God's not looking."

HOSTED BY
Dylan Gelula and Broti Gupta

GENRE
Education

FIRST EPISODE
"Jim Thorpe/PB&J"
(September 18, 2020)

INFLUENCES
Chopped Junior,
MasterChef Junior (Gelula);
Project Runway: Junior,
Shark Tank Junior (Gupta)

WHERE TO LISTEN
Patreon

SEAN'S PICK
"pinocchio//flat stanley"
(April 13, 2023)

Stuff You Should Know

STUFF YOU SHOULD KNOW

PODCAST

On the website for its industry-leading annual awards, the Ambies, the Podcast Academy writes, "Each year, the Governors of the Podcast Academy will select the winner of that year's Governors Award. This award will be bestowed to an individual, a show, a network, or a company that has contributed in a meaningful way to the growth of the podcasting industry." In 2023, Chuck Bryant and Josh Clark became only the fifth and sixth people to receive this top honor, a sign of just how influential their education podcast, *Stuff You Should Know*, had become since its debut fifteen years earlier (the first four—Marc Maron, Brendan McDonald, Sarah Koenig, and Julie Snyder—also appear in the pantheon).

Clark—a writer for HowStuffWorks who started as *SYSK*'s sole host before Bryant, his colleague at the website, joined three months later—suggests that in the show's nascency, it was impossible to understand just how many people were vibing with the podcast. That may have been in part because, rather than lean on a high-concept hook or dive deeply into one specific topic, the iHeart production tackled just about every phenomenon under the sun: shark attacks, dehydration, fight clubs, junk mail, microexpressions, lucid dreams, Romani culture, kleptomania, sinkholes, and on and on. It was, as advertised, simply a thing about . . . stuff.

There was also the matter of its impossibly short episodes, which offered a barrage of factoids intended to seed the listener with just enough expertise to bring a topic up at the dinner table in five minutes or less. As a result, it wasn't until "we first ventured out into the real world for live appearances," Clark explains, that the scale of his, Bryant, and longtime producer Jeri Rowland's true reach actually began to reveal itself. "We were happily overwhelmed by the response we got."

In reality, despite the somewhat moseying pace and fuzzy sound quality of its early episodes, *SYSK* was blowing up like no educational podcast before or since. "Josh and I were lucky enough to be allowed to simply become better at what we do while doing it," admits Bryant, who became famous with listeners for his myriad mispronunciations and misreadings. Within a couple of years, the pair's conversations had expanded in scope and length (reaching just under an hour, where they have since largely remained) and had begun incorporating a question-and-answer segment for fans as far abroad as India, Australia, and Europe. Soon after came the accolades: first a slew of Webbies and Podcast Awards, then a TV adaptation on the Science Channel, and finally their own categories of Trivial Pursuit and *Jeopardy!* By 2023, Apple had named it the tenth most popular podcast in the United States.

According to both hosts, however, the ultimate proof of *SYSK*'s irreplaceability in the wider history of podcasting came with a Governors Award. "I have thought more and more about our 'legacy' as I've gotten older and especially now, having become a parent. Sometimes I think about people listening to [the podcast] long after I leave the earth and it's both weird and wonderful to ponder," Bryant says. Clark concurs. "I've never made 1,500 of anything," he says humbly. "I'm pretty proud of what we've accomplished."

HOSTED BY
Charles W. "Chuck" Bryant and Josh Clark

GENRE
Education

FIRST EPISODE
"How Grassoline Works" (April 17, 2008)

INFLUENCES
Ira Glass, Click and Clack (Bryant); the Bathroom Readers' Institute, *MAD* magazine, Terry Gross, *1491*, *1493*, Nick Bostrom, Toby Ord, the Future of Humanity Institute, Zachary Crockett, Takashi Kokubo, Bill Evans (Clark)

WHERE TO LISTEN
iHeart

SEAN'S PICK
"Can You Control Your Dreams?" (June 23, 2009)

The Red Nation Podcast

Can a podcast save Mother Earth?

This is the driving question at the heart of *The Red Nation Podcast*, the propulsive audio project of the Red Nation, "a coalition of Indigenous activists, educators, students, and community organizers advocating Native liberation and addressing the marginalization and invisibility of Native struggles within mainstream social justice by foregrounding the targeted destruction and violence toward Native life and land." Launched by Red Media, the nonprofit media arm of the Red Nation, on Indigenous Peoples' Day 2019, the show is grounded by the twin concepts of decolonization and Land Back—not only with regard to the original peoples of the so-called United States but also on behalf of all peoples living under the conditions of settler colonialism across the planet.

As led by hosts Jen Marley, a scholar of queer Indigenous studies at the University of New Mexico, and Nick Estes, an assistant professor in American Indian studies at the University of Minnesota and the lead editor of Red Media, each episode of *TRNP* is vigorous, expansive, and staunchly revolutionary. Individual conversations with guests like Tohono / Akimel O'odham campaigner Napoleon Marietta, Tlingit/Haida antiwar activist Phoenix Johnson, and Kānaka Maoli land defender Shelley Muneoka often touch on hundreds of years of history and politics in the span of about an hour. "We interviewed Quechua medical doctor Vivi Camacho at a café in La Paz, Bolivia," Estes, whose recordings of events and teach-ins from within Indigenous movement spaces and communities served as the base materials for the podcast, offers by way of example. "She told us the story of how she lived and worked. Capitalism is killing in the Global South of hunger and killing in the Global North of sadness."

Estes and Marley joined forces soon after the latter's 2017 arrest for the successful abolition of the Entrada, a reenactment of the Spanish conquistador Don Diego de Vargas's racist and genocidal reconquest of what is today known as Santa Fe, New Mexico. Marley says that the

HOSTED BY
Nick Estes, Jen Marley,
Elena Ortiz, and Melanie Yazzie

GENRE
Education

FIRST EPISODE
"What Is Wild? Manoonim (Wild Rice) Harvesting
w/ Courtney & Kathy" (October 28, 2019)

INFLUENCES
"Bad-ass Native women" (Yazzie)

WHERE TO LISTEN
The Red Nation

SEAN'S PICK
"Native Veterans against War w/ Phoenix
Johnson" (March 9, 2020)

Red Nation cadre, made up of mostly Native women, agreed that co-hosting with Estes would help both to combat the "bro-dominated" reputation of podcasting and to better center the individuals and issues raised on the podcast, given Marley's increasingly public profile. Once paired, the hosts vowed to adhere to the same "journalistic principles" that gird their off-mic scholarship. "In the early days when Nick and I started recording together, we spent a lot of time reading and researching before each episode," Marley recalls. "We reviewed new books and interviewed authors, and we spent time learning about current events and trying to sharpen our analysis."

Indeed, from their first full release—an exploration of the centrality of manoomin (wild rice) in Anishinaabeg culture and prophecy led by harvesters Courtney Calia and Kathy Smith—knowledge has been the soil from which the podcast attempts to cultivate an expanded public consciousness. Media and its role in the continued genocide of First Nations peoples are also key concerns: The podcast's feed is shared by *Red Power Hour*, an ongoing dialogue between hosts Elena Ortiz and Melanie Yazzie on pop-cultural texts like Martin Scorsese's *Killers of the Flower Moon* and Denis Villeneuve's *Dune*. As a whole, the feed now serves as an archive for hundreds of hours of Native history, culture, and expression—all of which, notes *East Is a Podcast* host Sina Rahmani, serve to defy the campaign of terror waged on Indigenous people and their BIPOC comrades for generations. In an interview with theologist Cornel West, Estes says, "The larger project of decolonization begins with your mind, your spirit, your heart." If you wish to join him, listening to *The Red Nation Podcast* is a good first step.

Hello from the Magic Tavern

J. R. R. Tolkien. C. S. Lewis. George R. R. Martin. These are just a few of the renowned fantasy authors whose collected works look like nothing so much as child's play next to *Hello from the Magic Tavern*.

I'm being glib, of course, but it is true that within this delightful improv podcast exists a fictional universe as expansively imagined as any created by those writers, if perhaps just a touch less originally. That's because the characters, mythologies, and other elements of *HFTMT*'s lore all borrow consciously from *The Lord of the Rings* and *Game of Thrones* in service of creating hour-long improvisational scenes. Where Lewis had Narnia and the Pevensies, *HFTMT* has the magical land of Foon and Arnie Niekamp, a human who (in lieu of an enchanted wardrobe) fell through a portal behind a Burger King and into the Vermilion Minotaur tavern. It is from there, primarily, that Niekamp—in real life, the show's co-founder and a veteran improviser—riffs week in and week out on the fantastical comings and goings in Foon with Chunt, a shape-shifting badger voiced by Adal Rifai; Usidore the Blue, a Gandalfian wizard voiced by Matt Young; and a rotating cast of creatures, mages, and villains all voiced by comedy heavyweights like Jason Mantzoukas, Mary Holland, and Joel Kim Booster.

Since the podcast launched on Earwolf in 2015 (it has since moved to Patreon), the mythos of Foon has grown vastly; that it continues to feel real for fans of both fantasy and comedy speaks entirely to the chemistry and intelligence between Niekamp, Rifai, and Young. Each episode carries forward the story of Arnie and crew's battle with the so-called Dark Lord, and their collective ability to recall the details of previous encounters with his myriad minions while generating a raft of one-liners, puns, and inside jokes—all while remaining in character—is astonishing to behold. In fact, as Niekamp reveals to me, such high-level improv talent sometimes leaves those joining the show for only an episode or two a little hesitant. "Sometimes our guests are nervous about 'breaking' the show in some way," he says. "But breaking the show is sort of the point, and the fun is for us all

Fantasy

to collectively make some kind of sense out of the nonsense together. It's better to break the show than to be too safe or precious about it."

Still, after years of world-building, Niekamp knows that the continuity of the universe in *Hello from the Magic Tavern* means a lot to a lot of people these days. In addition to featuring on multiple best-of lists by NPR, *The A.V. Club*, and *The Guardian*, among others, the series has secured many famous fans. Niekamp identifies *Crazy Ex-Girlfriend* star Rachel Bloom in that cohort because she agreed to appear as a tree wench in season three. "She told me that she'd discovered the show by googling 'Funny podcasts?' and we came up," he says. "Thank god she added that question mark at the end, otherwise we might not have been in the search results."

HOSTED BY
Arnie Niekamp,
Adal Rifai, and Matt Young

GENRE
Fantasy

FIRST EPISODE
"Hello from the Magic
Tavern" (March 9, 2015)

INFLUENCES
"If an audio drama was
more like a chat show,
would it be easier to pay
attention?" (Niekamp)

WHERE TO LISTEN
Patreon

SEAN'S PICK
"The Singing Sword"
(May 23, 2016)

Add to Cart

How we each spend our one short life—and *what* we spend during it—is the topic every week on SuChin Pak and Kulap Vilaysack's *Add to Cart*, a genre-breaking rumination on the tenets of emotionally healthy consumerism. Ostensibly, this podcast from Lemonada is about goods: the cosmetics, furniture, decor, technology, media, and food and drink we buy into (both literally and metaphorically what we "add to cart"), as well as what we develop the courage to leave in the dust forever (or "remove from cart").

Not infrequently, such talk expands into something altogether more existential about how, as citizens of capitalism, hoarding resources—wealth, goods, energy, happiness—can serve as both a balm and a torment, profoundly satisfying and anxiety-inducing—and how letting go of everything we once found important can have the same effect.

Yet it is far removed from the dry, heady advice often doled out by other podcasts in the interrelated realms of fashion, beauty, and finance. "The best episodes we have are those that swing from obsessing over toothbrushes to digging into something we're struggling with in our lives," Pak, a former correspondent for MTV News, says in a statement. Long-term listeners, dubbed Carters, know that Pak represents the more reticent and cautious shopper: She tracks every purchase in her head, like expensive sparkling waters she cuts with regular water to justify their cost, and worries about the ramifications of doing away with something on the off chance she might use it again, like an electronic Kegel exercise machine. Revealing such personal habits can be quite exposing, she admits: "I've spent my entire career very carefully guarding myself from emotion when I'm working. This experience is almost solely tapping into emotion. So there were many times, maybe even the entire first year, where I would call Ku and have her talk me into not cutting out vulnerable moments."

"Auntie KuKu," by contrast, refers to herself as a "buy first, not think about it later" person. She is foremost an advocate for any choices made in the interest of self-care, particularly if they are Christmas-themed. For Vilaysack, producing a podcast concretely committed to bettering its listeners' lives is one such choice. "It's been soul fulfilling to have a platform to fully be ourselves as Asian American mothers in our forties with serious shopping issues," she admits. But Vilaysack is also a natural clown, having cut her broadcasting chops as the longtime host (with Howard Kremer) of *Who Charted?* and the creator of *Bajillion Dollar Propertie$*. When she and Pak conduct interviews, Vilaysack announces their guests—regardless of whether they're celebrities like Jada Pinkett Smith and Ricki Lake, life-style experts like Jonathan Van Ness and Tabitha Brown, or the hosts' own husbands, Mike Bender and Scott Aukerman—with the pomp of a carnival barker against the roll of a drum. "My goal always is to entertain," she says. "Sure, sure, sure, I have benefited greatly from the high-level tips I get and my skin looks outstanding . . . but the item is a conversation starter and a way to get to know each other."

In fact, there is such humor and warmth between the hosts ("SuChin was a friend before [the podcast], but has become much more than a friend to me since, she's a beloved family member," Vilaysack clarifies) that it can be hard to remember that *Add to Cart* is a product in and of itself. If Vilaysack's and Pak's own idiosyncratic choices prove anything, it is that adding something to your own cart may require removing something else: In this case, perhaps another podcast already in rotation or the opportunity to catch up with new music. Personally, at least, that choice seems like a no-brainer. I give it a five-star review.

HOSTED BY
SuChin Pak and Kulap Vilaysack

GENRE
Fashion and Beauty

FIRST EPISODE
"Salvaging Christmas with Poise (Pads), a Kegel Goose, and a Majestic Water Buffalo" (November 17, 2020)

INFLUENCES
DailyCandy (Pak); SuChin Pak, *Who Charted?* (Vilaysack)

WHERE TO LISTEN
Lemonada

SEAN'S PICK
"Intermittent Fasting Friends with Hayes Davenport and Sean Clements" (August 2, 2022)

Throwing Fits

Here is how loyal the Throw Gang is:

On an early episode of *Throwing Fits*, host James Harris randomly (and recklessly, he now concedes) blurted out that he and co-host Lawrence Schlossman should throw a barbecue in the park. Anyone could attend, so long as they could make it to New York by July 17, 2021. But when Harris and Schlossman arrived to "the grills by Driggs Ave." with some doughnuts, shit was already popping the fuck off. "Someone took a red-eye from Alaska and slept for a few predawn hours on a park picnic table to get us dibs on a grill; a friend worked with a chef from Albany to tap into a wholesale supplier, and together they whipped up a feast; a pizzeria owner pulled up with a ton of pies and handed them over the fence." It was, in Harris's words, "chaotic and beautiful and probably illegal"—in other words, "kinda like the podcast itself."

Throwing Fits has been around, at least in its current form, since January 2020, when "Jimmy" and "Larry" resurrected it from the ashes of . . . well, another podcast endeavor that, to protect the sensitivities of the Throw Gang, "shall not be named." Schlossman, who first made waves as the author of the blog *Sartorially Inclined*, says that when they "involuntarily manslaughtered" their previous show and "the totality of our intellectual property" with "some good ol' fashion hot mic riffing" (the details of which are transparently explained in the pilot episode), "we felt deep down in our plums that returning to our roots and breaking back out on our own was the only path forward."

The resulting effort was, ostensibly, a listener-supported fashion interview podcast, complete with regular "Fit Checks" that deep-dived into every guest's outfit. The first, with Vampire Weekend's Ezra Koenig (Harris: "the former prince of prep, the alpha dog of anime, the guitar guru, the champion of chill vibes!"), consisted of a limited-edition Mordechai Rubinstein fleece, Stone Island joggers, a Sunnei jacket purchased at 90 percent off, Henrik Vibskov socks, a Noah tote, and a long-sleeved soccer-patterned Peace Frogs shirt, all of which inspired a thirty-minute detour into Big Dogs couture and the merits of corduroy ("the poor man's velvet"). It

HOSTED BY
James Harris and
Lawrence Schlossman

GENRE
Fashion and Beauty

FIRST EPISODE
"Failing Upwards Is Now Throwing
Fits or: Two Grown Dirtbags
Fumble the Bag at the 1 Yard Line"
(January 16, 2020)

INFLUENCES
"My mom and dad, Katt Williams
circa 2006, pushing back against
the American emasculation of the
Asian male" (Harris); "Howard Stern,
Cum Town, my college fraternity
LISTSERV" (Schlossman)

WHERE TO LISTEN
Patreon

SEAN'S PICK
"If You Know Me You Know Me Pt. I
with Naomi Fry" (March 17, 2020)

was also, unsubtly, a declaration of these Zyn-loving self-professed dirtbags' intention to grill every fashionable celebrity they could with questions more impertinent than most would risk. How much, pray tell, does Alison Roman make in a year? (None of your business.) What, they might ask, does Mia Khalifa think of the internet's obsession with Sydney Sweeney's buxomness? ("Stolen valor.") And how, if you please, does Diplo combat mad diarrhea on tour? (By washing his toothpaste in local water.)

With this gambit, the show took Reddit, Instagram, and Discord by storm, earning its hosts reputations outside New York as caustic but accurate arbiters of menswear writ large. Soon they were lending brand authority to a number of fine-taste collabs on lines with Clarks and MR PORTER, and receiving glowing write-ups from *Esquire*, *GQ*, and Naomi Fry, their "fairy podmother" at the *New Yorker*. Even so, the strongest indicator that things were coming together came from the Throw Gang. Whenever episodes published (for free on Tuesdays and via Patreon on Thursdays), social media lit up with memes about Harris and Schlossman's favorite "jawnz" (Très Bien belts, Anonymous Ism socks, BRADY underwear "on the cock and balls"). Then there was the impromptu barbecue. "I hesitate to use the ultracommodified and hollow concept of community," Harris says, "but I don't know how else to explain what happened on July 17th." Honestly, neither can I—but you have to admit it sounds Gucci as hell.

The Thrilling Adventure Hour

Acker & Blacker Present... THE THRILLING ADVENTURE HOUR

Here's the long and short of it: In March 2005, writers Ben Acker and Ben Blacker began running a staged comedy show "in the spirit of old-timey radio" at M Bar, Los Angeles's famed alternative-comedy hub. Then called *The Thrilling Adventure and Supernatural Suspense Hour*, the show featured a rotating cast of improv-trained actors—the WorkJuice Players—like Marc Evan Jackson, Paul F. Tompkins, Busy Philipps, and Annie Savage playing the kinds of characters once found only on the Mutual Broadcasting System: Sparks Nevada (Jackson), a Buck Rogers–type Martian marshal with a trusty extraterrestrial sidekick (Mark Gagliardi); Frank (Tompkins) and Sadie Doyle (Paget Brewster), hard-drinking paranormal experts pitched one notch above Dashiell Hammett's Nick and Nora Charles; and Jefferson Reid, Ace American (Nathan Fillion), a Marvel-esque anti-Nazi supersoldier.

LA Weekly described the show as "comedy theater for geeks." A contributor to what was then *The Huffington Post* called it "tongue and cheek [*sic*]" and "contagious." Soon, audiences were cramming into M Bar, forcing Acker, Blacker, and director Aaron Ginsburg to look into larger rooms that might allow them to record some performances. So in 2010, renamed and ready to level up, *The Thrilling Adventure Hour* moved to Largo at the Coronet "in Hollywood, Los Angeles, California, America"—and a classic comedy podcast was born.

Acker, it should be said, had reservations about the whole thing. "*I don't think we can do it*," he recalls clammily. "It's one thing to have the actors come out and get direct claps and laughs from the audience. But taking what they do and giving it to the whole world?!" But Blacker, having started his solo podcast, *The Writers Panel*, to some success mere months earlier, tried to reassure him. Ultimately, it was Chris Hardwick (whose podcast, *Nerdist*, had recently made waves of its own) who settled their differences. After taking on *The Writers Panel*, Hardwick offered their new venture a distribution home with his company, Nerdist Industries. Nerdist released the first episode of the podcast, "Hell Is the Loneliest Number," in January 2011.

The Thrilling Adventure Hour worked on several levels at once. Unlike most scripted podcasts, which are recorded in-studio, it was performed live with actors using primarily their voices (some began wearing costumes, but everyone remained on book during recordings). As both an affectionate, scholarly homage to vintage audio programming and a searing satire of its familiar canned effects and overpitched dramatic arcs (such as the perpetually unresolved love triangle between Sparks Nevada, Croach the Tracker, and the Red Plains Rider), it managed to have its cake and eat it too. It remained mercifully short, with most episodes barely breaking half an hour. And most importantly, the majority of its core cast stuck with the show as it transitioned to downloadable content.

Blacker insists on this final point as the reason *TAH* stayed so popular with listeners despite jumps first off Nerdist to Forever Dog in 2018, and then again to Patreon. Regardless of whether they listen

CREATED BY
Ben Acker and Ben Blacker

GENRE
Fiction

FIRST EPISODE
"Hell Is the Loneliest Number"
(January 9, 2011)

INFLUENCES
Never Not Funny, the Second City, *The Kids in the Hall*, *Army of Darkness*

WHERE TO LISTEN
Patreon

SEAN'S PICK
"Sparks Nevada, Marshal on Mars, 'Do the Fight Thing'"
(February 6, 2012)

from Canada, Italy, or Australia, fans have come to consider *TAH*'s regulars podcast superstars. "Everyone shares a sensibility," Blacker says. "We never told everyone how to dress or where to stand or things like that—they started putting that all together themselves because they knew what this could be, maybe even before we did." Still, despite an increasingly fervent cult of international followers, both Blacker and Acker say there are still higher goals to reach. Acker explains that his one true goal besides casting Bill Murray was to impress Blacker. "It's that Second City philosophy that you should make your scene partner look good." Blacker chimes back: "We were always ever writing the show that we wanted to see. We were just lucky that other people found it and wanted to see it, too."

Black Men Can't Jump [in Hollywood]

If not for Martin Lawrence, the finest film-criticism podcast of its generation might never have come into existence.

It started with an argument between James III and Jonathan Braylock, two television writers and improvisers from the Upright Citizens Brigade, on Facebook: Why didn't Lawrence's performance in the 1999 cop comedy *Blue Streak* turn him into the next big thing in Hollywood? The chat got heated fast, with Braylock name-dropping *Bad Boys* as proof that Lawrence already *was* a megastar. Suddenly the comments section felt a little too small for this kind of conversation. Then an idea started to emerge . . .

On their website, James, Braylock, and fellow host Jerah Milligan describe this as the moment when their show, *Black Men Can't Jump [in Hollywood]*, was "forged." At the time, Braylock "was on a sketch team in New York with my friend Nic Rad, who had previously mentioned that he was interested in producing podcasts." Inspired, Braylock remembers, he reached out to Rad, who was in the process of developing programming for Headgum. In the end, all it took was a sample episode and Rad's endorsement to secure *BMCJIH* a home at the network founded by Jake Hurwitz and Amir Blumenfeld.

The podcast launched on July 26, 2015, with a quick explainer episode: The goal of the show, its hosts announced, was to review Hollywood movies starring Black men and analyze whether those movies helped or hurt the cause of getting more Black men into leading roles. At each episode's end, they would all vote, using a "Black fist" to indicate that, yes, the film in question helped the cause; a "white palm," indicating neither help nor harm done; or nothing at all, symbolizing a failure to do the right thing.

It took four episodes before the team got around to critiquing *Blue Streak*, with detours to discuss *Beverly Hills Cop* and *Barbershop*. This was an important strategy, because doing so allowed audiences to adjust to the men's ferociously funny rat-a-tat patter while also proving that the larger idea behind the podcast was a trenchant and necessary one. Listen today via their new network, Forever Dog—particularly to their anger at Sean Patrick Thomas's underuse in *Barbershop* and their belief that co-star Michael Ealy is the film's nuanced beating heart—and you can hear the beginnings of the kind of protective populism that they would come to represent for many cinephiles over the next ten years.

Not that every early idea worked. Braylock's insistence on comparing each movie with Will Smith's *Hancock*, for instance, was deemed an utter mistake. Milligan also nods to an oddball segment from that era called "The Swirl," the point of which "was to show how often Black male leads were not made the love interest if there was a white woman co-lead," he explains. More often than not, however, Milligan became so frustrated by how rarely stars like Eddie Murphy were allowed to appear in intimate scenes with the likes of,

say, the "milky" Denise Richards that he couldn't keep the segment on track.

Needless to say, "The Swirl" was swiftly dropped as the cohort developed more studied opinions on mainstream cinema. Milligan provides this example: "I quickly learned as I progressed in Hollywood on my own journey that I need to give the Black directors/writers some grace, as getting a film made with Black leads is incredibly hard to do. So the fact that they got the film made is a big win." Prophetically, roundtables about movies that fit that bill—such as Gina Prince-Bythewood's *Love & Basketball*, with guest Phoebe Robinson, and *Judas and the Black Messiah*, with guest Mamoudou N'Diaye—have become essential companion pieces as the podcast has grown in stature. And to think we might have none of it without one Martin Fitzgerald Lawrence.

HOSTED BY
James III, Jonathan Braylock,
and Jerah Milligan

GENRE
Film

FIRST EPISODE
"Inaugural Episode" (July 26, 2015)

INFLUENCES
*"How Did This Get Made?,
Blank Check with Griffin & David"*
(Braylock)

WHERE TO LISTEN
RedCircle

SEAN'S PICK
"Blue Streak" (August 21, 2015)

How Did This Get Made?

The greatest misnomer in audio surely belongs to Earwolf's flagship movie-discussion podcast, *How Did This Get Made?* While the show advertises itself as attempting to "make sense of the movies that don't make sense," hosts Jason Mantzoukas, June Diane Raphael, and Paul Scheer spend far more time joking about how broken the world's worst films are than actually investigating how they got broken in the first place. Sure, some guests try to understand why the motion picture they were forced to watch prerecording got greenlit, à la Michael Showalter and *Gymkata*, but by and large, these mile-a-minute conversations are given over to Mantzoukas's and Scheer's raucous declarations of shock at just how *literally* unwatchable something like *From Justin to Kelly* is (with Raphael more often a voice of patience and composure).

Scheer—a dedicated cinephile who also co-hosts the more positive (and ruly) *Unspooled* with critic Amy Nicholson—tells me that he and his teammates have plenty of good reasons to avoid actually answering the titular question. "We'd love to have fun gossiping about [a] movie," he says. "But we learned it's not easy to do in front of a microphone; you have relationships and experiences with the cast and crew."

Scheer recalls inviting actor Jack O'Halloran to spill the goods on his experience playing Kryptonian villain Non in a live episode dedicated to the widely panned *Superman II*—and spill O'Halloran did. "It was like the Boston Tea Party on that Largo stage," he describes. "[O'Halloran's] stories were so eye-popping that when we walked offstage, our producer was like, '*We can't air any of that. Jack will be sued for libel.*'" Ultimately, they were forced to chop the episode to bits before releasing it to protect O'Halloran from himself: "As much as it pains me to say it, no one will ever hear the full interview."

On another occasion, Vanilla Ice agreed to discuss his feature acting debut, *Cool as Ice*, not knowing that the 1991 teen musical was about to be completely bodychecked by Scheer, Mantzoukas, Raphael, and guest

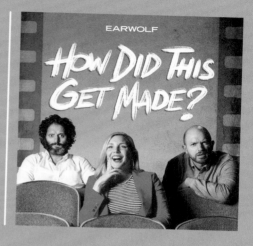

HOSTED BY
Jason Mantzoukas,
June Diane Raphael, and Paul Scheer

GENRE
Film

FIRST EPISODE
"Burlesque" (December 21, 2010)

INFLUENCES
"Dinner with friends. The actual thing,
not the Jon Favreau show." (Scheer)

WHERE TO LISTEN
Earwolf

SEAN'S PICK
"Geostorm: LIVE!" (April 12, 2018)

Brian Huskey. Here's Scheer again: "If we have a guest in a movie we have talked about, we don't want to make them feel bad . . . It's like having someone come on and publicly shit-talk their family." But *Cool as Ice* was notoriously bad, having so drastically underperformed at the box office and with critics to the point that director David Kellogg disowned the film altogether. So Scheer and the others figured that Ice "would be down" to lean into a study of its many peculiarities and peccadilloes, such as the scene where Ice races a horse on a motorcycle. "We set it up, we call out how ridiculous this opening is, but he's not on the same page. He thinks it's 'dope.'" They were left with no choice but to switch gears and turn the episode, number 30, into a full-blown Vanilla Ice career retrospective.

If the ever-increasing scope of *HDTGM*'s international tours and global adaptations is any barometer, such misfires have done nothing to dampen the people of Earth's fervor for episodes since the first premiered in 2010. Nor has Mantzoukas yelling "What's up, jerks?" at virtually every live recording kept august bodies like the Ambies and Webbies from naming it one of the best comedy and TV and film podcasts of the last fifteen years. As for Scheer, he remains in no rush to figure out how legendarily terrible works like *Hudson Hawk* and *Glitter* got made, so long as he, Mantzoukas, and Raphael get to keep talking about them with guests such as Seth Rogen, Jessica St. Clair, and Paul F. Tompkins. After all, he admits, "the answer, most of the time, isn't that scandalous."

On Cinema
at the Cinema

Around 2011, actor-director-musician Tim Heidecker (of the comedy duo Tim & Eric) and Gregg Turkington, the polymath best known for his leeeeegendary sleazebag alter ego, Neil Hamburger, were shooting Rick Alverson's *The Comedy* when they got to talking about an irritating new trend. As Heidecker remembers it, "We were lamenting about the tsunami of podcasts, where comedians would blather on about nothing, and it seemed very self-absorbed and useless to us." Their reaction was to create their own show, "just another voice in the endless deep well of pointless content being dumped online for free."

So began *On Cinema at the Cinema*, the podcast that launched an unlikely media empire that today encompasses a feature film (*Mister America*), a five-hour special (*The Trial*), a spin-off series (*Decker*), and more than a dozen seasons of television. Ostensibly a movie-review program featuring Heidecker as a distractable, highly combustible version of himself and Turkington as Tim's haughty "special guest," *OCATC* was primarily an excuse for the former to prod the latter into "droning on about nothing," like *Siskel & Ebert* hosted by an imperious video store clerk. By design, it was boring, vanilla, a slog; early episodes, Heidecker recounts, were recorded on an iPhone's Voice Memos app. Even some fans of Hamburger or Heidecker's influential Adult Swim series *Tim and Eric Awesome Show, Great Job!* were baffled, wondering if what they were watching was a sincere, if lousy, attempt to get into film analysis. This greatly amuses Heidecker. "There was a real special joy in making something so quickly and thoughtlessly," he says.

The metatextual world that Heidecker and Turkington created, however, continued to metastasize. Barely a year after launching, *On Cinema* released a webseries adaptation that situated the hosts in their first of several movie theater sets and incorporated early iterations of what would become their signature visual gags: Tim's ever-changing hairdo and volatile outbursts, Gregg's collection of vintage Hollywood hats. Guests, also playing distorted versions of themselves, soon entered the fray: Joe Estevez, the brother of Martin Sheen; Ayaka Ohwaki as Heidecker's on-again, off-again lover; Mark Proksch as a browbeaten celebrity impressionist. To those watching, it soon became clear that the podcast was no longer the "quick and thoughtless" nothingburger it had been designed to be. Instead, it was to serve as the urtext for a complex new ecosystem of droll multinarrative comedies.

The never-ending growth of the On Cinemaverse surprised Heidecker too. "It was all so natural and organic. I don't think there was an 'aha' moment where we all figured out what we were doing," he admits. But that has not stopped him and Turkington; for more than a decade now, they have continued to write and release new seasons, specials, and paid bonus content in character. Astonishingly, the Tim and Gregg characters have only become more endearing over the years, having endured tragedy after tragedy together, such as Proksch's coma and Heidecker's accidental (?) murder of twenty teenagers via Luther San's poison vapes at the Electric Sun Desert Music Festival. Fans of the show know to greet each other with "Hey, guys!" in homage to Turkington, and many get Heidecker's face, with its myriad changes from season to season, tattooed on their bodies. Trying to understand this massive world without listening to the podcast first would be a fool's errand. Just be sure not to miss it—it's a true five-bagger.

HOSTED BY
Tim Heidecker and
Gregg Turkington

GENRE
Film

FIRST EPISODE
"Ghostbusters"
(September 20, 2011)

INFLUENCES
Albert Brooks, Andy
Kaufman, David Letterman
(Heidecker); "Albert Brooks,
Phil Hendrie, *National
Lampoon Sunday Newspaper
Parody* (an absolute master-
class in world-building!)"
(Turkington)

WHERE TO LISTEN
HEI Network

SEAN'S PICK
"Star Trek II: The
Wrath of Khan"
(November 21, 2011)

The Flop House

If first impressions were enough to kill podcasts, *The Flop House* might never have survived. Listen back to that first episode—a savage deconstruction of the 2005 AWOL AI thriller *Stealth*—and your ears might bleed. Not only is the audio unlistenable (or, rather, unhearable, with Dan McCoy, Stuart Wellington, and original co-host Simon Fisher chatting in what sounds like an underground bunker), but it also comes across as an artifact very much of its time, replete with both overeager contrarianism and a smattering of misogynistic commentary about women movie stars.

Yet if ever there were a podcast that rewarded listeners' patience, this would be it. As one of the longest-running film podcasts in the medium's history, *The Flop House* has spent its more than a decade and a half on the internet shape-shifting into arguably the most influential entity in "bad movie" discourse, as well as capturing its hosts' slow but immense intellectual and social growth. Along with Fisher's successor, Elliott Kalan, McCoy and Wellington have whittled away at the qualities that constitute a "good-bad movie," a "bad-bad movie," or a "movie you kinda liked" in conversation after conversation, using cult classics (*The Wicker Man*), blockbuster hits (*xXx: Return of Xander Cage*), and forgotten disasters (*Zarkorr! The Invader*) alike as their case studies.

In so doing, the Peaches—so named for the Rockford Peaches in *A League of Their Own*—evolved into politically conscious civilian scholars with a shared, heightened awareness of the power of depictions both cinematic and auditory. According to Kalan, this was no accident. While "a bad movie is a thing you can step back from and laugh at derisively," he theorizes, "a bad podcast is more intimate—like the experience of hanging

out with people you don't like." Having acknowledged that "many listeners feel that way about *our* show," the hosts set out to attract far fewer edgelords and far more serious film lovers with their perspectives on supposed flops. That shift toward conversations fueled by enthusiasm, affection, and allyship, Kalan says, has helped drive the team's outrageous longevity: "We've been around long enough that I think we feel we owe it to our fans to put out a fun, enjoyable show."

Listeners have responded by anointing the Peaches as respected thought leaders in film culture, even though they still remain somewhat peripheral to "establishment showbiz," as McCoy puts it. "For most of the run of *The Flop House* I've been working as a bartender in New York," says Wellington, who also co-owns Brooklyn's Hinterlands Bar. "These days, it's a weekly occurrence to have fans show up to my bar hoping to say hi and talk movies."

As for whether any of those fans enjoy *The Flop House* as ironically as the Peaches like, say, *Tango & Cash*, McCoy insists such a thing is impossible. The novelty of a great-bad movie, he jokes, "is almost like taking a hallucinogenic drug." But a "good-bad podcast?" That, says McCoy, "would just be like listening to a boring conversation, and I have enough of those in my life already."

HOSTED BY
Elliott Kalan, Dan McCoy, and Stuart Wellington

GENRE
Film

FIRST EPISODE
"Stealth"
(September 6, 2007)

INFLUENCES
Mystery Science Theater 3000, MAD magazine (Kalan); *Mystery Science Theater 3000, Jordan, Jesse, Go!* (McCoy); "Drinking" (Wellington)

WHERE TO LISTEN
Maximum Fun

SEAN'S PICK
"Tango & Cash" (April 21, 2012)

You Must Remember This

To describe historian Karina Longworth's epic cultural project, *You Must Remember This*, as a film podcast would be like calling Everest a tall mountain. Since 2014, Longworth has committed countless hours to investigating "the secret and/or forgotten histories of Hollywood's first century," turning her laser focus on an underexplored cultural figure for increments of forty-five minutes or so each week. Howard Hughes, Judy Garland, Frank Sinatra—each has come under Longworth's perceptive microscope, sometimes for years at a time (especially in the case of Hughes, on whom Longworth centered both a miniseries, "The Many Loves of Howard Hughes," and a book-length study, *Seduction: Sex, Lies, and Stardom in Howard Hughes's Hollywood*).

But while her gaze often lingers upon the cinema of her subjects, Longworth has become renowned for entwining their accomplishments in music, vaudeville, theater, and comedy, among other art forms, into her analyses. No other film podcast touches so many facets of pop culture so frequently, or so deftly. This is no accident: Trained as a critic, with a master's degree in cinema studies from New York University, Longworth founded the podcast in an environment then unsuited to her multipronged approach. "When I started *You Must Remember This* in 2014," she says over email, "I had never heard a podcast that was quite like what I wanted to do, so I didn't really have any direct inspirations."

Where other shows studied the impact of individual movies or industry stars, Longworth envisioned a program that helixed the accomplishments of one figure or film into American history writ large, as she told *New York* magazine's Nicholas Quah in 2020. For a deep diver such as herself, that required some flexibility: "The process of writing and researching differs from episode to episode," she says. "Generally, I just try to read every source I can. I take notes, then turn the notes into sentences. Eventually, it becomes an essay of eight thousand to one hundred thousand words, with notes interwoven throughout about movies or other audio clips that I want inserted."

With the help of an editor, these raw materials eventually become a bricolage of archival testimonials, character performances by actors like Noah Segan (who portrayed Hughes, among many others) and Maggie Siff (for ten episodes, the voice of the unjustly sidelined filmmaker Polly Platt), and Longworth's own hypnotic, erudite narration. The result, whether it lasts for one episode or a season's worth, is as stimulating aurally as it is intellectually. No surprise, then, that *You Must Remember This* has earned its host what Quah calls "cult status" among audiences and podcasters alike. Join her, won't you?

HOSTED BY
Karina Longworth

GENRE
Film

FIRST EPISODE
"The Hard Hollywood Life of Kim Novak" (April 1, 2014)

INFLUENCES
N/A

WHERE TO LISTEN
Spotify

SEAN'S PICK
"It Wasn't Sexism, Then" (May 25, 2020)

Doughboys

In the legacy of *Diner*, *Reservoir Dogs*, and *Seinfeld*, Mike Mitchell and Nick Wiger offer the kind of entertainment best suited to people who don't mind hearing their friends chewing in old-timey leather booths. *Doughboys* is a rare hybrid of food and comedy podcasting, a sincere celebration of the unsung power of chain restaurants told mostly through sidelong observations and dueling insults. It isn't that Mitch (a.k.a. Spoonman) and Wiges (a.k.a. Burger Boy) aren't truly friends off mic (on the contrary, they're peas in a pod)—it's more that both simply realize how funny it can be to make merciless fun of someone whose mouth is full of french fries.

"It's absurdist, I think, the way that we go on tangents or will just tell a completely made-up anecdote or just run a bit into the ground over not just an episode but years. We have a tendency to live with the absurd," Wiger says over Zoom in an attempt to explain just what has made *Doughboys* the crossover hit it is. He's not wrong: The banter between the two, who started out as comedy writer-performers for (in Wiger's case) Funny or Die and (in Mitchell's case) the Birthday Boys sketch group, bears much in common with that of Conan O'Brien and Andy Richter, the preeminent absurdist duo of the late 1990s (when both *Doughboys* hosts were impressionable teenagers). "We try to get silly," Mitchell agrees, "but I don't think we're *actively* thinking about it."

That gels too. Though every episode opens with Wiger reading a pre-written bit of fast food–centric poetry (From the intro to episode 120, "HomeTown Buffet with Toni Charline": "6939 AD—that's the distant year the Westinghouse Time Capsule is scheduled to be unearthed and opened . . ."), the podcast is driven primarily by rambunctious, free-flowing conversations about the variable joys of eating with Mitch and Wiges's producers, Emma Erdbrink and (formerly) Yusong Liu; friends from the Los Angeles sketch and improv scenes, including comedians like Jon Gabrus, Michael "Mookie" Blaiklock, Alana "the Knife" Johnston, and Evan Susser; and people like wrestler Colt Cabana, food writer Farley Elliott, and whatever Bug Mane is. The only condition for entry is that each guest be as willing as the hosts to let listeners pay for their meals. The resultant listening experience is a grand vicarious delight, an invitation to fuck around in the McDonald's ball pit with two guys playing "chubby bunny" with chicken nuggets for five bucks a month.

For some of us, that's too good an offer to pass up. As of 2024, more than twelve thousand people were members of the Golden Plate Club, a Patreon subscription tier that offers ad-free access to the show along with a bonus weekly recording known as *Doughboys Double*. That excludes many who listen for free via Headgum, *Doughboys*' distributor since 2018, as well as attendees of any of the live events enumerated on the show's expansive fan-run wiki. Though their partnership is nearly a decade deep, Spoonman and Burger Boy still sound a little stunned by the scale of it all, particularly considering that their Patreon account—which regularly cracks the list of the top twenty creators in the world—is known among other podcasters as a model for how to succeed on one's own terms.

"The night we launched the Patreon, Nick and I went out for caviar and cigars," Mitchell laughs. They returned to find the pod besieged with subscriptions. That moment, Wiger says, remains among the most transformative of their lives. "It went from 'This is a thing where we go out of pocket for fast food and gas, but have fun doing it' to 'Wait, this can pay our bills,'" he says. "If it hadn't, I don't think we'd still be doing the show."

HOSTED BY
Mike Mitchell and Nick Wiger

GENRE
Food

FIRST EPISODE
"Chili's with Eva Anderson" (May 20, 2015)

INFLUENCES
Late Night with Conan O'Brien, *The Simpsons*, Adam Sandler, the Coen brothers, Jesse Thorn, Bill Simmons

WHERE TO LISTEN
Headgum

SEAN'S PICK
"Nugget Power Hour with Nicole Byer & Jon Gabrus" (April 20, 2017)

DOUGHBOYS
WITH NICK WIGER AND MIKE MITCHELL

Gastropod

To listen to Cynthia Graber and Nicola Twilley's *Gastropod* is like being invited to a dinner party in heaven. An utterly (there is simply no other word for it) delicious stew of food science, world history, and cooking tips, *Gastropod* has long been culinary audio's qualitative yardstick (a fact supported by its many award wins from the International Association of Culinary Professionals and other esteemed bodies). Every episode thrums with Graber and Twilley's hunger for discovery, both for tastes unfamiliar and knowledge yet unknown. To use a cheesy simile, it is most like a fine cheddar: sharp, distinctive, and rare.

Graber (a print reporter and radio producer who teaches in MIT's graduate program in science writing) met Twilley (a contributor to *The New Yorker* and the author of *Frostbite*, a fascinating history of refrigeration) at a meetup of food and farming journalists in 2013. A year later, they independently launched the podcast out of "curiosity, frustration, and wanting to hang out," they tell me. At the time, food journalism was largely controlled by a small number of establishment publications, the resources for which were dwindling as rapidly as their staffs. In podcasting, by contrast, a niche for their kind of long-form, research-intensive reporting was newly springing.

The first episode, an exploration of the history and science of cutlery titled "The Golden Spoon," launched on September 6, 2014. The episode lays bare the intense chemistry between Graber and Twilley, which plays out in rapid-fire talking-over-each-other patter, as well as in their mutual delight over having their minds blown by such minutiae as the weights, shapes, and sizes of salad forks. Their interviews with food historian Bee Wilson and Zoe Laughlin, co-founder of the Institute of Making at University College London, ripple with wonderment, and perhaps even more remarkably, when they eat on mic (as they do so often throughout the series), it sounds enjoyable, not repulsive.

It is no surprise that by 2017, *Gastropod* was attracting accolades from the likes of the Radio Television Digital News Association (the disseminating body of the Edward R. Murrow Awards), as well as one hundred

HOSTED BY
Cynthia Graber
and Nicola Twilley

GENRE
Food

FIRST EPISODE
"The Golden Spoon"
(September 6, 2014)

INFLUENCES
"Curiosity, frustration,
and wanting to hang out"
(Graber/Twilley)

WHERE TO LISTEN
Spotify

SEAN'S PICK
"Pumpkin Spice Hero:
The Thrilling but Tragic
True Story of Nutmeg"
(November 7, 2023)

thousand downloads per biweekly episode, according to Adweek's David Griner. Still, it wasn't all fine dining and awards ceremonies. "There were many challenging moments," Graber and Twilley say. "For one episode [season twelve's 'Eat This, Not That: The Surprising Science of Personalized Nutrition'], we volunteered ourselves as human guinea pigs for a two-week-long experiment that involved eating electric-blue muffins (the dye made them recognizable when they came out the other end), wearing all kinds of sensors, and submitting various samples of bodily fluids that we collected ourselves." Graber experienced "gut-twisting pain" during the experience, while Twilley became uncontrollably hyper.

That two people who radiate such love for their craft would also suffer for it only helps to burnish *Gastropod*'s bona fides as a food lover's paradise. But even those who don't think of themselves as particularly culinarily inclined will be grateful for the chance to hang out with these true epicureans. "People who love to eat are always the best people," Julia Child once said. How prescient she was.

The Sporkful

Over the last thirteen years, eaters (*not* foodies, as podcast host Dan Pashman will be quick to tell you) around the world have become intimately familiar with Pashman's origin story. Laid off from six commercial radio jobs in eight years, including a 2:00 A.M. morning gig at a studio whose CEO he once discovered shredding documents, Pashman decided to make a more personal investment in a new audio medium. So, like his colleagues Marc Maron and Brendan McDonald, he snuck into the offices of the talk radio network Air America in the fall of 2009 to record pilots for what would become his beloved podcast, *The Sporkful*. He posted the first of them—a deep, delicious dive into the history of grilled cheese—the following January.

"In those early years, I edited *The Sporkful*, wrote the blog posts, took the photos, did the social media, composed the theme music in Garage-Band, sold what few ads we got, set up a pre-Patreon-type subscription service through PayPal (which maybe fifty people signed up for), and did the marketing and PR for the show," Pashman recalls today. Despite the generosity of several celebrity guests, such as former Air America colleague Rachel Maddow, it would still be four years before his podcast went legit, joining WNYC Studios in 2013. Even then, Pashman says wryly, "they still didn't have a desk for me. For six months I worked at the corner table of the lunchroom. I felt like the nerdy public radio version of a mobster who sits in the back of a restaurant taking meetings all day."

Two James Beard Awards, a Webby, and several million downloads later, *The Sporkful* is far away from those scrappy early days when its future hung "on a buffalo wing and a prayer." The food world's most renowned figures, including former *New York Times* critic Pete Wells, cookbook author Dorie Greenspan, and restaurateur extraordinaire David Chang, now regularly jostle for slots on the show. Pashman, too, has become a force in the industry as the host of Cooking Channel's *You're Eating It Wrong* and the author of *Eat More Better*, a guide to "making every bite more delicious." He even invented a new pasta shape, cascatelli, a take on the Italian word for "waterfalls."

Yet all this success has not much changed the host or his show itself. Thanks to Pashman's adherence to journalistic protocols and his long-standing commitment to spotlighting a diversity of tastes from around the world, *The Sporkful* continues to expand its listeners' palates one episode at a time. For those who love to grill, grind, roast, rub, boil, blend, bake, sear, sauté, powder, pan-fry, or just learn about what goes into our bodies, it remains the food podcast world's crème de la crème.

HOSTED BY
Dan Pashman

GENRE
Food

FIRST EPISODE
"Grilled Cheese"
(January 15, 2010)

INFLUENCES
Ira Glass, Alex Blumberg,
Marc Maron, Jon Stewart,
Z100 Morning Zoo comedy

WHERE TO LISTEN
Amazon Music

SEAN'S PICK
"Going Undercover with
NY Times Restaurant Critic
Pete Wells" (May 13, 2019)

THE SPORKFUL

The Splendid Table

Preparation Time: Thirty Years
Serving Size: More Than Eight Hundred Episodes

Ingredients:

- Two "unusually big-hearted, intelligent" food connoisseurs like Lynne Rossetto Kasper and Francis Lam, equally equipped to share with the public their infinite enthusiasm for the magic of a good meal and their vast stores of ideas for how to make one.
- A dedicated, long-serving executive producer like creator Sally Swift, still focused on maintaining "the founding values" of her show three decades in.
- A guest list culled from the food world's most storied figures, including iconic restaurateurs like Jacques Pépin, Jamie Oliver, and Prue Leith; celebrity chefs like Nigella Lawson, Carla Hall, and Ina Garten; and rising culinary stars like Fête's Robynne Maii, *Veg-Table* author Nik Sharma, and filmmaker George Motz.
- A global base of listeners (like me) that have spent the bulk of their lives relying on new episodes for guidance on what to cook for any event, including bar mitzvahs, Spanish class presentations, multiple first dates, and Friendsgiving 2015.

Directions:

1. Take the "uber-talented, curious and spirited" Kasper's landmark cookbook, *The Splendid Table: Recipes from Emilia-Romagna, the Heartland of Northern Italian Food*, and connect it with "one of those people who start thinking about dinner when I am brushing my teeth in the morning" and consider their kitchen "my creative space and refuge," like Swift.

HOSTED BY
Lynne Rossetto Kasper
and Francis Lam

GENRE
Food

FIRST EPISODE
"Now You're Cooking"
(January 4, 1997)

INFLUENCES
"The quiet corner of the
cocktail party" (Lam)

WHERE TO LISTEN
TuneIn

SEAN'S PICK
"People Who Taste Shapes"
(October 18, 2003)

THE
SPLENDID
TABLE®

≡ APMstudios

2. Have Swift and Kasper meet over lunch and decide to adapt it into a "magazine-style" weekend show for Minnesota Public Radio that will break the mold for food programming by centering interviews on such vastly different food topics as the emergence of soda poppers (as explained by regular contributors Jane and Michael Stern) and how some synesthetes experience taste as visual "fireworks" (as discussed by Dr. Richard Cytowic in episode 203); live call-in sessions with Kasper ("The lines are officially open!") about her current favorite preparations and world cuisines, like Moroccan-style rabbit with Italian green olives and couscous in episode 363; and conversations with farmers, distributors, cultural historians, and food scientists about cooking and baking recipes.

3. Maintain that singular standard for more than twenty-two years, honoring "the range of experience of our listeners, from a first-time cook to a chef to a young family with four kids to a person cooking for one" and encouraging them to

"understand the pleasure and power of feeding yourself," as Swift and Kasper did until 2017.

4. In the short period of adjustment after Lam—a two-time James Beard Award winner and contributor since 2010—takes over for Kasper as host, "re-focus" your show to suit him and the younger audience his presence brings. Do this by releasing a podcast version no less centered around "the belief that the way a person eats and cooks tells us a lot about the rest of their lives," as Swift puts it; by letting Lam deepen the scope of conversations about food to address systemic inequities in its availability, the ramifications of colonized foodways, and how to use food as a balm against the plague of loneliness infecting society; and by rejiggering the host's conversations such that two guests, rather than four or more, now fill every episode.

5. Share cute stories, like the one about that time the legendary Julia Child got caught "blithely reading the paper, as WE COULD HEAR, because she was incredibly noisy when she turned the pages" in the middle of one of Kasper's opening segments in the early days (even if, per Swift, "it was hilarious. The woman could get away with anything, and deservedly so").

6. Serve your podcast, *The Splendid Table*, to millions of foodies and reap the accolades, including being named to too many top-ten and "best of" lists to count and inspiring families like mine to lovingly eat their way through the world, for generations.

7. Enjoy!

While podcasting is a famously auditory medium, an expansive visual record of its first twenty years has already begun to form. Some creators use photographs to keep track of their shows, both in terms of what they release to the public and what happens behind the scenes; others use original graphics or artwork. What follows is a small sampling of images from those in the pantheon, including some that have never before been published.

1 Chemda Khalili and Keith Malley in the early days of *Keith and the Girl*.
2 Keith Malley and Chemda Khalili with guest Adam Conover.

3

4

5

6

3 *Criminal* episode 153, "The Max Headroom Incident."

4 *Criminal* episode 260, "The Dial Painters."

5 Jerah Milligan, far left, James III, and Jonathan Braylock of *Black Men Can't Jump [in Hollywood]*.

6 Brendan O'Hare, left, and Cory Snearowski outside Branchburg, NJ.

7 Dan Pashman of *The Sporkful* with chef Pietro Lonigro, one of the inventors of spaghetti all'assassina.

8 Paul Gilmartin hosting *The Mental Illness Happy Hour*.

7

8

9 The Fantasy Footballers on tour. From left: Andy Holloway, Jason Moore, and Mike Wright.

10 *Nocturne*'s "3-2-1!" from September 2021.

11 *Nocturne*'s "Into, Under, Through" from July 2015.

12 *Nocturne*'s "Rest for Them" from December 2020.

13 M, of *How to Be a Girl*.

14 Matt Young as Usidore the Blue at a *Hello from the Magic Tavern* live show.

15 Andy Carey, left, as Noah Paine with Adal Rifai as Chunt, the talking badger, at a *Hello from the Magic Tavern* live show.

16 *Uhh Yeah Dude* fan art.

17 *Add to Cart* hosts SuChin Pak, left, and Kulap Vilaysack with guest Jason Mantzoukas.

14

15

16

17

18

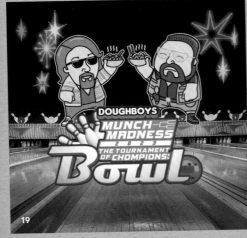

19

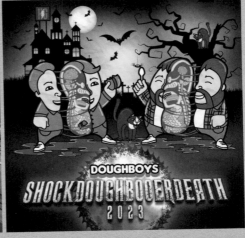

24 Marc Maron and Barack Obama from episode #613 of *WTF.*

25 Marc Maron and Robin Williams from episode #67 of *WTF.*

26 *The Witch Wave* host Pam Grossman.

27 Krista Tippett in dialogue with Bishop Desmond Tutu.

28 A bad snowman in Night Vale.

29 The iconic Glow Cloud from *Welcome to Night Vale.*

30 Hopefully we can find everything lost, and reunite everything found.

31 Poster for one of *The Fantasy Footballers* blockbuster megala-tours.

32 Dan Taberski, left, with producer Henry Molofsky outside the late Richard Simmons's childhood home in New Orleans.

28

29

30

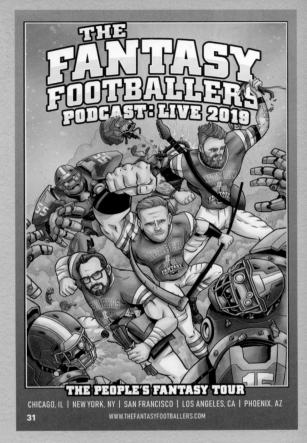

31

32

33

34

33 Pera and Dann in a conversation of sorts with guest Carmen Christopher.

34 *Drifting Off* host Joe Pera, left, with an assist from collaborator Ryan Dann.

35 *Twenty Thousand Hertz* creator Dallas Taylor tinkers with sound.

36 The art of sound design as heard in *Twenty Thousand Hertz*.

37 The world of hacking as explored on Jack Rhysider's *Darknet Diaries*.

38 Marc Maron with Bruce Springsteen from episode #773 of *WTF*.

39 An early advertisement for what would become Naomi Ekperigin and Andy Beckerman's podcast *Couples Therapy*.

40 Ekperigin, left, and Beckerman sharing hosting duties.

35

36

37

38

IN STEREO
TWO COMICS, ONE STAGE

July 21st
FREE
Hosted by Naomi Ekperigin
& Andy Beckerman
39   The HiFi Bar (Ave A & 11th)

40

Wait, Wait . . . Don't Tell Me!

If consistency were akin to godliness, then the production team behind NPR and WBEZ's *Wait, Wait . . . Don't Tell Me!* would be living it up on Mount Olympus. For more than twenty-five years, *Wait, Wait* has stood tall as the preeminent quiz show of the listening world, thanks to the Trebek-like chops of Peter Sagal, its witty, erudite host, and his Johnny Gilberts—the late Carl Kasell and, since 2014, Bill Kurtis. Originally developed by creator Doug Berman for radio, the show began broadcasting in 1998 with host Dan Coffey as a tie-in with Berman's other mega-hit, *Car Talk*. Sagal, a panelist on that first episode, came aboard full-time four months later and has steered the ship ever since, including when the January 28, 2006, episode with guest Tim Meadows went down in history as the first to be made available in podcast form by NPR.

"A good part of our first few years on the air was spent establishing what our sound would be, week to week," Sagal tells me. That included perfecting what has since become the program's well-known and oft imitated format. Each week, Sagal leads an assemblage of quick-witted celebrity panelists—typically comedians (Paula Poundstone, Hari Kondabolu), journalists (P. J. O'Rourke, Richard Roeper), and writers (Mo Rocca, Sue Ellicott)—through a run of games designed to slyly catch listeners up on recent news. "Who's Bill This Time?" requires contestants to identify the sources of real-world quotes read by Kurtis; in "Listener Limerick Challenge," Kurtis references the week's main events through humorous poems devised by Philipp Goedicke; and at the end of each episode, panelists compete in trivia speed round "Lightning Fill in the Blank."

Though it remains popular on the radio (averaging four million listeners an episode, according to a 2017 report by *The Ringer*), *Wait, Wait* continues to engage new generations of listeners who know it primarily from its regular presence on the podcast charts (that same *Ringer* report noted it as the year's tenth-most-downloaded program). Sagal credits that to the producers' constant efforts to dip into a larger well of guests and panelists over the years. "The best way to get a new comedic take on the news is to have new people provide them," he says. "Of course, there are things that a Black or female or Asian or young or queer comedian can say that I (an increasingly middle-aged white guy) can't, but more importantly, there are things they know that I don't."

That the show still moves like perfect clockwork with younger talent behind and in front of the mics is entirely on purpose. "Finding new and more diverse panelists who can still do the improvisational triple sal-chows that our odd format requires has been difficult at times," Sagal admits. "But it has paid off brilliantly, and I think is the primary reason our show continues to keep its audience."

HOSTED BY
Dan Coffey and Peter Sagal

GENRE
Game Show

FIRST EPISODE
Untitled [featuring Roy Blount Jr., Roxanne Roberts, and Peter Sagal] (Radio: January 3, 1998; Podcast: January 28, 2006)

INFLUENCES
Groucho Marx's *You Bet Your Life*

WHERE TO LISTEN
NPR

SEAN'S PICK
"Isabella Rossellini" (February 1, 2020)

Happier with Gretchen Rubin

As the means of production have grown more accessible, so too has the modern podcast scene become littered with scummy, self-appointed gurus peddling toxic positivity and reheated affirmations to desperate solace seekers. They are just as often as not exposed as predatory manipulators of a democratized system, breeding a culture of mistrust among dedicated health and/or fitness podcast listeners.

So in 2015, Gretchen Rubin, a globally recognized expert on "happiness, good habits, and human nature," and her sister, television writer-producer Elizabeth "Liz" Craft, created *Happier with Gretchen Rubin*, a much-needed counterpoint to the standard blowhards with microphones. In each episode, Rubin and Craft pinpoint a specific spot of sensitivity (a.k.a. a "happiness stumbling block"), such as how to wrestle with one's cravings for workplace doughnuts or maneuver around a serious bodily aversion to taking pills. They develop implementable practices for listeners to "Try This at Home" and report back. ("When we started, we just had a basic 'Listener Question' segment, but over time, we started more and more to incorporate listeners' ideas, resources, and questions pervasively," Rubin clarifies.) The hosts then balance their own perfect mood pHs by trading off "Happiness Demerits" (ways in which they undercut their own happiness, like Rubin's stress from driving) and "Gold Stars" (sources of comfort, like Craft's loyal writing partner, Sarah Fain).

For Craft, Rubin's "happiness guinea pig," and Rubin, Craft's "happiness bully," happiness is not an intangible buzzword reserved for the monkish and mindful; it is the holistic experience of satisfaction and contentedness that occurs when somatic, psychic, and environmental ecosystems align. It can be acquired, grown, and maintained when four interlocked resources are conscientiously employed: "cutting-edge science," "wisdom of the ages," "lessons from pop culture," and our "own life experiences."

Sometimes, the "Happiness Hacks" (Rubin, you may now sense, has a biologist's flair for assigning her tools succinct names) proffered are

HOSTED BY
Liz Craft and Gretchen Rubin

GENRE
Health

FIRST EPISODE
"The One-Minute Rule" (Feb. 24, 2015)

INFLUENCES
Car Talk, Satellite Sisters,
The Howard Stern Show, 99% Invisible

WHERE TO LISTEN
Audacy

SEAN'S PICK
"Give Yourself a Derby Name, an Easy Way to Give
Yourself a Treat, and a Conversation with 'The Good
Place' Creator Mike Schur" (January 26, 2022)

as simple as lubricating the throat with cold water before taking supplements, making the bed before leaving a hotel, or introducing pleasant smells into personal spaces. Other times, they are geared toward longer-term concerns. One particularly affecting episode, "Write Your Manifesto (& Bring Your Own Condiments)," finds Craft detailing how compiling her own personal manifesto informed her career in the unforgiving halls of Hollywood: "Take the meeting. Write into the fear. Don't stop. Stay human." These rules, she explains, are essential to winning "a war of attrition"— that is, the impulse to give up in the face of constant rejection and missed opportunities.

Rubin, too, maintains her own manifesto as a podcaster. "Beware of banter" is one of its key points, she reveals to me, and she and Craft adhere to it strictly: *Happier* and its offshoots, *More Happier* and *Little Happier*, are uniformly tight as drums and hot air–free. Rubin also copies the words "Practical, Funny, Transcendent, Revealing, Research, Sisters, Evergreen, Loose, Fun, Vulnerable, Differences, Community, Suspense, Authenticity" onto every episode's outline "to help us remember our aims." Such acts of scientifically grounded discipline have prevented them from making the same mistakes as some of their more opportunistic peers and have for years preserved their spot atop numerous podcast charts. If they stick with these manifestos, there is no reason to believe they won't keep heading "onward and upward" ad infinitum.

The Accessible Stall

THE ACCESSIBLE STALL PODCAST

Kyle Khachadurian and Emily Ladau's podcast, *The Accessible Stall*, is the epitome of "edutainment." In one sense, it is a vector for greater empathy with disabled folks that never scolds those who have unwittingly internalized the privileges of the status quo for their ignorance or complicity in the reinforcement of ableism. In another, it is a pure treat, a free offer of a seat at a table with two good-spirited, hearts-on-their-sleeves hosts.

Each episode explores a different facet of disabled life: its costs, financial and emotional; its many privileges and delights; the daily comedy and tragedy it entails. Naturally, some installments get intensely personal, as in Khachadurian and Ladau's analysis of their experience at the 2018 NYC Disability Pride Parade. But they can also be more overarching, as in the hosts' informative, long-in-the-works explainer of the Americans with Disabilities Act conducted with attorney Andrew Bizer.

Where the series moves past easy categorization is in episodes that sway fluidly, back and forth, between these modes, such as their one hundredth, "Disabled Bodies Are Weird." It opens gleefully, with Ladau chuckling to herself about "pee math" ("how many hours you have between accessible bathrooms") and the awkwardness of letting her partner clip her toenails ("I'm definitely not saying there's anything wrong with being interdependent. I'm more just saying that disabled bodies are kind of a mess sometimes," she clarifies). Later, the episode gives way to what Khachadurian calls a genuine "teachable moment" about the Moro reflex, a startle reflex that infants typically outgrow but which he and others with cerebral palsy (CP) must contend with into adulthood. "You can clap your hands in front of me loudly and tell me exactly when it's going to come, and I will startle," he describes frustratedly. "It's very annoying."

Given the historically poor treatment imposed on disabled people, Khachadurian and Ladau would have been well within reason to create a

HOSTED BY
Kyle Khachadurian and Emily Ladau

GENRE
Health

FIRST EPISODE
"Oranges" (April 18, 2016)

INFLUENCES
"Lawrence Carter-Long (disability media expert), *Penn & Teller: Bullshit!*" (Khachadurian); "Ellen Ladau (my mom), Judith Heumann (disability rights activist)" (Ladau)

WHERE TO LISTEN
Patreon

SEAN'S PICK
"Disabled Bodies Are Weird" (February 1, 2022)

podcast far less patient in nature. But this never seemed to cross their minds. "I love talking about disability issues—so much so that I often joke I'm a 'professional disabled person,'" Ladau tells me. Her co-host concurs: "Once we put the show out into the world and got our first few listens, that was the justification I needed to make more episodes. It's been a labor of love ever since." Knowing what it entails, none of the thousands of listeners who discovered *The Accessible Stall* through glowing write-ups in *Forbes*, Autostraddle, and MoMA's *Magazine* take that labor for granted. On the contrary, it makes the opportunity to walk in these good souls' shoes all that much sweeter.

Behind the Bastards

I would argue that, contrary to the well-known aphorism, history is not written by the victors—at least not exclusively. Quite often, the great losers of the world are just loud enough to merit recording their terrible deeds for posterity, lest future generations attempt to repeat them. For proof, consider the eponymous lowlifes of *Behind the Bastards*, the investigative history podcast hosted by journalist Robert Evans and produced by Sophie Rae Lichterman: While Osama Bin Laden, Coco Chanel, and Helena Blavatsky all failed to win the big game of life, for instance, they still fall under Evans and Lichterman's aegis for being among "the very worst people in all of history."

Regular listeners to *BtB* know that Evans only studies a Bastard when he has a compelling argument to do so. Trained as an editor and investigative reporter, Evans spent the better part of the late 2010s and early 2020s writing from conflict zones and recording podcasts to better understand what drives human beings to commit harm. But once he settles on a subject, there are few lengths to which he will not go in the name of research. "During the 2020 riots," Evans explains, referring to a series of violent events organized by racist hate groups in Portland, Oregon, "I wrote parts of at least two episodes while sitting around what had actively been declared either a riot or civil disturbance." When Evans was reporting, his hand was broken by a member of the Proud Boys, and he watched firsthand as local law enforcement officers protected perpetrators like his attacker while conducting state violence of their own against counterprotesters, including antifascist activists and members of the Black Lives Matter movement. "It turns out it's remarkably easy to write about the worst police abuses of power in history when you're watching people get tear-gassed!" he says ruefully.

According to Lichterman, her colleague first pitched the idea for the pod "on a phone call where the reception was terrible" and she "could only hear about every other word." ("It was the greatest pitch call I've been a part of and [I] immediately asked to produce the show," she clarifies.) Lichterman and Evans set out to reshape the public conversation through impeccable research into history's most famous pieces of shit, particularly those whom amateurs and experts alike might think they already know everything about. In the pilot, Evans presented several lesser-known aspects of the young Adolf Hitler, with particular attention paid to his overabundant flatulence and the cocktail of mood-altering pharmaceuticals he took throughout his rise to power; the following month, he unveiled the *Jackass*-style pranks that Joseph Stalin played on his terrified underlings (tomato in the pocket, anyone?).

Even then, Evans's delivery dripped with disgust, setting the tone for the show to unabashedly center itself in social justice and the fight for human rights. This approach turned *Behind the Bastards* into a breakout hit for iHeart. In 2021, the company put its weight behind Evans and Lichterman's network, Cool Zone Media, which in addition to *Bastards* also produces over a dozen righteous and radically intellectual podcasts, including *It Could Happen Here* and *The Women's War*. For the latter, Evans again tapped the same bona fides that made him a podcast superstar to study how the citizens of a de facto autonomous region in northeast Syria known as Rojava built a feminist oasis amid a collapsing government. "My trip there was funded entirely by fans who were paid back for their donations with a long podcast series about the history of the American Nazi movement," he says. Sounds like a fair trade to me.

HOSTED BY
Robert Evans

GENRE
History

FIRST EPISODE
"Farting Hipster Hitler" (April 24, 2018)

INFLUENCES
"The *Dollop* guys (in terms of comedy) and Popular Front (in terms of journalism)" (Evans); Jamie Loftus and "our entire team at Cool Zone Media" (Lichterman)

WHERE TO LISTEN
iHeart

SEAN'S PICK
"Hitler: Y.A. Fiction Fan Girl" (May 22, 2018)

Citations Needed

"The US media are alone in that you must meet the condition of concision. You've got to say things between two commercials, or in six hundred words. And that's a very important fact, because the beauty of concision—you know, saying a couple of sentences between two commercials—the beauty of that is that you can only repeat conventional thoughts."
—Noam Chomsky

If a 100 percent listener-supported podcast that addresses "media, PR, and the history of bullshit" sounds like it requires too much focus, consider its value proposition. Adam Johnson and Nima Shirazi's *Citations Needed* is a ferocious corrective against propaganda and its dissemination into the media ecosystem, as well as a rebuke of the bad-faith actors responsible. Each week, Johnson and Shirazi disassemble corporate and state-sanctioned communiqués across decades of ideological warfare against civilians, reaching into ever-more-fatuous texts and ripping out their truer, more venal implications. The hosts' analyses are principled, contemptuous, outraged—and obviously brilliant. "Occasionally, someone on Twitter will say, 'Adam, you've ruined my day,' and I'm like, 'My work here is done,'" Johnson acknowledges in the third episode, "The Rise of Superpredator 2.0," a study of media narratives surrounding the rise of so-called gang raids. "It is the highest compliment. If you want to have your day not ruined, go fucking watch Lifetime. You want to be reaffirmed, go do something else. It *is* depressing. It *is* sad. There is no law of nature that says life should be good and warm and positive."

The program began in 2017 with a barn-burning excoriation of the charter school system and the misinformation promoted by its most prominent advocates, including the team behind the award-winning 2010 documentary *Waiting for Superman*. In conversation with guest Jennifer Berkshire, the hosts railed against the film's almost "sadistic" adherence to "bootstrap, victim-blaming" language used under LBJ to demonize public education advocates and teachers' unions. At the time, Shirazi and Johnson were both living and working in New York City, the former as a nonprofit communications strategist and an editor at *Muftah Magazine*, the latter as an analyst for the media watchdog Fairness & Accuracy in Reporting (FAIR) and a columnist for *The Nation* and the *Los Angeles Times*. As they and senior producer Florence Barrau-Adams, producer Julianne Tveten, and assistant editor Trendel Lightburn collectively explain: "We recorded our episodes in person, sitting across from each other—sometimes in Adam's living room, sometimes at Florence's dinner table, mostly sneakily from a conference room that Nima snuck us into in an office building overlooking the entrance to the Holland Tunnel and raiding the fully stocked fridge during breaks."

Note the shared, sly pride at this subterfuge. Indeed, while their charter school takedown gave an early indication of the solemnity with which they'd treat the insidious deceit of "freedom of choice" rhetoric in health-care policymaking, the deleterious impacts of *The West Wing* on civic discourse, and other information asymmetries in American media over the course of two-hundred-plus episodes, it also revealed a mischievous sense of play that would come to undergird even Johnson and Shirazi's most vehement criticisms. (In the following episode, a look at how Orientalist mythologizing of North Korea led to a culture of nuclear fear, Shirazi joked, "How can we stop the cycle?") This marriage of humor and righteous anger remains profoundly seductive to anyone interested in fighting the tides of antidemocratic and

authoritarian media behavior, as evidenced by the caliber of guests, such as filmmaker Oliver Stone, *Guardian* journalist Hussein Kesvani, and human rights lawyer Derecka Purnell. If that also includes you, reader, then there is no better deal on the market in terms of value delivered for your attention.

HOSTED BY
Adam Johnson and Nima Shirazi

GENRE
History

FIRST EPISODE
"The Charter School Scam" (July 12, 2017)

INFLUENCES
Fairness & Accuracy in Reporting, Ida. B. Wells, Jacques Ellul, Edward Said, *That Mitchell and Webb Look*, Howard Zinn, James Baldwin, *Newswipe*, Noam Chomsky

WHERE TO LISTEN
Patreon

SEAN'S PICK
"Attacks on Affirmative Action and the Commodification of Diversity" (October 3, 2018)

Slow Burn

Slow Burn, Slate's history anthology, is a shape-shifter. In its first season, co-creators Leon Neyfakh and Andrew Parsons explored the lesser-known edges of the Watergate political scandal with pulse-quickening intensity, offering a sort of audio supplemental to Woodward and Bernstein's *All the President's Men* and Ron Howard's *Frost/Nixon*, influenced by 1970s crime dramas. Their second season, by contrast, approached the Clinton-Lewinsky scandal of the 1990s from a more grounded angle, doing away with the abject thrill seeking that infested the contemporaneous news cycle in order to argue for Lewinsky as the story's true, still-undersung hero. Then came the third season—a bouncy, often existential dance through the twin tragedies of Tupac Shakur's and Biggie Smalls's murders with host Joel D. Anderson stepping in for Neyfakh—which so differed from its predecessors' tones that it felt like a kind of challenge to listeners: *You thought you knew what kind of podcast this was, but you didn't.*

Unlike the innumerable other history podcasts that apply tried-and-true formats to each episode or season, *Slow Burn* is defined by such constant aesthetic reinvention. It utilizes a stew of archival material, scripted narration, and exclusive interviews with key figures in some of America's best-known cultural crises, like the 1992 Los Angeles riots (covered in season six) and *Roe v. Wade* (season seven), to explain how they unfolded. Parsons, now an executive producer at Prologue Projects, notes that this multimedia approach emerged in response to the fact that "there wasn't really an understanding of what it would take to pull together a documentary-style podcast so quickly." (Parsons and Neyfakh produced season one in just a few months, he says.) But Josh Levin, the podcast's editorial director and host of season four, was dead set on gathering both the best archival tapes available and the right people to fill in gaps where such footage was unavailable. "History isn't inevitable," Levin says. "It's the product of a bunch of small choices, made by fallible human beings. Those moments weren't always obvious at the time and weren't necessarily captured by TV cameras or newspaper reporters."

Under Levin, the series has rarely trafficked in big revelations, twists, or surprises; it simmers where others prefer to explode, conjuring the feeling of a stick of dynamite perpetually about to blow (hence its title). This is a braver strategy than it might sound on paper, as doing so risks losing the kinds of listeners who value consistency and dependability over all else. "Making a show 'pop' from nothing requires so many things to go right: so many good decisions, so much luck," says Neyfakh, who since making the show has gone on to produce *Fiasco*, a fellow narrative-history series, and *Think Twice: Michael Jackson*, an acclaimed ten-episode study of the infamous musician. "But if you pull it off once, and you find an audience, you can address that same audience next time you have something new."

Neyfakh certainly knows what it means to find—and keep—his audience. Since premiering in November 2017, *Slow Burn* has been used to adapt multiple hit documentary and fiction series for Epix (now MGM+), Starz, and FX, with its eighth season (an Anderson-hosted four-parter on Supreme Court Justice Clarence Thomas's rise to power) winning Podcast of the Year at the 2024 Ambies. Despite the fact that every one of its seasons is distinct from the last, it has remained a stalwart both atop the most popular podcast charts and on many critics' lists of the greatest podcasts ever for the best part of a decade. Clearly, the public remains hungry for this particular kind of stew.

HOSTED BY
Joel Anderson, Christina Cauterucci,
Josh Levin, Noreen Malone,
Susan Matthews, and Leon Neyfakh

GENRE
History

FIRST EPISODE
"Martha" (November 28, 2017)

INFLUENCES
"*S-Town*, Ike Sriskandarajah and Kate Osborn,
Why Oh Why, everyone who read at Refresh
Refresh Refresh, J. Anthony Lukas" (Neyfakh)

WHERE TO LISTEN
Slate

SEAN'S PICK
"A Very Successful Cover-Up" (December 12, 2017)

Lore

"*Lore* is much more than just a podcast," intones host and creator Aaron Mahnke at the end of each episode. Quite so. Since launching independently in 2015, this goliath hit dedicated to "the darker side of history, exploring the creatures, people, and places of our wildest nightmares," has been adapted into a two-season series for Amazon Prime Video and a three-book set from Penguin Random House. And in their wake, the company that *Lore* helped build, Grim & Mild, has also launched two sharp new podcasts: the short-form *Cabinet of Curiosities* and *Unobscured*, which features season-long explorations of important subjects. All have helped to position Mahnke's voice among the most widely heard on the internet; at one point, he was reported to have five million listeners a month. Not bad for someone who, in his own words, "fell into the world of narration for audio programs a bit accidentally."

In a 2017 interview with *The Economist*, Mahnke stated that he founded the podcast to help market his "supernatural thrillers." Essayistic and structurally spare, with no celebrities or costly studio gimmicks to buoy his half-hour-or-so historical monologues, *Lore* could have slipped through the cracks of pop culture as easily as hundreds of thousands of similar programs. "I don't have the same sort of bag of tricks that a professional voice-over artist might," Mahnke informs me. "I tend to jump right into the booth whenever I need to record something and cross my fingers that my voice will hold up."

Instead, serendipitously, the show caught fire. Unlike other podcasts about macabre and grotesque mythologies, *Lore* is unusually literary. Poe, Lovecraft, and Stoker, forerunners of an aesthetically familiar Gothic imaginary, are common reference points in Mahnke's tales, but so are Thoreau and Hawthorne. As host, he is particularly gifted with metaphor (ever wondered how the Leaning Tower of Pisa represents John Wilkes Booth's character flaws?) and adores pronouncement of antique wisdom. "Sometimes the hardest thing to deal with in life . . . is life," he says in one episode. And while his subjects of choice can be brutally well researched (the squeamish should steer clear of episodes like "The Bloody Pit" and

HOSTED BY
Aaron Mahnke

GENRE
Horror

FIRST EPISODE
"They Made a Tonic"
(March 19, 2015)

INFLUENCES
Paul Harvey's *The Rest
of the Story*, Rod Serling's
The Twilight Zone

WHERE TO LISTEN
Spotify

SEAN'S PICK
"Assumption"
(March 4, 2019)

"Cutting Ties"), Mahnke is never base, or provocative. "Surprisingly, I'm not a fan of horror myself," he reveals, "and I do try to limit the amount of gore and violence on my show. I don't think being graphic necessarily makes a person a better storyteller."

Such respect and enthusiasm for the simple power of campfire-style oration can make exploring this 250-plus-episode backlog a breeze. After all, Mahnke's second most common refrain is "I have one more story I'd like to tell you." The first is a reminder that if any of his tales capture your imagination enough to compel you to listen to a second episode, it is important to write in and say hi. He likes it when people say hi.

Welcome to Night Vale

The sensation of sleep paralysis has never been so acutely captured as in *Welcome to Night Vale*, the quasi-horror podcast created by Jeffrey Cranor and Joseph Fink in 2012. Set in a humdrum Roswell-style community distinguished only by the otherworldly and alien elements surrounding it, each episode welcomes into an ever-expanding milieu those creatures once restricted to nightmares and urban legends: mysterious black masses emitting piercing frequencies; cats floating unbidden through rooms; a glowing sentient cloud capable of possessing all who see it.

So spooky and atmospheric is the sci-fi-inflected world built by Cranor and Fink that unexposed listeners may be shocked to learn that it is constructed primarily through misdirection, paraprosdokians, and droll wordplay. Though it is certainly, to use a term favored by its fans, creepy, *Night Vale* doubles as a sly, pointed satire of suburban boredom told in bimonthly monologues by "the voice of Night Vale," actor Cecil Baldwin. As loyal regional radio host Cecil Palmer, Baldwin delivers such standard local news segments as "Traffic," "Lost & Found," and "Community Calendar" with the smirking, sinister edge of Orson Welles à la "The War of the Worlds": "And now for a brief public service announcement: Alligators—can they kill your children? *Yes.*"

It is a tour de force performance in its capacity to frighten, amuse, and romance, and Palmer's role in the mythology has only expanded over the years, with Cranor and Fink adding a time-warped lover named Carlos and several unfortunately fated radio interns. Complementing the narration is ambient electronica artist Disparition, who produces and composes the score running beneath Palmer's dispatches. His music is droning, unnerving, and hypnotic—the very embodiment of the supernatural evils lurking around every corner. In context, Disparition's music brings to mind the 1980s horror soundtracks of John Carpenter and Tangerine Dream, particularly when it comes to the theme song that plays after every episode intro. ("Weather," another recurring segment, incorporates music from other sources.)

The podcast's creators cite the experimental prose of Deb Olin Unferth's novel *Vacation* and Will Eno's revolutionary one-man show, *Thom Pain*

Horror

124

(Based on Nothing), as dual influences on *Night Vale*. And as with those texts, reviewers often struggle to describe the singular vibe cultivated on the podcast without contradicting themselves. For its combination of finely drawn local yokels in spooky environments, Cranor and Fink are sometimes compared to Garrison Keillor and Stephen King, or to H. P. Lovecraft and Douglas Adams—often in the same sentence.

Not that such indescribability has put much of a damper on their popularity. "Our one-year anniversary celebration for the podcast was held at an upstairs bar in the East Village that a friend let us use after-hours. About a hundred and fifty people came. It felt like the pinnacle of my creative life," Fink reflects. Still working a day job at the time, Fink left the event early to talk

down his furious boss and slipped on his apartment stairs, breaking his tailbone. "A year later, we had another anniversary celebration. This one was at a Broadway theater, where we were the headlining act. We had two shows that night, because the first one had sold out in seconds," he says. In addition to the flagship podcast, the *WTNV* universe now includes five books, an endless string of live shows, and a Patreon campaign offering Zoom hangouts and exclusive bonus episodes. As a model for success in fiction podcasting, theirs is now the standard-setter, an unthinkable outcome for the young Fink forced to nurse a broken tailbone. "If I could go back to the version of me in my twenties," he says, "I don't know what I would tell him. I guess I would just say, 'Be careful on the stairs.'"

HOSTED BY
Cecil Baldwin

GENRE
Horror

FIRST EPISODE
"Pilot" (June 15, 2012)

INFLUENCES
Vacation by Deb Olin Unferth; *Thom Pain (Based on Nothing)* by Will Eno

WHERE TO LISTEN
Patreon

SEAN'S PICK
"First Date" (July 15, 2013)

WELCOME TO NIGHT VALE

Bullseye
with Jesse Thorn

The ethos guiding the venerated podcaster Jesse Thorn's landmark interview show, *Bullseye*, is one of unabashed celebration, affection, and openness. In the vein of "the New Sincerity," a term made popular by David Foster Wallace in 1993, Thorn's style disavows the smarm and aloofness preferred in supposedly "unbiased" media spaces in favor of an unconcealed respect for his subjects. This can leave interviewees vulnerable. Some of the people Thorn speaks with are shocked when he dares to express deep personal connections to their work on air. Others cry. That luminaries like Dolly Parton, Dale Earnhardt Jr., Mavis Staples, Kareem Abdul-Jabbar, and John Waters keep returning to his studio overlooking beautiful MacArthur Park even so is due solely to one widely accepted fact: that Thorn is as good as hosts get.

Thorn has led some form of *Bullseye* since 2000, when it was still called *The Sound of Young America* and broadcast at the University of California, Santa Cruz radio station KZSC-FM (which NPR has distributed since 2013). Along with co-hosts "Big Time" Gene O'Neill and Jordan Morris (with whom he also created the *Jordan, Jesse, Go!* podcast), Thorn was given free rein to do "pretty much whatever we wanted" with the station's early morning slot, an opportunity that forced them to "reverse engineer" *The Sound* from scratch. "The only creative guidance that anyone gave us was 'Do something that is not like the other shows on the air if you want to get airtime,'" Thorn explains by phone. And so they did, staging a half-hour radio drama one day only to feature the hosts trialoguing over whale song on another. "Santa Cruz," he chuckles, "is a place where people listen to weird shit."

As the trio continued to hone their voices, such esoterica slowly gave way to soulful, good-humored conversations that refuted the shock doctrines favored by other broadcasters of the era. Though *The Sound* had once been forced to book the likes of Bill Withers, Andrew W.K., and Chuck D with the slyly misleading "We're a public radio show in the Bay Area," Thorn says, celebrity guests soon began to appear with increasing frequency. After becoming the sole host in 2004 (the same year *The Sound* was among the first-ever series to be made available as a podcast), he became more aggressive in booking comedians like *Mr. Show* creators Bob Odenkirk and David Cross, Upright Citizens Brigade founders Matt Besser and Matt Walsh, and Sarah Silverman. It's the one thing he tells me he's willing to take credit for: "It is hard for some to imagine, but there was no comedy media when we started. The fact that we actually cared about comedy and knew about it and thought it was worth having discussions about it? I certainly didn't know of anybody who was doing anything like that."

In 2012, Thorn renamed the show *Bullseye*, an apt metaphor for his outsize ability to strike at the heart of his subjects. Like *The Sound*, it was produced through his podcast network, Maximum Fun, which also counts on its roster a number of other culture-shifting shows such as *Baby Geniuses*, *Judge John Hodgman*, and *The Flop House* (see p. 86). In June 2023, MaxFun employees voted to convert the network into a cooperative that is 100 percent co-owned by Thorn and his fellow worker-owners. It was a momentous occasion for both the history of podcast labor and the company's founder personally: "The special thing is to be able to show our work, and say this really is a group of people working together on this and benefitting from it. It's not just a 'take-my-word-for-it' situation."

Despite its revamped organizational structure, however, *Bullseye* remains the network's flagship and Thorn its greatest attraction, combining as he does the erudition and preparedness of a Terry Gross or Ira Glass with the comic lightness of his idol, David Letterman. Perhaps more impressively after twenty-five-plus years of broadcasting, Thorn still only platforms those who deserve the respect and sincerity he is famous for developing. Of his longevity, he explains, "You DO have a responsibility to your audience to give a shit. Otherwise, why are you an entertainer?"

HOSTED BY
Jesse Thorn

GENRE
Interview

FIRST EPISODE
Untitled (Radio: 2000; Podcast: 2004)

INFLUENCES
Terry Gross, Ira Glass, David Letterman, Norm Macdonald, *Seinfeld*, Tenacious D, *The Larry Sanders Show*, *Mr. Show with Bob and David*, A Special Thing

WHERE TO LISTEN
Maximum Fun

SEAN'S PICK
"Jack Handey, Author, TV Writer, and Creator of Deep Thoughts" (May 30, 2008)

Fresh Air

Lawyers have the Code of Hammurabi. Clergypeople have the Dead Sea Scrolls. And podcasters? Well, they have *Fresh Air*.

It's true that *Fresh Air* was originally created for radio by David Karpoff, program director of Philadelphia's WUHY (now WHYY), in 1973. The earliest broadcasts of Karpoff and his successor, Judy Blank, were dedicated "primarily to local affairs and guests," according to the Radio Hall of Fame. (The broadcasts remain largely inaccessible to the public.) But that changed when Karpoff hired WBFO's Terry Gross to take over the two-to-five afternoon slot in 1975. "When I came to Philadelphia, David gave me the freedom to do what I wanted with *Fresh Air*, and he offered his support and friendship at a time when I really needed it," Gross explained in 2015. While her version of the talk show still centered on ferociously intelligent conversations with guests like Johnny Cash, James Baldwin, a young Spike Lee, and Maya Angelou (twice!), Gross's interviews were also distinguished by her unerring personal investment in the answers—the expression of which was still considered verboten among professional (and, of course, largely male) broadcasters of the era. Soon, *Fresh Air* and its host were being heralded as among the most innovative in radio history, earning the first of two prestigious Peabody Awards in 1993 (the second was awarded in 2022).

Not much has changed in that regard since NPR began distributing *Fresh Air* as a podcast on February 12, 2007. Executive producer Danny Miller, who joined the program in 1978, acknowledges that there were early concerns internally that releasing a podcast version might "cannibalize" the show's theretofore loyal radio audience and hurt the member stations that carried it (in a press release, the company said the show was syndicated to 624 such stations). But after only "a year or two," such fears had evaporated, he writes me: "We realized that the podcast numbers were growing at such a rate that on an aggregate basis (broadcast and podcast), our listenership was growing substantially." In 2016, *Fresh Air* was the most downloaded podcast on Earth.

"Our podcast has pretty much been our radio show," Miller continues, though he does highlight some small changes that help explain its gargantuan reach. He cites "the huge advantage of being able to listen to [the podcast] when it's convenient in your schedule," as well as what he calls its "more relaxed format." As a downloadable, "the show would be heard with fewer 'cutaways' for local stations," though those who wanted them could still hear ads read by the familiar voices of NPR's Chioke I'Anson and Jessica Hansen between segments. Miller also argues that *Fresh Air*'s unmatched reputation for conducting "thoughtful, well-prepared interviews" helped attract guests who might have otherwise been too busy to give two hours of their time to a podcast recording.

More than half a century in, the combined heft of its successes as both radio show and podcast have positioned *Fresh Air* as one of contemporary audio's seminal texts, with Gross yet to be dethroned as the greatest of her generation. Change, however, is looming. In 2023, Gross began splitting hosting duties with co-host Tonya Mosley and guest host Dave Davies, who share some of her inherent sense of attunement to the tenor and pace of conversation. Mosley, the founder of podcasting company TMI Productions and host of the podcast *Truth Be Told*, says she tries not to let Gross's irreplicable career distract from the larger goal of bringing daily delight to *Fresh Air*'s many, many listeners. "I feel a great responsibility to maintain the strong reputation of the show while bringing my own sensibilities and my full self in the way that Terry does," she says. Tonya, you've got your work cut out for you.

HOSTED BY
Terry Gross and Tonya Mosley

GENRE
Interview

FIRST EPISODE
Untitled (Radio: 1973;
Podcast: February 12, 2007)

INFLUENCES
N/A

WHERE TO LISTEN
NPR

SEAN'S PICK
"Gene Simmons"
(February 4, 2002)

Here's the Thing
with Alec Baldwin

Certain podcasts enter the pantheon because they set listener records. Others are pioneers in their genres, the first or best of a kind. Then there are those that claim spots through sheer aesthetic excellence.

Into this final category falls *Here's the Thing*, an otherwise well-produced interview show made enthralling by one of the rarest gifts in all of broadcasting, the vehicle par excellence for the conveyance of guile, poise, and humor: Alec Baldwin's voice. As audiences around the world first learned through his roles on screen and stage, it can be hard to turn away from Baldwin at his most charismatic. Yet I would argue that it is in podcasting where the Academy Award nominee has found his truest métier.

After more than a decade in service to *Here's The Thing* (first for WNYC Studios and later for iHeart), Baldwin's mellifluous narration has become as inextricable from its auditory ecosystem as the Miles Davis riff that opens and closes each segment. As the cliché goes, you could listen to him read from the phone book. This is no accident, Baldwin tells me; on the contrary, he diligently prepares his instrument for each recording: "I try to eat very little on the days that I'm tracking, which is the announcing in and around the conversation." When he needs to, he sucks on Vocalzone lozenges to protect his throat. He also mentions that he tries to think of what he calls the "billiard break" question, meaning "the question that opens up the conversation to several other questions," on interview days. "And I'm not always successful," he admits.

This helps explain why, though Baldwin often speaks with the most famous newsmakers of our time—his taste in guests ranges widely, from political figures like Bernie Sanders and Katie Porter, to respected medical experts like Anthony Fauci and Robert Lustig, to timeless stage and screen stars like Patti Smith, Barbra Streisand, and Dustin Hoffman—it is only the rare occasion indeed in which his voice falters. "Hopefully, I've gotten somewhat better at not intruding on the conversation," he says, though he confesses to still "get[ting] somewhat excited from time to time." Without that brazen, almost academic curiosity, *Here's the Thing* would not work as well as it does. Even those few guests who do test Baldwin's patience and perspicacity, like disgraced ex-congressman Anthony Weiner or Hall & Oates's Daryl Hall (who stubbornly called the host "Alex"), are treated to a profound, respectful fascination. "It is not my goal to have people on the show who only share my perspective," Baldwin says. "That can be rather dull."

Still, if this podcast can be said to have a main attraction, it remains the artist who has been its voice since it first premiered in 2011. "Enjoying this conversation?" Baldwin still asks before cutting to commercial. Invariably, the abiding answer is yes.

HOSTED BY
Alec Baldwin

GENRE
Interview

FIRST EPISODE
"Michael Douglas"
(October 24, 2011)

INFLUENCES
Dick Cavett, Steve Kroft,
Johnny Carson

WHERE TO LISTEN
iHeart

SEAN'S PICK
"Anthony Weiner on
Term Limits and Text
Messages" (May 9, 2016)

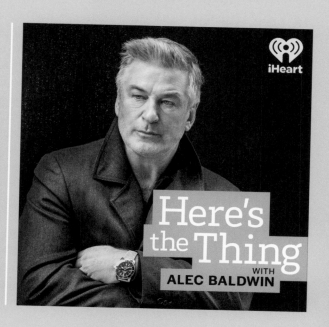

iHeart

Here's
the Thing
WITH
ALEC BALDWIN

WTF with Marc Maron

"Lock the gates!" When Marc Maron first yelled those words in Cameron Crowe's *Almost Famous*, he never could have expected them to become an anthem for hundreds of millions of listeners around the world. For decades, Maron struggled to convert the acclaim he had received as a stand-up comedian into true success. He bounced from TV pilot to TV pilot, marriage to marriage, and even attempted to pivot full-time to radio when his comedy career stalled. By 2009, however, all that was gone, and Maron was again alone, out of work, and nearly bankrupt.

With nowhere left to turn, Maron and Brendan McDonald, his producer and friend of many years, used their old key cards to sneak into a former employer's radio studio to record an unmistakably human conversation between Maron and the comedian Jeff Ross. Provocatively titled *WTF with Marc Maron*, the podcast centered on Maron's attempts to make good with some of the people he'd hurt, all while trying to find his way back into an industry that had chewed him up and spit him out. "My biggest influence in starting the podcast was desperation," he divulges, because "[back then], there was no podcast industry, there weren't a bunch of famous podcasters to emulate, and there was no real money to be made. There was just the sense that my career was going nowhere, that I was good on a radio mic, and that podcasts were things that a couple other comics I knew were doing."

The Ross episode landed online in September 2009 with hardly a blip, like so many other of Maron's projects. But as he welcomed increasingly famous guests to the converted garage he used to record the podcast, a.k.a. the Cat Ranch—Jim Gaffigan, Ben Stiller, and Sarah Silverman all visited in the first year—the world began taking notice. Soon Maron was starring in his own series for IFC and hosting the likes of Bruce Springsteen, Alicia Keys, and even the leader of the free world, Barack Obama, in the same rooms as old comic friends like Maria Bamford, Zach Galifianakis, and Rich Vos.

"When a president comes over to your house, a lot of things happen," Maron explains to me. "When President Barack Obama came over to record a podcast interview in my garage, these things happened: A sniper was put on my neighbor's roof; a tent was built over my entire driveway, eliminating

WTF with MARC MARON

HOSTED BY
Marc Maron

GENRE
Interview

FIRST EPISODE
"Jeff Ross"
(September 1, 2009)

INFLUENCES
"Desperation"

WHERE TO LISTEN
Acast

SEAN'S PICK
"Lorne Michaels"
(November 9, 2015)

direct sight lines; my guest room became a mobile comms center with ominous buzzing machinery; a Secret Service person prepared the president's tea and water to make sure it was not lethal." Suddenly, the Cat Ranch was a landmark in international diplomatic relations. "Oh yeah, they also gave me an instruction sheet to leave by my phone in case a bomb threat came in." However, he clarifies, "none of this happened when Patton Oswalt came over."

After over fifteen years and fifteen hundred episodes, *WTF* is now among the most popular broadcasts in history, with proud Whatthefuckheads, Whatthefucktuckians, and Whatthefuckniks from around the globe downloading two new episodes every week. The original garage is long gone, but Maron's new studio is no less a mecca for filmmakers, musicians, actors, artists, and all manner of notable figures looking to engage with his trademark combination of cutting intelligence and radical vulnerability for an hour. If any further proof was needed to cement Maron's importance to podcasting, his breathtaking 2010 interview with Robin Williams was inducted into the Library of Congress's National Recording Registry in April 2022. Still, being revered as the greatest interviewer of his generation hasn't done much to quell the host's trademark angst: "It would be better if I just allowed myself the space and didn't have a current of self-flagellation surging through me," Maron laments. "But that is what it is."

Dirty John

Christopher Goffard was a decade deep into staff writing for the *Los Angeles Times* when his editor contacted him with an odd new assignment: "We're doing a podcast, so go buy a recorder and get your interviews on tape." Being a "career print guy," as he puts it, Goffard "just didn't know how audio reporting was done—the physics of sound, how glass walls give you a hollow sound and padded walls a good one, background noise." Asking around for the best setup "for podcasting" was no use either. He immediately returned the studio equipment that his local electronics store had sold him, since he'd only be conducting boots-on-the-ground reporting. "I was clueless!" he says, laughing.

Somehow, a complete and total lack of experience was not enough to stop Goffard from making what would soon become one of the most listened-to nonfiction series in the history of downloadable audio. *Dirty John*, created in partnership with the *Los Angeles Times* and podcast network Wondery, centers on Debra Newell, a Southern California entrepreneur whose family life was upended by a man calling himself John Michael Meehan. Over six harrowing episodes released in 2017, Goffard explores how Meehan—the titular "Dirty John"—snaked his way into the Newells' lives through manipulation and mistruths, culminating in a devastating conclusion heard by more than ten million listeners in the show's first month of release. It was, by any calculation, a true (crime) phenomenon.

But Goffard was less surprised by the podcast's global success than one might expect. He was aware of the ground broken by such predecessors as *Serial* and *S-Town*, but *Dirty John*'s wrenching intensity was more influenced by antique radio shows, such as *The Shadow* and *The Adventures of Harry Lime*, which shaped the cultural imaginary for many Americans in their eras. In fact, Goffard's intelligent and authoritative narration—an essential factor in the show's instant popularity—was a direct tribute to lionized broadcasters like the young Orson Welles. "Those old shows gave me a sense of how compelling a well-structured audio drama could be," he applauds. "Of course, *Dirty John* is strictly nonfiction, but some of the same techniques (foreshadowing, pacing, scene building, etc.) can be used."

Nearly a decade on, *Dirty John*'s singular impact continues to ripple across the wider entertainment industry. In addition to a raft of other hit podcasts, it inspired an award-winning television series of the same name, setting the stage for a blossoming true-crime pod-to-screen adaptation industry that shows no signs of shrinking. Further, it reinforced a worldwide appetite for in-the-field reporting in audio, a gift not lost on the "career print guy" who helped put it on the map. Originally, Goffard says, "a lot of the making of the show had that stumbling, learn-as-you-go feel." Now that he's a hitmaker, the student has become the master.

HOSTED BY
Christopher Goffard

GENRE
Investigative Journalism

FIRST EPISODE
"The Real Thing"
(October 2, 2017)

INFLUENCES
Orson Welles,
This American Life, *Escape*

WHERE TO LISTEN
Wondery

SEAN'S PICK
"Terra" (October 8, 2017)

Headlong: Missing Richard Simmons

The central mystery of *Missing Richard Simmons* is not, as the title suggests, why Richard Simmons sought privacy from the public after decades in the limelight. Nor is it an effort to force the late, but beloved, fitness guru out of so-called reclusion to tell his own story. Rather, at the core of this heartbreaking investigative podcast is the constant niggling ache one feels when a trusted friend retreats into a smaller world that doesn't include them—and never says goodbye.

This first installment in the (retroactively named) *Headlong* series was produced by Topic Studios, Pineapple Street Media (now Pineapple Street Studios), and Stitcher and released in six parts in early 2017 (with a few bonus half episodes following later) to frenzied acclaim. It was co-created by Henry Molofsky (of the similarly brilliant *Still Processing* and *Wind of Change* podcasts, among others) and Dan Taberski, a filmmaker and producer for *The Daily Show*. The latter, a former student at Simmons's Slimmons Studio, spent years getting to know the star, only to find their relationship suddenly over when Simmons "disappeared" into his palatial estate in the Hollywood Hills in 2014.

Originally, Taberski remembers, he intended the project as a feature film to be made in collaboration with his famous friend: a nonfiction narrative inspired equally by "scrappy documentaries about regular people" like *Hands on a Hardbody* and *American Movie* as by the "musical and incredibly funny and incredibly tragic and just obscene and sensitive" aspects of *Hedwig and the Angry Inch*. But as Taberski began looking more deeply into the circumstances surrounding Simmons's newly quiet life, it quickly became clear that he was already too close to his subject. "It's really hard to make a documentary where the director is part of it," he says. "It feels very self-indulgent."

Instead, Taberski and Molofsky turned to podcasting, a format in which "being the narrator and being able to ask questions" could be "really help-ful" to telling a story, rather than distracting from it. The result was like

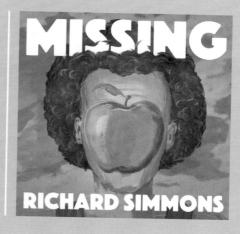

HOSTED BY
Dan Taberski

GENRE
Investigative Journalism

FIRST EPISODE
"Where's Richard?" (February 15, 2017)

INFLUENCES
Hands on a Hardbody: The Documentary,
Hedwig and the Angry Inch, *The King of
Kong: A Fistful of Quarters*, *American Movie*

WHERE TO LISTEN
Topic Studios

SEAN'S PICK
"The Maid and the Masseuse"
(March 1, 2017)

nothing else of its era: a serialized audio documentary told with ripped-from-the-tabloids suspense—was Simmons being held hostage? was he even alive?—yet suffused with the personal pain of its host. In several episodes, Taberski speaks candidly about how interviewing those close to the guru, like fellow Slimmons student Gerry "GG" Sinclair and Simmons's brother, Lenny, offered a kind of therapy, even though none can explain Richard's true intentions. By the final episode, it becomes clear that Taberski is as much the subject as Simmons himself.

This truth begot certain consequences. The release of *Missing Richard Simmons* prompted a global discourse around ethics in downloadable audio, with *New York Times* writer Amanda Hess deeming it "the morally suspect podcast" and Aja Romano of *Vox* calling it "an experiment in privacy invasion." Taberski says that while such potent criticism was "nerve-wracking, upsetting, and scary as fuck" as it was happening, it also helped shape his approach to several follow-up projects, including *Surviving Y2K* and his 9/11 podcast, *9/12*, which was named Best Podcast at the 2022 Ambie Awards. These days, he no longer gives interviews about Simmons, who died in 2024, but he remains proud of his and Molofsky's work on the show and grateful that it continues to find new listeners with every passing year. "As scary as it is to get criticism, there is also this other layer of 'I can't believe you're talking about what I made,'" Taberski confesses. "It is really incredible to hear and to see and to read."

S-Town

When John B. McLemore wrote to *This American Life* in 2012 about what he believed to be the murder of Dylan Nichols, he set off a chain reaction that would unwittingly impact tens of millions of people and shake the podcasting industry to its core. Following McLemore's tip, reporter Brian Reed traveled in 2013 to Woodstock, Alabama, where he discovered that the crime in question was more of a misunderstanding but nevertheless began a correspondence with the troubled clock repairman that lasted until McLemore's death by suicide in 2015. Two years later, on March 28, 2017, Reed, co-creator Julie Snyder, and the teams behind *TAL* and *Serial* released a seven-episode saga about McLemore and the denizens of the fourteen-hundred-person hometown he spitefully referred to as Shittown. Then the world exploded.

Here are some of the international articles that followed in *S-Town*'s immediate wake:

- ► "New Podcast from *Serial* Makers, *S-Town*, Breaks Download Records"
- ► "*S-Town* Has Exceeded 40M Downloads, Which Is Truly a Ton of Downloads"
- ► "*S-Town* Makes History"

Here are some other think pieces:

- ► "Was the Art of *S-Town* Worth the Pain?"
- ► "It's Hard to Recall a More Touching, Devastating Podcast"
- ► "*S-Town* Is a Stunning Podcast. It Probably Shouldn't Have Been Made."

From the first, this Peabody Award–winning show has divided audiences with its brilliantly reported yet ultimately shattering depiction of mental illness, sexuality, and poverty in the context of the American South. It has been referred to as "trauma porn" and "audio voyeurism," as well as "binge-ready art" and "a monument to human empathy." Dissertations and journal articles have analyzed everything from the decision

Investigative
Journalism

138

to out McLemore as queer, to the impact of Daniel Hart's original music on the podcast's popularity, to the beautifully intuitive design of the website on which every *S-Town* episode remains available for free. And while Reed has since gone on to co-host *The Trojan Horse Affair*, another investigative miniseries rich with scandal and criminality, it is for his narration, interviews, and producing work on *S-Town* that he will be rightly recognized for the remainder of his life.

"The responses *S-Town* has inspired in the seven years since it came out mirror the multi-faceted reality [that] the show was documenting: They've been delightful, surprising, moving, funny, vulgar, dark," Reed said in the spring of 2024. One response on his mind at the time was from Cheryl Dodson, who after *S-Town*'s release quit her job to become the executive director of the Alabama Suicide Prevention & Resources Coalition. According to Reed, the organization has since trained ten thousand Alabamians in suicide prevention. "Cheryl begins each training she leads by talking about her friend, John B. McLemore, who she lost to suicide, and the podcast that through his story connected people around the world to the joys and struggles of her small town," he says. Given that, perhaps *S-Town* was, to answer one writer's question, worth the pain. One thing is more certain, though: If not for McLemore's email, the world would be a lonelier place.

HOSTED BY
Brian Reed

GENRE
Investigative Journalism
(*Content Warning: Suicide*)

FIRST EPISODE
"Chapter I" (March 28, 2017)

INFLUENCES
"Edward P. Jones; *Stoner*; Flannery O'Connor; John B. McLemore's high-low style of speaking" (Reed)

WHERE TO LISTEN
STownPodcast.org

SEAN'S PICK
"Chapter III" (March 28, 2017)

Serial

Maybe no single podcast has done more to popularize the medium as a whole than *Serial*, the investigative mega-hit from the producers of NPR's *This American Life*. The show, a nonfiction story told in literary-style chapters, was co-created by Julie Snyder, a veteran narrative radio producer, and Sarah Koenig, who also hosted. "I got the idea from listening to books on tape during long drives I was taking at the time from where I lived in PA to NC for a story I was working on," Koenig tells me. "I hate to fly, so I was driving these ridiculous distances."

Season one told the story of Adnan Syed, a Baltimore teenager imprisoned for the alleged murder of his ex-girlfriend, Hae Min Lee. With its masterful reporting, themes of racial injustice, and a memorable score, the season spent months as the main character in most watercooler talk, leading to documentary spin-offs, viral parodies on *Saturday Night Live*, and a Peabody Award in 2015. It even made "Mail . . . Kimp?" unforgettable.

Given their sudden celebrity, Koenig and Snyder could have cashed in and dropped a new season of lesser quality immediately. "It's true that we did expect a smaller audience for *Serial*," Snyder says, laughing at the suggestion, "but I don't think we thought of ourselves as toiling in anonymity when we were making these shows." Instead, they leaned into their *TAL* experience for the next fourteen months to report the complex story of Bowe Bergdahl, a US Army sergeant who was deemed AWOL after being held by the Taliban. Released in 2015–2016, the season secured *Serial* the all-time world record for episodic podcast downloads, permanently inscribing it into the annals of media history.

In the years since they dropped seasons three (a multi-faceted look at the Cleveland judicial system) and four (a reported history of Guantánamo Bay), true crime continues to dominate the streaming and download charts—a phenomenon largely attributable to Koenig and Snyder. But their full legacy as creators extends beyond simple statistics. In 2022, Syed was freed from prison after twenty-three years, thanks in part to details uncovered by *Serial*'s reporting. It may be the first instance of a podcast directly helping to achieve justice in a real-life murder case. *Serial* Productions was also purchased by *The New York Times*, leading to a bounty of spin-off series inspired by Snyder and Koenig's standard-setting work. Whenever, inevitably, there are new seasons, the whole world will be tuning in.

HOSTED BY
Dana Chivvis and Sarah Koenig

GENRE
Investigative Journalism

FIRST EPISODE
"The Alibi" (October 3, 2014)

INFLUENCES
"Books on tape" (Koenig); "*The Staircase* (documentary)" (Snyder)

WHERE TO LISTEN
The New York Times

SEAN'S PICK
"A Bar Fight Walks into the Justice Center" (September 20, 2018)

The Dropout

If ABC News's *The Dropout* proves anything, it's that old-school boots-on-the-ground journalism is alive and thriving in audio. Created and hosted by Rebecca Jarvis, the chief business, technology, and economics correspondent for ABC News, the six-episode documentary fuses the investigative pushiness of *60 Minutes*' Mike Wallace with the compassionate curiosity of *Serial*'s Sarah Koenig to riveting effect.

The dropout in question is Elizabeth Holmes, who left her undergraduate studies at Stanford to found blood-testing company Theranos, only to later be convicted of defrauding investors with false claims about the company's revolutionary technological capabilities. Holmes's case—the subject of myriad articles, books, and films in the late 2010s—is a widely known white-collar crime sensation. But in the hands of Jarvis and producers Taylor Dunn and Victoria Thompson, this tale of a modern-day Icarus blossoms into a saga of cultural and fiscal proportions so expansive that it becomes clear just how lightly other projects skimmed the subject's surface.

Jarvis writes that "when we started investigating Elizabeth Holmes and Theranos, it was long before the SEC and DOJ charges" that ultimately landed the founder with an eleven-and-one-quarter-year prison sentence. At first, Jarvis shares, the podcast was "about this interesting person who'd defied so many odds, with some of the world's most notable people in her orbit, but who also withheld a lot of key pieces about what could've been an extremely consequential medical technology." Creating it entailed one-on-one interviews with players in the case, including whistleblower Erika Cheung, lab consultant Kevin Hunter, and biophysics pioneer Phyllis Gardner, as well as actually "knocking on doors" at key locations, like Theranos's Palo Alto headquarters.

While in a "spooky Airbnb in the middle of the woods" in Palo Alto, Dunn, Thompson, and Jarvis also acquired a series of deposition tapes featuring Holmes and Ramesh "Sunny" Balwani, the disgraced COO of Theranos. Jarvis calls them "the missing element" that the production required: "We were all mesmerized. We couldn't stop. It was the first time Elizabeth Holmes was being shown in a completely different light, having to answer all the questions." Indeed, these recordings of the once confident Holmes on the precipice of a Shakespearean fall from grace lend the podcast the intensity of such classic courtroom thrillers as *12 Angry Men* and *Inherit the Wind* without needing actors like Henry Fonda or Spencer Tracy to deepen the stakes.

Such vigorous drama firmly demonstrated the impeccability of the creator and producers' reportage, as many outside this book have already remarked upon. (Credit is also due to Evan Viola's exciting theme song and Teddy Blanks's eye-popping artwork, which helped define the show aesthetically.) Following the podcast's launch in January 2019, Jarvis, Dunn, and Thompson received a number of prestigious accolades, including an Edward R. Murrow Award for outstanding achievement in audio journalism. It was also adapted into an acclaimed Hulu miniseries that later received six Emmy nominations, including for Jarvis, Dunn, and Thompson as executive producers.

Jarvis and company have stayed abreast of the case in the intervening years, releasing several follow-up episodes about Holmes's time on trial and her life post-scandal. "Covering Elizabeth Holmes and Theranos was all about the questions—the questions I couldn't shake, that kept me up at night, and just seeing where that would lead," Jarvis says today. Ultimately, where it led was directly into the podcast history books. Presumably that makes it a little easier to sleep.

HOSTED BY
Rebecca Jarvis

GENRE
Investigative Journalism

FIRST EPISODE
"Myth-Making"
(January 23, 2019)

INFLUENCES
Serial, The Jinx

WHERE TO LISTEN
ABC Audio

SEAN'S PICK
"The Whistleblower"
(February 12, 2019)

The Last Days of August

In 2017, pornographic actress August Ames died by suicide in Camarillo, California, at the age of twenty-three. Ames was a rising star in the industry, a Canadian expat, and an AVN Award winner with over a hundred credited scenes to her name. But her mental health, which had proved precarious on previous occasions, again turned drastically after she was taken to task for a tweet she'd posted regarding gay porn performers. Her body was found two days later.

Ames's death and the circumstances surrounding it are the ostensible subjects of *The Last Days of August*, a seven-episode nonfiction series from writer Jon Ronson and producer Lina Misitzis (who coined the title). The topic was a natural one for the pair, whose previous collaboration, *The Butterfly Effect*, was, in Ronson's words, "a much more upbeat show about the porn industry, about the consequences of the tech takeover of porn." Ronson was also something of an expert in the treatment that Ames endured, having written a book, *So You've Been Publicly Shamed*, about others who had experienced mass castigation.

Last Days might have devolved into either sleazy docudrama or a misguided hero's journey under different circumstances. But Ronson and Misitzis's approach was studied and compassionate, resulting in as intimate and humane an exploration of the violent collision between social media and sex work as audio has ever produced—by design, Ronson says four years after its release: "In a way, I see *The Last Days of August* as a critique of true-crime podcasting—how the genre isn't too far away from conspiracy theories." While *Last Days* never takes its eyes off what Misitzis calls the "unhappy story" of Ames's untimely passing, it also refuses to play her tragedy for cheap thrills, instead interrogating the exploitative habits of fellow podcasters who might, if given the chance, "take a sliver of information and run with it, creating false narratives born from magical thinking."

That Ronson and Misitzis still manage to paint a vivid portrait of their subject without collapsing into tired tropes may be why their production

Investigative
Journalism

144

is revered among both the audiophile and sex worker communities as the limited series par excellence. Like *The Butterfly Effect* and Misitzis's Pulitzer Prize–winning episode of *This American Life*, it is also gorgeously produced and performed. But making it as good as it is, Ronson concedes, took a toll: "On a personal level it had a negative impact on my health, and in fact for the first time in my life I needed to take time off work afterwards." He's "not sure [he'd] want to make something as dark and difficult" again, he tells me, but Misitzis says she continues to draw inspiration from Ronson's writing in episode two: "'*I don't want this to be one of those shows that creates narrative tension by fueling suspicions that someone might be a murderer . . . this will not turn out to be a murder mystery.*' Which I can't take any credit for; that was all Jon! But I think it's classy, and thoughtful, and even a bit hopeful."

HOSTED BY
Jon Ronson

GENRE
Investigative Journalism
(*Content Warning: Suicide*)

FIRST EPISODE
"Episode One" (April 11, 2019)

INFLUENCES
Holly Randall Unfiltered

WHERE TO LISTEN
Audible

SEAN'S PICK
"Episode Seven" (April 11, 2019)

How to Be a Girl

When the pseudonymous Marlo Mack started her podcast, *How to Be a Girl*, in 2014, her daughter, M, was six years old. At three, M announced that she was a girl and had been incorrectly assigned male at birth. At the time, Mack writes by email, "the idea of a transgender child was utterly alien to practically everyone I knew. I might as well have been claiming that my child was a dragon or president of the United States." It took her a year to acknowledge that this was a simple fact of M's life, not a phase, and to begin practicing gender-affirming parenting with her daughter. Two years later, she launched the podcast.

At first, Mack says, "I was pretty obsessed with privacy. I wanted to let [M] decide when she was older what she shared about herself with the world." To protect both her daughter's safety and authority over her own narrative, Mack assumed a pen name, invited friends to read for her "part," and considered hiring a local professional actor to host the podcast, lest she be recognized. But it didn't take. "In the end, it didn't really sound authentic," Mack admits, "and my friends in the local podcasting community convinced me that my own voice was going to be more powerful."

We have those friends to thank for this wondrous docuseries, then. For more than a decade, Mack has shared in her own voice the most intimate moments of her life as the parent of a trans daughter: the nervous excitement over M's first big switch to a new school in "Episode IX: School (Part I)"; the paralyzing fear at the introduction of an anti-trans "bathroom bill" in M's home state in "Episode XI: Bathroom Bill"; the swirl of thoughts accompanying the implantation of a puberty blocker in "Episode XXXII: The Medical Stuff." The episodes, which publish sporadically on Patreon, are primarily constructed from conversations with members of M and Mack's chosen community (including M's father, doctors, and close friends), as well as with publicly visible trans celebrities like Laverne Cox and Jazz Jennings, all layered over the sounds of M singing, playing, and offering her own intermittent commentary. Many were recorded among what Mack calls the "massive horde of stuffies" in M's bedroom to allow for "excellent acoustics."

Beautiful production work is not *How to Be a Girl*'s sole accomplishment. In 2017, it was nominated for a Peabody Award and named Best International Podcast by the British Podcast Awards; later, it was adapted into both an audiobook and then a memoir of the same name. Even so, in December 2023, Mack revealed on the podcast that her then-teenage daughter no longer wanted to participate in the show (or in write-ups about it, like this book). Yet M allowed Mack to preserve the previous thirty or so episodes as an oral record of her abundantly joyous, gender-euphoric childhood. This way, listeners can always access the full archive even when Mack has not released a new episode in months (or years).

HOSTED BY
Marlo Mack

GENRE
Kids and Family

FIRST EPISODE
"Episode I: Mama, I'm a Girl" (June 7, 2014)

INFLUENCES
"My remarkable kid; the many transgender adults who have emailed me their support and their stories; Jan Morris; Jazz and Jeanette Jennings; Jennifer Finney Boylan; Mary Karr; Third Coast founder Julie Shapiro; my super-supportive Seattle audio community; the Jack Straw Cultural Center; my number one cheerleader, my dad" (Mack)

WHERE TO LISTEN
Patreon

SEAN'S PICK
"Episode XIII: Play Date" (October 19, 2016)

"The most moving emails are from people who tell me that our story made them feel like they weren't alone," Mack says. That includes "parents of young kids like mine," as well as other children as young as nine. "They say our story has given them hope, even saved them from making a very dark choice. Knowing we've had this impact is the honor of a lifetime."

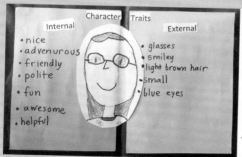

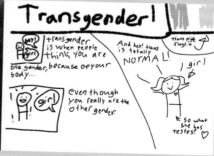

Story Pirates

Lost touch with your inner child?
Need to laugh and laugh until tears stream down your face? Look no further than *Story Pirates*, the family podcast from the renowned media company of the same name. Created by Lee Overtree and Benjamin Salka, the show turns stories written and submitted *by* kids into comedy *for* them—though not exclusively. In fact, it is the Story Pirates' commitment to treating every listener like a grown-up that makes their program such a delectable and consistent treat, even for those of us, like myself, without young ones.

Each episode spans three realms: an imaginary world conceived of by children based on prompts known as "Story Sparks"; the narrator's world, in which Overtree, co-host Peter McNerney, and their fellow comedians perform as cartoonish versions of themselves; and the real world, in which Overtree drops character altogether to interview the story writers, who range in age from four to around twelve. Though this structure is as quietly complex as Christopher Nolan's *Inception*, the stories themselves are often chosen for their digestible simplicity. In one premise, bumblebees have overtaken the roads of Manhattan; in another, (all) eight unicorns fresh from the "mane salon" meet for their regular trot. My personal favorite features the Statue of Liberty as a Batman-style vigilante.

Working with music directors Brendan O'Grady, Eric Gersen, and Jack Mitchell and sound designer Sam Bair, Overtree and Salka's staff convert selected submissions (culled from tens of thousands) into hooky songs and musical sketches with hints of *Sesame Street*, Terry Gilliam movies, *Saturday Night Live*, and Philippe Gaulier. To call it a winning formula would be to seriously undersell it: As of 2024, the podcast has netted over eighty-five million downloads* and remains a constant player on the Kids and Family podcast charts.

But as Salka messages me, what appears to be an "overnight success" was actually "a million tiny moments over a number of years that contributed to us finding our audience." First, there was the launch of the Pirates' live sketch show in the basement of New York's Drama Book Shop in 2004. In 2009 came a mythic performance at the Kennedy Center to commemorate President Barack Obama's inauguration and, not long after, a radio show recorded completely live ("including music and SFX," Overtree says) for SiriusXM's Kids Place Live. In 2013, Overtree and Salka began releasing the Sirius recordings for download, beginning with a six-year-old's story about marshmallow launchers at a day camp. Suddenly, parents could play old episodes for their offspring outside the confines of their daycare commutes.

A significant following began to develop. Within four years, they'd moved to Gimlet with the promise of a "real budget" and an expanded vision for the podcast. The partnership resulted in a gigantic back catalog—more than 150 episodes across six seasons—of comedy bits becoming available. Celebrities began requesting guest spots. "Fairly early on, we booked Dax Shepard to do a part on the show, and his wife Kristen Bell, with no prompting from us, did an Instagram story about how she was jealous," Salka recalls. Soon, major stars like Julie Andrews, John Oliver, and Claire Danes were guesting too. "Our already sizable audience quadrupled in the span of a few months," Salka says.

It also made important memories for its creators. Overtree notes a particularly moving submission from an eight-year-old named Lyla that arrived as an audio file, "which at first was confusing (stories are usually written or typed) until we realized that Lyla was blind." For the production team, adapting Lyla's story "about an evil clock with a dreadful secret" into "an almost-horror comedy piece with immersive audio and high-production-value sound design, scoring, and voice acting" was a turning point in how they saw the comedy they made, Overtree says. "Working on that one story made concrete for us the real-world value of validating the imaginations of the kids."

HOSTED BY
Lee Overtree and Peter McNerney

GENRE
Kids and Family

FIRST EPISODE
"I Love a Ghost / Fred the Carrot"
(November 20, 2017)

INFLUENCES
Looney Tunes, Monty Python, *Homestar Runner*, commedia dell'arte

WHERE TO LISTEN
Spotify

SEAN'S PICK
"All 8 Unicorns / Riding a Seagull Was Good" (November 30, 2017)

---

* And counting: "This number changes fast," Overtree warned me when I asked for recent stats.

Death, Sex & Money

When Anna Sale announced that *Death, Sex & Money*—her podcast about "the things we think about a lot and need to talk about more"—was ending its run with WNYC Studios in 2023 after more than four hundred episodes, "gasps rang throughout the world," wrote *Lifehacker*'s Lauren Passell. Those who had grown accustomed to hearing Sale dive into topics like poverty, aging, disease, pregnancy, et alia every week since the first week of May 2014 begged the network to reconsider. Fans were so distressed by the cancellation (a result of extensive budget cuts, as with many other podcast cancellations that year) that at a live event eulogizing the show (and featured in the final WNYC episode, "Four Interviews and a Funeral"), Sale had to soothe the crowd, according to *The New Yorker*'s Sarah Larson. "I'm not dead, the members of the *Death, Sex & Money* team are not dead, and we don't even know if the show is dead," Sale reportedly said.

She was right to be optimistic: In early 2024, the beloved interview show was picked up by *Slate* to bolster its already sturdy podcast network. "Not only am I personally a fan of the show and Anna's work," CEO Dan Check wrote, "but it is a perfect fit for *Slate*'s listeners, who come to us every day for engaging, revealing, and often personal discussion about the topics most affecting their everyday lives."

"Engaging," "revealing," "personal": Check's words get to the core of why audiences flock in such droves to *DSM*, regardless of its distributor. Take its modern-classic second episode, "This Senator Saved My Love Life," in which Sale discloses in extreme detail how a protracted breakup with her boyfriend, Arthur Middleton, was turned around through the intervention of Wyoming senator Alan Simpson and his wife Ann Schroll (after which Sale and Middleton married and had two children). Her telling of the tale is fearless, and helps the episode walk an impossible tonal line between intense and funny, broad and specific. Understandably, it went viral when it first aired, prompting the production team to continue pursuing engaging, revealing, and personal stories about other so-called verboten topics.

After the *Slate* announcement, I touched base with Sale to ask about her favorite experiences broaching topics as brutal as murder, cheating, abuse, and class warfare on the show. One of the episodes she cited—"Big Freedia Bounces Back," from her 2015 series "In New Orleans"—speaks to her one-of-a-kind recipe for podcast greatness. For it, she interviewed musician Big Freedia on the block from which Freedia was evacuated during Hurricane Katrina, only to have a porch swing give out during their conversation. Though the episode touches on poverty, race, and infrastructure, Sale found the biggest laugh of her career in it: "We jumped up thinking it was coming down with us in it. A perfect moment of punctuation from the universe."

As for the other episode she notes, "Who's Driving Your Uber?"—a look at the finances and family lives of Uber drivers in the Bay Area from 2017—Sale says it offers an important reminder about "how many [*DSM*] episodes are moving around me every day if I pause and ask a few questions." With any luck, she will never forget to pause again.

HOSTED BY
Anna Sale

GENRE
Lifestyle

FIRST EPISODE
"How to Be a Man with Bill Withers" (May 5, 2014)

INFLUENCES
Studs Terkel, Barbara Walters, Terry Gross

WHERE TO LISTEN
Slate

SEAN'S PICK
"This Senator Saved My Love Life" (May 7, 2014)

DEATH SEX & MONEY

WITH ANNA SALE

WNYCSTUDIOS

Drifting Off
with Joe Pera

Old teak floorboards creaking under the weight of a soft loafer. Grandfather clocks chiming from behind panes of weighted glass. Dewy wisps of wind lashing the loamy edges of an Irish cliffside.

These are among the hypnotic sounds conjured in the making of *Drifting Off with Joe Pera*, a delicate, otherworldly sleep podcast from the eponymous comedian's company Chestnut Walnut. In his television series *Joe Pera Talks with You*—a sort of training ground for the nonnarrative dreamscapes he would later create—Pera displays an outsize affinity for images reminiscent of a calmer, more grounded era in human life: trellises overladen with beans, a lake glazed over with the early winter frost. One episode's climax centers on a pumpkin floating down a roaring white river.

In *Drifting Off*, launched just over a year after the final *Talks with You* episode, the narrativity and character arcs disappear. Yet the Thoreauvian musings—and the piquant little interjections that are Pera's signature as a humorist—remain. "The show comes together differently each month depending on our schedules and that of the guest composers," Pera says of this somewhat experimental process. "Our" refers to Chestnut Walnut producer Grant Farsi and composer Ryan Dann, whose ethereal scores punctuate many of Pera's pet projects. Together, the team sources guest composers like Dan Deacon and Julianna Barwick to supplement Dann's original music, then wind both together to help Pera lull the listener into a trance with talk of, say, childhood clarinet lessons (episode eight) or a Hans Christian Andersen Christmas poem (episode ten).

For Pera, whose distinctive andante delivery masks a spry wit, it's the teamwork that literally makes those dreams work. "After doing TV together, it's nice to be able to take an idea from conception to a fully formed piece in a matter of weeks or days and immediately be able to share it with an audience," he says. Regular collaborators like Jo Firestone and Carmen Christopher, who wrote for and starred in the Adult Swim series,

Meditation

HOSTED BY
Joe Pera

GENRE
Meditation

FIRST EPISODE
"Soup (Ft. Jo Firestone)"
(February 5, 2023)

INFLUENCES
"Rebecca Reider's *Dreaming
the Biosphere*; Glenn Gould's
"The Idea of North" and his other
audio series; ambient composers;
audiobooks about animals,
history, and fish" (Pera)

WHERE TO LISTEN
Patreon

SEAN'S PICK
"An Audio Tour of Ireland Ft.
Julianna Barwick & Dr. Art
Hughes" (May 7, 2023)

also make guest appearances here. Dann even creates an extended eight-hour version of each new episode for Patreon subscribers seeking the "full night experience."

Unsurprisingly, many have sought out just that, including critics for *The Guardian* and *The Atlantic*, which named *Drifting Off* one of 2023's best podcasts. However, if any readers think that means they are in for a lullaby, think again. Though its host's voice is certainly enchanting, this jewel of a show is also searingly, sometimes even distractingly, funny. Pera, after all, is a comic by trade, having debuted his first hour-long special, *Slow & Steady*, within months of the podcast's launch. He seems at times to be pulled by two instincts. Just as the cold grip of sleep starts to creep into a recording, there he is with a one-liner of unexpected vulgarity. It can be shocking from a man once cast to play a sluggish tree in Pixar's *Elemental*. "I'm sorry," he's been known to say after the most mischievous of these. No apology necessary, Joe—just let the poor folks get their rest.

Analyze Phish

Jam bands are kind of like cilantro: Some people love them completely, while others are repulsed by their mere existence. Even those who have never actually given the Grateful Dead, moe., or the String Cheese Incident their fair shakes nevertheless have strong opinions on their music. This was the starting point for *Analyze Phish*, a deceptively profound ten-episode series about the psychedelic rock band Phish released by Earwolf between 2011 and 2014. The podcast was the brainchild of Earwolf co-founder Scott Aukerman and Phish-obsessed comedian Harris Wittels. Wittels, a rising writer and producer for *Parks and Recreation* and *The Sarah Silverman Program*, proposed the series while guesting on Aukerman's landmark improv show *Comedy Bang! Bang!* (see p. 36). In it, he would serve as the listeners' "tour guide through the cosmos," while the more resistant Aukerman would try to get over his issues with the band with help from famous guests, like actor Adam Scott, writer Nathan Rabin, and musician Nick Thorburn.

Had the series' ending been planned, it might have been remembered only for the ground it broke creatively. At the time, while Aukerman was widely known as a podcast pioneer and luminary, Wittels was still best known for inventing the term "humblebrag" on his legendarily droll Twitter feed. It was not a collaboration that many would have expected to completely reshape podcasting. In one striking experiment halfway through their run, the hosts suddenly converted the *Analyze Phish* feed into a two-part series about "analyzing fish" like Jaws (from *Jaws*) with Paul F. Tompkins, Howard Kremer, and Shelby Fero. ("We thought that was a funny trick to pull on the audience," Aukerman giggles.) In another, "Phish Live in NY," Wittels coached Aukerman through a ganja goo ball–filled Phish concert at Madison Square Garden in real time. Aukerman believes this to be "one of the first examples of gonzo podcasting" in history, an audio-only version of the form Hunter S. Thompson made popular. "No one had really been doing anything like that at that point," he says by Zoom. "It felt like we were breaking new ground."

Off mic, Wittels's love for the band dovetailed none too comfortably with his personal life as a struggling addict. In one 2013 episode, he and

Aukerman hold a frank conversation about Wittels's attempts to get sober after what Aukerman now calls a "darker" experience going to see Phish at the Hollywood Bowl. In a perceptive 2017 analysis for *Vulture*, Rabin captures the Hollywood Bowl saga's power perfectly: "It's riveting as a portrayal of a brilliant, troubled man in a state of transition and a singularly deep and fascinating friendship that led to a quietly masterful body of collaborative work that was, on some level, an exploration of the nature of friendship."

Though not as formally innovative as the Madison Square Garden episode, that conversation remains revelatory in its intimacy and intensity today, in part because it became a prophecy not long after. In 2015, at the age of thirty, Wittels died of a drug overdose. His passing was decried as the loss of a burgeoning genius who had been cut short before he could reach the superstardom for which he was destined. Whether their collaboration might have continued in different circumstances is a mystery; in fact, according to Aukerman, Wittels left the recording of their last episode pissed that the former had been "too much of an asshole" about the latter's favorite band. But Aukerman insists that *Analyze Phish*'s greatest legacy is in serving as a repository for Wittels's most brilliant ideas as a game-changing podcaster and voice-of-a-generation comedian. "I do love that those ten episodes are this documentation of him as a comedian and an artist that never put out a Netflix special, and whose stand-up wasn't really recorded," Aukerman says proudly. "People can go back and hear his voice anytime they miss him or just want to laugh."

HOSTED BY
Scott Aukerman and Harris Wittels

GENRE
Music (*Content Warning: Overdose*)

FIRST EPISODE
"Phish 101" (August 8, 2011)

INFLUENCES
"Our relationship on *Comedy Bang! Bang!*" (Aukerman)

WHERE TO LISTEN
Earwolf

SEAN'S PICK
"Hollywood Bowl" (June 25, 2014)

Cocaine & Rhinestones

Tyler Mahan Coe's Homerian epic of a podcast, *Cocaine & Rhinestones*, requires focus. Dense as mom's matzo balls and obsessively researched in its consideration of twentieth-century country music ("and the lives of those who gave it to us"), it is poorly suited to workouts, white noise, or falling asleep. Instead, when it comes time to consume Coe's sprawling, spirally storytelling, treat it like landing a plane: with extreme concentration and a dedication to reaching the end safely, come hell or high water.

Coe has said that single episodes can take him around a hundred hours to produce, which explains why so few (less than forty at the time of writing) have been released since the first debuted in the fall of 2017. Each comes complete with a seemingly unrelated prologue, a "game" of slow reveals that Coe plays to "keep [the podcast] engaging." Then it's on to his real subjects, which have so far included Mariana Trench–deep dives into the wider cultural impact of essential country artists (Wynonna Judd, the Louvin Brothers, George Jones), "complete and total examinations" of seminal songs (Merle Haggard's "Okie from Muskogee," Bobbie Gentry's "Ode to Billie Joe"), and rescue missions on behalf of countless lost and forgotten stars (Owen Bradley, Glenn Barber, Sonny Fisher, Justin Tubb).

In his pièce de résistance, Coe delivers a three-episode revisionist history—at a length of three hours and fifty-nine minutes—on how record producer Shelby S. Singleton, songwriter Tom T. Hall, and singer Jeannie C. Riley collided in the cloud of genius that was their 1968 mega-hit "Harper Valley PTA." The series has borrowed from a range of resources—each studiously bibliographized, as with every episode, on his blog—and Coe goes so far as to accuse Riley of fabricating details about the saga in her book about her life. (Riley, for her part, admits in an interview for *this* book that some personal experiences, such as the events of her divorce from her first husband, Mickey Riley, and her attitudes toward fellow country stars like Loretta Lynn, were indeed altered "for drama." However, she states: "I would like for it to be known that the things in my book *From Harper Valley to the Mountain Top* that really matter about my life are very true. My testimony is still sound.")

Another factor in the relative scarcity of Coe's output—and a slightly ironic one, at that—is that he has spent successive years in wild demand. So creatively accomplished was season one (Coe's first entrée, stunningly enough, into podcasting, though he has since gone on to co-create *Your Favorite Band Sucks* with Mark Mosley) that the autodidactic creator-narrator-writer was invited to conduct research at the Country Music Hall of Fame and Museum. This significantly broadened his access to rare documentation and other archival materials, and the show followed suit: Where season one's episodes were capped at two hours maximum, season two followed no such rules, with several installments breaching 140 minutes. Not that this hindered the show's popularity with its dedicated Patreon patrons: On the contrary, Coe adapted the season into a book for Simon & Schuster in 2024.

As both country music connoisseurs in such nations as Germany, Sweden, and

HOSTED BY
Tyler Mahan Coe

GENRE
Music

FIRST EPISODE
"CR001—Ernest Tubb: The Texas Defense" (October 24, 2017)

INFLUENCES
The Rest of the Story, Herman Melville, Robert Anton Wilson

WHERE TO LISTEN
Castbox

SEAN'S PICK
"CR007—Harper Valley PTA, Part 1: Shelby S. Singleton" (December 5, 2017)

Finland and more casual fans alike continue to discover *C&R*, Coe's fame has grown to the point where he is now recognized in public, at least partially. "The funniest thing about being a podcaster with a somewhat popular show (or two) is that most people don't really know what you look like but there are a lot of folks who become deeply familiar with the sound of your voice," he declares. "Most times I go to Honky Tonk Tuesdays at the American Legion here in Nashville, if I'm in the always-crowded sidebar talking to a friend, there'll be someone making their way through the room who hears my voice and stops to ask if I'm the guy from that country music podcast." It's been mostly "nice," Coe says, to have that "instant familiarity" with strangers. Just don't ask him when the next season comes out. "I don't know," he is liable to answer. "I have to make it first."

Punch Up the Jam

The road to immortality for *Punch Up the Jam* has been long and strange. Founded in 2017, it was headlined for its first two years by creators Demi Adejuyigbe and Miel Bredouw before Adejuyigbe left to pursue other projects. Bredouw held down the fort without any dip in quality control over the following year, partly solo and partly with Chris Fleming as guest co-host, before they, too, departed in 2020, leaving the podcast's devoted fans wondering if it was gone for good. The news that Headgum planned to revive the show in 2021 with newcomers Andrew and Evan Gregory at the helm was greeted with trepidation at first, then with increasing joy as the brothers proved to be every bit their predecessors' equals as master parodists. Sadly, this, too, was not to last.

In its Adejuyigbe-Bredouw era, the show delivered high-concept entertainment at a rare level of consistency. Each episode required the duo to "punch up" (industry lingo for fixing or making better) a well-known song by changing its lyrics, its melody, or both. Looking back at early installments, which covered tunes as universally beloved as Vanessa Carlton's "A Thousand Miles," "Your Song" by Elton John, and (how dare they) Phil Collins's "In the Air Tonight," one sees just how brazen the concept was at the time—and why, by extension, it attracted such a committed fan base so quickly. While the remixes may have been made all in good fun, they also effectively disrupted the monoculture by suggesting that established, epochal hits could still be seen as flawed. It was antiestablishment podcasting disguised as musical comedy.

Surely the concept would have grown stale quickly if not for the sophistication of Adejuyigbe and Bredouw's punch-ups. Often, these were less superficial edits than full-blown remixes requiring extensive production hours from the hosts, who alternated between singing and playing various instruments. "It was very much an idea that felt unique and involved an amount of work that made it something hard to replicate," Adejuyigbe remembers. In some cases, that work—or finding the time to complete it—was even prohibitive, as with unaired episodes centered on Prince's "Sexy MF" and Black Eyed Peas' "I Gotta Feeling." To this day, Adejuyigbe still has "a genuinely insane, long-winded but well-founded theory about the Charlie Daniels Band's 'The Devil Went Down to Georgia' being a metaphor for rock and roll being stolen from Black people" that never made the podcast, much to his chagrin.

It took courage for the Gregory brothers to try to fill his, Bredouw's, and Fleming's shoes (Fleming's "W.U.G. [Wildly Unlikeable Guy]" is incapable of being punched-up). Where Adejuyigbe and Bredouw talked a mile a minute, Andrew and Evan moseyed. They were generous in their love for artists like Bob Dylan and "Weird Al" Yankovic, more often choosing to celebrate their subjects than to pillory them. Their edges were softer. But in time, they demonstrated an aptitude for light jabbing not unlike that of Yankovic, who guested on their inaugural vivisection of Paul McCartney's "Wonderful Christmastime." Without that, the second *PUTJ* incarnation might not have survived as long as it did.

Despite that, after only fifty-two episodes, the Gregorys announced their own indefinite pause on December 22, 2022, exactly five years and a day after the first episode premiered. Whether the podcast will ever return remains up in the air. "It's a lot of effort to do it right and to make something unique that isn't just 'It's friends hanging out!'" Adejuyigbe admits. But with nearly two hundred episodes, it is hard to feel anything besides gratitude for the work these podcasters left behind . . . unless, of course, you wrote "Crash into Me." Then you're actually probably pretty pissed.

It was December 2017, lemme recap
See I was posted up like Santa with a shawty on my lap
I said c'mere baby girl, you're my present lemme open ya,
she leaned over and whispered "send help to ethiopia"

I asked her what was wrong, she said it's hot as an oven
We gotta pray for West Africa before we get to lovin'
Cause In Africa, it doesn't ever rain or snow
Instead of eggnog, they drink like, the blood of a crow, or somethin

Instead of turkey, they swallow their pride
You could turn their damn tears into a water slide
So take a good look at that bling on your wrist
'Cause every single child in Africa is Oliver Twist (but black!)

Cmon cmon, and send 'em some cash
Take this sad tear puddle, we can make it a splash
Cause in Africa, a bell is a death chime
Now raise your motherfuckin' glass, cause it's Christmastime

HOSTED BY
Demi Adejuyigbe, Miel Bredouw, Evan Gregory, and Andrew Rose Gregory

GENRE
Music

FIRST EPISODE
"'Little Drummer Boy' by Jack Halloran Singers" (December 21, 2017)

INFLUENCES
"Weird Al" Yankovic, JibJab, the Lonely Island, *Snacks and Shit* (Adejuyigbe)

WHERE TO LISTEN
Headgum

SEAN'S PICK
"'A Thousand Miles' by Vanessa Carlton (w/ Jon Cozart)" (August 9, 2018)

Song Exploder

At the root of Hrishikesh Hirway's *Song Exploder,* Hirway explains, is a simple desire: "to bring some insight into what artists are thinking while creating their music." This is easier said than done, of course; in capturing how the guts of songs come together into final, full tunes, one must wrestle not only with understanding their chord progressions, melodics, and intricacies of tone but also with the egos, attitudes, and celebrity of those who created them. Take, for example, a nearly catastrophic incident from the making of episode ninety-three, about Metallica's song "Moth into Flame." As Hirway remembers it, his long-in-the-works interview with Metallica singer James Hetfield was nearly ruined by the sound of a buzz saw next door just moments before Hetfield's shiny black SUV rounded the bend in front of his Los Angeles home. Frantic, Hirway was forced to run next door and plead for the workers there to hold.

Here's more from him: "Luckily, these guys looked like they might be really into Metallica. So I pointed at the car and said, 'That's James Hetfield from Metallica. Would you please let me get a clean recording with him?' They agreed to it, but one of them asked if I could get them an autograph in exchange. At the end of the interview, I told the whole story to James, who kindly obliged. I ran back over and gave the guy the autograph. But it turned out I'd misheard him, and it was addressed to the wrong name."

That Hirway makes this nightmare of a memory now seem pleasant—delightful, even!—is part and parcel of why *Song Exploder* has emerged as an island of singular pleasure in the music podcast realm. Like its host and founder's, the series' functional qualities are curiosity, excitement, and a desire to learn. Every episode is tight and digestible, running about twenty minutes, with not a single overlong or bloviating exception since January 2014. And Hirway's taste in the music worth dissecting piece by piece—which runs the gamut from pop (Kesha, Madonna, Santigold) to hip-hop (Common, Run the Jewels, Meek Mill) to country (Maren Morris, Brandi Carlile, Jewel)—is impeccable and vast.

HOSTED BY
Hrishikesh Hirway

GENRE
Music

FIRST EPISODE
"The Postal Service: 'The
District Sleeps Alone
Tonight'" (January 1, 2014)

INFLUENCES
Sergei Prokofiev's *Peter and
the Wolf*, *WTF with Marc
Maron*, *The Memory Palace*

WHERE TO LISTEN
PRX

SEAN'S PICK
"The Magnetic Fields:
'Andrew in Drag'"
(September 24, 2015)

This has made Hirway something like podcast royalty as one of the most prolific and most recognizable figures in the field. By current count, he has hosted or produced eight podcasts, including the Spanish-language spin-off, *Canción Exploder*, and the much-beloved TV-recap podcast *The West Wing Weekly*, in addition to creating an acclaimed streaming adaptation of *Song Exploder* for Netflix. Nonetheless, it is this original podcast version that remains his crowning achievement for many, including members of the Academy of Podcasters, who awarded it Best Music Podcast in 2016 and 2017. Just don't ask Hirway to sign any autographs.

The Best Show

The town of Newbridge, New Jersey, tends to attract weirdos. Some of the creeps living there include Bryce Prefontaine, a Grateful Dead–obsessed pothead whose weed stench is perceptible from his lean-to behind a decrepit Lady Foot Locker; Gene Simmons of KISS, or some ball-busting alternate-universe version of him; and Roy Ziegler, a.k.a. Philly Boy Roy, a pain-in-the-ass lowlife and crook of proud Pennsylvania stock who coincidentally serves as Newbridge's criminal mayor.

Thankfully, none of these tools are real. They are merely the creations of musician Jon Wurster, who on his nights off drumming for bands like Superchunk and the Mountain Goats performs as one half of the comedy duo Scharpling & Wurster. The other half is Tom Scharpling, founder and host of *The Best Show* since its early life as a radio show on New Jersey's WFMU.

Originally slated for a 9:00 P.M. time slot, *The Best Show* began broadcasting its signature blend of live calls, music, and comedy in October 2000, only to expand to its now-classic three-hour format the next year. Since then, the show has featured Wurster as dozens of obnoxious residents of the fictitious Newbridge, all pretending to call in and bother poor fellow Newbridgian "Tom Scharpling." But Scharpling, the bemused straight man to Wurster's demonic characters, is hardly a victim; rather, he is the show's stalwart conductor and impresario, shifting out of Wurster's outrageous appearances and into serious conversations with stars like Aimee Mann and Paul Rudd like a dolphin catching waves. In between, he spins any tunes that catch his fancy—or asks the musicians who wrote them to perform them.

That sense of easy listening has made *The Best Show* a touchstone for many fellow musicians, comedians, and podcasters over more than twenty years, even after the show left WFMU and became a weekly independent podcast in 2014. Over a decade later, it remains a strange, surreal anomaly in podcasting: an epically long yet never boring synthesis of droll comedy, intuitive interviewing, and independent music (Scharpling's team of producers and engineers never misses). Fans hail Scharpling and Wurster for their relentless refusal to reach for the low-hanging fruit so favored by lazier comedians, an antagonism reinforced by the show's signature motto, "Steamrollin' Chumps." For Scharpling, who day jobs as a television writer for hit series like *Monk* and *What We Do in the Shadows*, *The Best Show* simply provides a bit of space for the weirdos of the world. As one of them, I consider this no small gesture.

HOSTED BY
Tom Scharpling

GENRE
Music

FIRST EPISODE
Untitled (Radio:
October 10, 2000; Podcast:
December 16, 2014)

INFLUENCES
SCTV, David Letterman,
Bob and Ray, Andy
Kaufman, *Saturday Night
Live*, Coyle & Sharpe

WHERE TO LISTEN
Forever Dog

SEAN'S PICK
"TOM CANNOT
COMPLAIN! THE VANCE
AND GARY SHOW!
ANDY BRECKMAN!"
(April 20, 2016)

The Take

When Alexandra Locke first joined Al Jazeera's current-affairs podcast, *The Take*, as executive producer, it was still being released in weekly increments. Malika Bilal, a former digital producer for *The Stream*, had just stepped in as interim host following the departure of the commanding Imtiaz Tyab. The show was still finding its footing with listeners, having just started its second season. "Time," Locke tells me, "was a luxury."

Less than a year later, Bilal returned to announce that *The Take* was moving to three episodes a week, with her on board as permanent host. Bilal, for her part, made the upgrade sound almost natural: Much of the world was frozen in place by COVID, and people were devouring information more conscientiously—and ravenously—than ever. But it paid humongous dividends: At the height of the pandemic, *The Take* emerged as one of the most trustworthy news programs in production, with Bilal as her generation's audio answer to Walter Cronkite.

"If there was one bright spot in that time period, it had to have been the recognition that podcasts were this lovely lifeline to the rest of the world that could withstand all that work-from-home culture threw at it," the host says today. "What other news medium could thrive like we could under lockdown conditions?" When COVID created an aggressive discourse around remote work in the United States, Bilal brought the late anthropologist David Graeber on to discuss labor inequality, essential workers, and Graeber's phrase "We are the 99%." When world leaders met at the United Nations Climate Change Conference (COP26) in Glasgow, she interviewed the former president of Kiribati, Anote Tong, about the threat that climate change posed to his sinking island nation. For listeners, such empathetic and informed conversations came to feel like essential correctives to inadequate coverage of these issues from more established news outlets.

Appropriately, in 2021, Bilal was named Best Podcast Host by the Gracie Awards, while the show won an Online Journalism Award in the Excellence in Audio Digital Storytelling, Ongoing Series category from the highly reputed Online News Association. Soon, Al Jazeera began releasing bite-size episodes (typically around twenty minutes long) covering "the real story on what you need to know about the world" on its website every single day. As Locke says, "Turning our show into a daily podcast took years of work under the hood and a team of serious talent ready to pounce on news before it hits the headlines." It meant adding intensive, deep-dive reporting on topics like the future of Indian space colonization and the global plague of loneliness to a coverage slate that already included conflicts in the Middle East, Ukraine, and Sudan.

But for anyone considering a listen, Bilal stresses that, for all the professionalism of its production team, *The Take* never went dire. "There was also joy, like in the conversation I had with two Black Iranian women over Zoom from the closet. They talked about what it's like to be a minority in Iran—from the beauty of it to the difficulty. The amount of laughter and levity, and perhaps therapy, that flowed in that interview was palpable."

HOSTED BY
Malika Bilal and Imtiaz Tyab

GENRE
News

FIRST EPISODE
"Syria: The Endgame"
(October 19, 2018)

INFLUENCES
Ira Glass, Anna Sale

WHERE TO LISTEN
Al Jazeera English

SEAN'S PICK
"In a New Space Race,
Who's In and Who's Out?"
(January 8, 2024)

Chapo Trap House

"You're listening to Chapo Trap House, attempting to wring content out of the cruel and futile spectacle of US electoral politics."

If it were up to the team that makes it, *Chapo Trap House* would never appear in a book like this. Accolades, acclaim, recognition—none of it gels with the irony-pilled personae that Felix Biederman, Matt Christman, Amber A'Lee Frost, Will Menaker, and (at one time) Virgil Texas have adopted as the voices of the current events show since 2016. On air, they have become vectors for the pain of the disenfranchised, furiously piling onto American politicians and shadow oligarchs for the physical and emotional harms they impose on people struggling day after day. Every conversation is like a roomful of Gatling guns aimed at cutouts of Dennis Prager firing simultaneously; sarcasm, contempt, and flippancy are their bullets.

For tens of thousands of so-called Grey Wolves (a mocking reference to a Turkish paramilitary group), subscribing to the podcast on Patreon for an average of around four bucks each month has come to feel like an act of protest against any infrastructure—religious, military, class-based—designed by the rich to make themselves richer while everyone else grows poorer. To contribute is to yawp along with the hosts at the wounded recognition of our shared unwitting subjugation. As Menaker, the group's de facto front man, joked in his 2021 interview with documentarian Adam Curtis, "'I'm not the object of propaganda . . . I'm smart. I'm of the group of people that . . . doesn't fall for that kind of thing.' Well, I mean, if you believe that . . . chances are you're absolutely the victim of propaganda." Through the shepherding of Chris Wade, who has produced *Chapo* since 2018, the hosts (reluctantly and excluding Christman, who was unavailable for comment at the time) revealed that their podcast's primary inspirations were not explicitly political but comic: *The Ricky Gervais Show*, *Mystery Science Theater 3000*, *The Flop House*.

"My parents in general were pretty generous with what media they allowed me to consume when I was a child, but my mom expressly thought Howard Stern was hilarious and interesting," says Biederman, the most eloquent and acrid of the original creators. "She bought me *Private Parts* when I was twelve, and I read it nonstop until our tyrannical blowhard gym teacher took it from me." Wade also cites the development of alternative distribution structures in the American hardcore and underground music scene of the 1980s as one pillar of the show's enormous success. Under his aegis, *Chapo* was ranked Patreon's third-most popular podcast creator as of September 2024.

Still, to dismiss the venture as a tongue-in-cheek bit ignores the immense respect it commands in the political podcasting sector. Along with the teams behind *Cum Town* and *TrueAnon*, Biederman, Christman, and Menaker are considered progenitors of a kind of civically engaged audio news program that eschews the fake politesse of broadcast cable in favor of a more explicitly angry and empathetic mode of discourse. Among the luminaries who have appeared as guests are six presidential hopefuls, New York gubernatorial candidate Cynthia Nixon, and political commentators like Briahna Joy Gray and David Sirota. That these free-flowing, often vulgar conversations are sometimes described as extensions of what's been termed "dirtbag leftism"—a nebulous designation for any personal politics anchored by a willingness to openly scorn opposing ideologies—reflects just how committed *Chapo* is to the very real work of damning any and every authority figure willing to inflict class violence on their fellow citizens in the name of capital. Or, to use Menaker's words: "For all our shit talk, we do love you."

HOSTED BY
Felix Biederman, Matt Christman, Amber A'Lee Frost, Will Menaker, and Virgil Texas

GENRE
Politics

FIRST EPISODE
"Episode 1—THA SAGA BEGINS" (March 12, 2016)

INFLUENCES
Loveline, *Mystery Science Theater 3000*, *The Ricky Gervais Show*, *Cum Town*, *Mike and the Mad Dog*, Howard Stern, *Our Band Could Be Your Life*, *The Flop House*, Fugazi, *The G. Gordon Liddy Show*

WHERE TO LISTEN
Patreon

SEAN'S PICK
"Episode 65—No Future Feat. Adam Curtis" (December 12, 2016)

Fake the Nation

If there is any justice, it will not be long before Negin Farsad is as well known in the Western world as Samantha Bee, Whoopi Goldberg, and Bill Maher. All operate in the sphere of political comedy, digesting headlines and the latest current events through conversations with wonky, civically minded peers. The key difference comes down to Farsad herself, a weapons-grade wit who over four hundred episodes of *Fake the Nation* has proved as capable of hosting a presidential debate for CNN as she is an episode of *Wait, Wait . . . Don't Tell Me!* (see p. 110).

From its inception, her series has focused directly on issues of grave seriousness without batting an eyelash—or losing its sense of humor. "As a child growing up in the desert of Southern California, I thought that if you lived in New York City, you would always be throwing dinner parties with the most fascinating people engaged in the most scintillating and hilarious conversation," Farsad, a filmmaker and actor with a master's degree in African American studies, shares. She was inspired to create the podcast, she adds, by the kind of imagery she saw on *Friends* and in high-society magazines: "Like you're witness to the coolest dinner party conversation with the smartest and funniest people. And that maybe Joey would fall off his chair for some reason."

Farsad got the chance to make a test pilot in June 2016. But the week she had selected to record it coincided with the deadly massacre at Pulse, a gay nightclub in Orlando, Florida. "*Fake the Nation* was meant to be a comedic show about news and culture, so I figured the network would let me skip mass murder," she recalls. "But no, they wanted to see how comedians handled appalling tragedy." Making the pilot called for a delicate balance of entertaining political analysis and respect for the families of those involved. Though it went unreleased, executives at Earwolf were impressed with Farsad's sensitive handling of the attack, greenlighting and launching the podcast the following month.

Like *The View* and Maher's *Real Time*, *Fake the Nation* is a panel show, just on a slightly smaller scale. Episodes typically feature two panelists along with Farsad as their de facto ringmaster, as demonstrated by the

Politics

168

HOSTED BY
Negin Farsad

GENRE
Politics (*Content Warning: Violence*)

FIRST EPISODE
"Beyoncé for Vice President" (July 8, 2016)

INFLUENCES
"An idyllic dinner party" (Farsad)

WHERE TO LISTEN
Headgum

SEAN'S PICK
"Avocado Tax (and Other Bad News)" (June 6, 2019)

ding-ding before each of three topic segments. Farsad calls the first the "amuse-bouche," as she invokes softer talking points meant merely to whet the appetite, such as whether a husband is entitled to give his wife the silent treatment after she disappears for five weeks (from the episode "Erudite OnlyFans") or if Taylor Swift deserved to be named *Time*'s Person of the Year ("F*ckbags Who Suck"). Then it's on to more pressing subjects for the last two segments: Are the United Nations Climate Change Conference's plastic waste reduction efforts sufficient ("The Economy of Your Heart")? What do the results of Super Tuesday say about American voters ("Sonny & Scare")? Which nations get to make space laws ("Ladies Brunch on the Moon")?

These are complex topics for anyone, much less professional entertainers, but under Farsad's aegis, punching down is strictly verboten. The guest list is a veritable who's who of comedians selected exclusively for their shared political literacy and intelligence: Akilah Hughes, Ted Alexandro, Judah Friedlander, Paula Poundstone, Margaret Cho, Mo Rocca. Bee, a grandmaster of political comedy, has also made several appearances, including on the fan favorite 2020 episode "The Smells of Christmas," in which she delivered a soaring monologue about parenting in the days before the pandemic. Metatextually speaking, her recurring presence feels something like the passing of a torch, a tacit acknowledgment that if there is anyone else on earth capable of making, say, an impassioned argument for politicians to do more to address the mental health epidemic both informed and hilarious (as she does in the episode "Ugly Time"), it is Farsad. Television executives would be wise to pay heed.

The Majority Report with Sam Seder

The duality of man is ne'er more evident than on the five-time award-winning *Majority Report*. Every episode is a study in contrasts, partly a dogged corrective against abject moral cowardice and partly an irreverent satire of modern political media. Where one segment might have Associated Press investigative reporters Margie Mason and Robin McDowell on to discuss prison labor, the "Fun Half" might feature Tim Heidecker impersonating antagonistic commentators like Steven Crowder or Tim Pool. Even its title is, "like most things I do," host Sam Seder described in 2016, "half a joke and half not a joke. You can't quite tell, and I don't really know either."

TMR originated with a one-off appearance that Seder and Janeane Garofalo made on Tom Scharpling's *The Best Show* (see p. 162) in February 2003. Featuring a live introduction by Seder's college friend H. Jon Benjamin (of *Bob's Burgers* and *Archer* fame), the two-hour block was charged with the comedians' anger at the media's burying of "voices of dissent" over the impending war in Iraq, which they argued was a direct result of the Supreme Court's decision to reject America's voting majority in their *Bush v. Gore* ruling. So electrifying and courageous was this position at "a time where there was no liberal talk radio, certainly not at a national level, and certainly nothing on television," in Seder's words, that Air America offered Garofalo (and, upon her insistence, Seder) their own program, which launched the next year.

Following Garofalo's departure in 2006, Seder took the reins full-time, guiding *TMR* through key changes to its personnel and audience. "I often speak of *The Majority Report* in its 'current iteration,' which I date to late 2010, when it became strictly an online show. In those early years, I vacillated between calling it a podcast and a show, because we have always been live but more listened to as a podcast or on demand," he explains a month after its twentieth anniversary. Speaking on transformative moments, he cites the 2013 addition of late producer and co-host

Michael Brooks, as well as the addition of his successor, Emma Vigeland, advertising head Kelly Carey, and producers Matt Lech, Matt Binder, and Jamie Peck. On top of fomenting a "clubhouse" culture, Seder notes, these teammates made the program funnier and kept it apace with the evolution of online political culture during the Trump presidency.

Despite such changes, *TMR* still delivers what it has always promised: a daily information antidote to misogyny-rich, climate-change-denying, genocide-supporting brain poison. "We try to create an environment where we are constantly learning new things along with the audience, where the show becomes an experience that educates and inspires but is imperfect and not intimidating," Seder says. This can sometimes seem futile, as when he and Vigeland "do their best to educate libertarians on just how hypocritical their backwards ideology is," a process so frequent that it inspired a nearly two-hundred-video-long playlist. But it also has its benefits: *TMR*'s YouTube channel has over 1.5 million subscribers, who propel it to more than 12 million views a month.

Given such massive consumer loyalty across two decades, it is impossible to overstate the show's impact on American politics. Since leaving, Garofalo has become regarded as a hero and pioneer for having been among the first public figures to speak out against the Bush administration. Seder, too, often hears "from young people who tell me they were headed down a right-wing path" until they discovered the podcast. He is living proof that a lifelong commitment to the protection of democratic freedoms, especially in the face of encroaching fascism, is a winning strategy for any broadcaster.

THE MAJORITY REPORT

WITH SAM SEDER

HOSTED BY
Janeane Garofalo and Sam Seder

GENRE
Politics

FIRST EPISODE
"A Call from Jarrett 'the Weight Loss Kid' from Dessert Town, Who Pushes the Toxic 'Chocologgedeon' on Tom. Later: The Debut of The Majority Report with Sam Seder, Julian Phillips of Fox News, and Janeane Garofalo" (Radio: February 11, 2003; Podcast: November 3, 2010)

INFLUENCES
The Howard Stern Show, Amy Goodman, Christopher Lydon, Janeane Garofalo, Bill Moyers, Dick Cavett, Phil Hendrie, the Replacements, Rush Limbaugh, AM talk radio

WHERE TO LISTEN
Majority Report Radio

SEAN'S PICK
"2094—The Handmaid's Tale Becomes a Reality w/ Benjamin Dixon & Things Get Awkward w/ H. Jon Benjamin" (May 17, 2019)

Another Round

It's long past time to buy a round for Tracy Clayton and Heben Nigatu, hosts of the dearly missed *Another Round* podcast. Despite creating an environment fertile enough for both perceptive commentary and shamelessly drunken banter about the multitudinous experiences of Blackness and brownness, BuzzFeed put the show on an inexplicable permanent hiatus in 2017. "Even after becoming an immediate hit, *Another Round* never received the respect or the fanfare it deserved from our employers and it made producing the show very difficult," Clayton and Nigatu write to me. "Not having your hard work seen or recognized makes you feel invisible, and feeling invisible causes a whole host of internal problems. We really struggled with that both as employees and as Black women."

Yet in cultural spaces, Clayton and Nigatu's work across more than 113 extraordinary episodes continues to leave ripples in listeners' brains. Their podcast remains so widely adored in no small measure because it is unclassifiable, a sumptuous cocktail assembled from equal parts clip show, talk show, music appreciation show, cultural salon, and call-in advice program. It was neither didactic nor impatient, the primary default modes for many dialogic spaces addressing race in a modern context. As Tracy put it in the "Citizen's Arrest" episode, "We're not here to be anybody's diversity counselors."

Another Round infused interviews with the likes of Quinta Brunson, Ava DuVernay, and Roxane Gay with the same searing level of wit and warmth carousingly brought to more tongue-in-cheek segments, like "White Devil's Advocate" and "Drunken Debates." A weekly program, it tackled topical, racially charged events (e.g., the whitewashing scandal around Marvel's *Doctor Strange* and the deadly "Unite the Right" rally in Charlottesville) without ever losing sight of how they reflected the more holistic marginalization of people of color every day in the global West. Unlike the show's corporate distributors, Clayton and Nigatu's peers expressed constant admiration for what this brought to the American cultural conversation. "When our one-year anniversary hit, we didn't expect any recognition," the hosts say, "but we got the best surprise in the world

Pop Culture

172

HOSTED BY
Tracy Clayton and Heben Nigatu

GENRE
Pop Culture

FIRST EPISODE
"Unlearning (with Durga Chew-Bose)" (March 24, 2015)

INFLUENCES
"The *Ricki Lake* show (the one from the '90s), Beyoncé, *In Living Color*, happy hour, Audie Cornish, Anna Sale, Black girls everywhere" (Clayton); "Oprah, the library, every time Carrie said, 'I couldn't help but wonder . . .' on *Sex and the City*" (Nigatu)

WHERE TO LISTEN
Spotify

SEAN'S PICK
"What's on Your Reparations Tab? (with Ta-Nehisi Coates)" (October 20, 2015)

when our Black friends and colleagues surprised us with flowers (a bouquet for each of us), a bottle of whiskey, and a huge handmade card filled with love and congrats and well wishes. Somewhere there's a picture of us holding them all, smiling from ear to ear, likely on the verge of tears. It meant so much."

Almost a decade since MacArthur "Genius" Nikole Hannah-Jones schooled and "DJ extraordinaire" Donwill serenaded Brooklyn's Bell House with satirical carols in the cathartic final "Kwanzaa Spectacular," *Another Round* still sounds peerless in its unapologetic and challenging analysis of difference ("Fuck politeness" is how Nigatu said it at the time). And while the show's pause appears to be never-ending, its hosts now know how far from invisible they truly are: "Hearing our people tell us that they see and appreciate us truly shifted our center of gravity and gave us a priceless reminder of why we were making the show. To borrow from Toni Morrison's comments about Ralph Ellison's *Invisible Man*: Invisible to whom? Not to them. That's what really mattered then, it's what matters the most now, and that knowledge is a weapon we need as we continue on through life. We still have the card! (We definitely drank the whiskey.)"

Uhh Yeah Dude

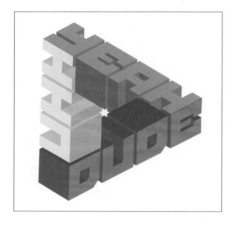

Who would you prefer burglarized your home: a little person dressed as Chucky or a fifty-nine-year-old in a Ghostface mask? How would you rather die: from a bloody encounter with a vagina dentata or at the hands of an angry John Rambo? Rick Moranis, John Corbett, and Peter Gallagher get into a prison fight—which one comes out alive?

Jonathan Larroquette and Seth Romatelli have spent sixty minutes of every week for twentyish years slow-killing each other's brain cells with dumbass prompts like these. Romatelli says, "I remember being at a birthday party in February of 2006"—the month the duo premiered their trailblazing podcast *Uhh Yeah Dude*—"and trying to explain to people there what me and Jonathan had just started doing. Nobody (including myself) had any idea what I was talking about." When he and Larroquette first got going, mocking MySpace (now Myspace) and reading Craigslist personals ("I was wearing a leather jacket. Did you notice me?"), they were navigating uncharted waters. Podcasting was still technologically rudimentary and far from tipping into popular culture. "At least for that period of time, it felt like a new thing. Something that was open and free to all to partake both in making and listening," Larroquette concurs.

Neither of them particularly minded being the Lewis and Clark of this broadcasting netherworld, making "radio for the cyber generation," as they once described it. Actually, that was sort of the point. "At its core, it's just the two of us, in a room, chopping it up," Romatelli summarizes. In that sense, *UYD* is *pure* core. Each episode runs one hour long, give or take a minute, and opens and closes with some vibey music. In between, "Sethro" and "Jah" talk about nothing and everything: deaths by lightning strike, overabundant 911 calls, undeserving Westminster Kennel Club Dog

Show winners (Rufus, you rascal!), the seven-year itch, sociopaths with low resting heart rates, New Balance cutting a little deal with Dunkin', the second-oldest woman in the world (RIP, Bessie Hendricks).

Occasionally, especially in the early days, it could dip into fucked-up territory: Pedophile rings, incestuous wet dreams, and queer-baiting "Rumors of the Week" about '90s TV stars all made appearances before the hosts locked into a more inclusive, less clumsily provocative modality. That was partly because there has never really been anyone to rein it in—*UYD* has no guests, no advertisers, and no rules (it is entirely supported through listener patronage). "Suffice to say, we didn't know what we were doing or who was hearing it or how, technically, the entire thing worked," Larroquette admits.

They learned better fast, though, and eventually figured out how to be just two "American Americans" in a room together at no cost to anyone. Even after listening to hundreds of hours of chatter, I still can't say when, exactly, they entered the ineffable flow state that defines an exceptional episode like "Episode 814 08/25/2020." Nor can I verbalize what it is about "big dog and his handler" going fully "off-chain" at 5:53 P.M., talking about cereal brands whose mascots don't make good enough eye contact, and FaceTiming with Larroquette's father, the actor John Larroquette, that works so assuredly. All I know is that at one point, when someone proposed titling a new Discovery+ series *I'm Sucking and Fucking a Mama's Boy,* I laughed so hard that I developed a semipermanent cough.

Oh, and for what it's worth, they don't think Moranis and Gallagher have the desperation necessary to go all the way. "John Corbett would bite you!" argues Romatelli. Disagree? Call them at 888-842-2357 and let them know.

HOSTED BY
Jonathan Larroquette
and Seth Romatelli

GENRE
Pop Culture

FIRST EPISODE
"Episode 1 02/11/2006"
(February 11, 2006)

INFLUENCES
"My father, John Larroquette" (Larroquette);
"My father, Joe Romatelli" (Romatelli)

WHERE TO LISTEN
Patreon

SEAN'S PICK
"Episode 814 08/25/2020"
(August 25, 2020)

Asian Not Asian

There is a moment in "Boys Night," a 2023 episode of Jenny Arimoto and Mic Nguyen's *Asian Not Asian* podcast, when Nguyen and guest Fumi Abe, the show's co-creator and former host, just stop talking altogether. For most of the conversation before that, Abe and Nguyen warmly catch up on Abe's burgeoning comedy career while both are easing back into the familiar roles of therapist and comrade. They sound jittery with excitement, swapping jokes and life stories at double speed. Then, suddenly, the zippiness of their reunion kind of . . . slows down . . . There is a beat . . . four . . . five . . . six seconds of silence.

Anyone who has ever felt held exactly where they are by a longtime friend will recognize this moment of comfort—yet it is the only time I can ever remember hearing such a thing on a podcast. It is the kind of space that Abe, Nguyen, and, more recently, Arimoto have worked to create and maintain for themselves and their unfortunately named fans, the ANALS, on their New York–based talk show. *Asian Not Asian* bills itself as a "dive deep into the weirdness which is the Asian American–ish experience" and a place to "discuss race, politics, media, funny stuff, food pics, peace signs, model minority myths, urban myths, and Urban Outfitters." And, yes, it is undoubtedly those things. "The podcast was the first and only public place where I've really talked about my dad's death," Arimoto offers by way of example. "It was in part a way to process my feelings (selfishly), but also because I trust our community of listeners and felt that it would be a safe space to be honest about what I was going through."

But according to Nguyen, who has steered the ship since its 2018 launch, it has also always quietly been a show about the intensity of friendship: "In a way, the podcast is/was an exploration of the relationship [Abe and I] had with each other. There have been several moments in the show where I'm essentially looking to him in order to assuage the vast amount of insecurities I have, and he, in a reversal of our usual student-senpai relationship, gives me the tough love I need." In early episodes, that dynamic propelled Abe and Nguyen's interviews to uproarious heights. Both are stand-ups by trade, and when they took turns soft-grilling Randall Park,

Ronny Chieng, and other guests about their lives as descendants of Asians, it often felt like they had their arms locked against the world.

The miracle of *Asian Not Asian* is that this still held true after Arimoto joined full-time in 2022. Under the nickname "the Asian Friends," she and Nguyen quickly cultivated a dynamic distinct from that of the first three years—one anchored in processing feelings and truth encountered in their daily lives—without abandoning the spry, sour humor that made the show so potent early on. This was particularly challenging for Arimoto, who before the podcast had just performed comedy in character. Only after years of co-hosting has she learned how to "become comfortable, perhaps a little too comfortable, being myself in front of an audience," she admits. No complaints from us, Jenny.

HOSTED BY
Fumi Abe, Jenny Arimoto, and Mic Nguyen

GENRE
Race and Society

FIRST EPISODE
"The Rice Cooker" (February 26, 2018)

INFLUENCES
"My therapy sessions, *Feeling Asian*" (Arimoto); "Desus and Mero, but Asian" (Nguyen)

WHERE TO LISTEN
ART19

SEAN'S PICK
"Big Dick White Girl Energy" (December 3, 2018)

Yo, Is This Racist?

The perceived fraughtness of engaging in honest, adult discourse around racism in US culture has kept many a podcast from even broaching the topic. For some fragile white podcasters, the imagined fear of saying something ignorant that lives online forever can induce a paralyzing spasm of wordlessness, whereas for BIPOC podcasters, it can feel exhaustingly like all anyone wants is a hot take on your identity politics or for you to offer up the pain of living in a still largely segregated and overpoliced state as entertainment. As a result, a lot of potentially meaningful audio art falls by the wayside.

That, at least in part, is why the *Yo, Is This Racist?* project has remained so singular since the comedy writer Andrew Ti launched it, on Tumblr, in 2011. From the first, Ti was a bold and fearless commentator on racism, capable of not only isolocating it in otherwise innocuous social behaviors but also of rendering his critiques of it pithily and hilariously. When his readers ask him to confirm if something is indeed offensive, he can be brutally direct. One such example from January 2, 2013, goes as follows:

"Anonymous asked: 'I met a white lady with twin adopted Asian daughters she named Jasmine and Jade. Those names seem pretty racist. Am I right?'"

"OH, I'M SURE IT'S JUST A RACIST COINCIDENCE."

Perhaps just as importantly, Ti—laser-focused and motormouthed and casually obscene—is also a born podcaster. When *YITR* first launched on the Earwolf network in the fall of 2012, Ti took listener calls and read emails along with guests whom he regularly outclassed in intensity, sometimes even challenging those who dithered or refused to take hard positions on what he saw as obviously stereotypical or bigoted behavior. For all his silliness, Ti took the gig profoundly seriously, he confesses: "In the early incarnation of the show, when it was just hosted by [me], the show ran as five ten-to-fifteen-minute mini-episodes a week, once daily, which helped get our episode count up exponentially compared to weekly shows." ("This makes us look like one of the longest-running podcasts in existence, but we're probably not," he disclaims.)

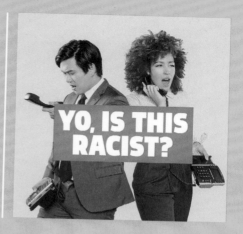

HOSTED BY
Tawny Newsome and Andrew Ti

GENRE
Race and Society

FIRST EPISODE
"Jimmies" (October 1, 2012)

INFLUENCES
"Hard to think of anyone else stupid
enough to tackle racism in this way" (Ti)

WHERE TO LISTEN
Sub-Optimal

SEAN'S PICK
"Dating Outside Your Class"
(March 5, 2013)

On that parenthetical, Ti is mistaken. Throughout its second decade, *YITR* has stayed a staunch and irreplaceable salon for critical thinking on race, even as larger conversations on the subject have edged their way deeper into popular discourse with the emergence of Black Lives Matter and the Stop Asian Hate movements. Much of that longevity is owed to Tawny Newsome, the musician and actor well known for improv-sharpened performances on *Space Force* and *Bajillion Dollar Propertie$*. With her seemingly boundless energy, Newsome infused the podcast with a much-needed bonhomie when she joined as Ti's slightly less cynical counterpart in 2018.

Their more balanced, two-headed approach (or, more accurately, three-headed, thanks to the regular appearances of producer Kevin Bartelt in later episodes) reshaped *YITR* for a new generation of more informed, more tolerant listeners. Not long after, Newsome and Ti launched Sub-Optimal Podcasts, an independent subscription site offering bonus content like *Yo, Can We Live?*, a sister series featuring "regular-ass" talk for anyone "sick of stories of Black and brown folks' trauma." The one thing it does not include are Ti's old Tumblr posts, which are still good for a quick, angry laugh:

"Hos-nax-deactivated20240116 asked: 'Is it racist to call out racism by somebody who's a different race from me?'"

"I guess it depends on some details, but broadly, DO THAT SHIT ALL THE TIME."

On Being

Vulnerability is the vehicle and grace the fuel for *On Being*, the main podcast organ of Krista Tippett's Minneapolis-based nonprofit, the On Being Project. And oh, what a sensitive, soft show that makes for!—A titanic attempt, in Tippett's gentle hands, to map the variegated contours of humanity's spiritual search.

Tippett, a Fulbright Scholar and journalist, launched what was then called *First Person* in 2001 as a monthly show with American Public Media; in 2003, as it transitioned to a weekly schedule amid a fast-widening listenership, it became *Speaking of Faith*, a title more directly reflective of what were essentially (and please understand, this is a simplification of tremendous proportions) fifty-minute dialogues on the personal purpose of belief for the likes of the Dalai Lama, Thich Nhat Hanh, Maya Angelou, and Elie Wiesel. The next twenty years are a blur of landmark moments: a Peabody Award in 2007; a final retitling to *On Being* in 2010; Tippett's founding of what would become the On Being Project in 2013; a National Humanities Medal awarded by President Barack Obama in 2014. Then, finally, in June 2021, came what Tippett refers to as "this last chapter": a defining move from public radio to a seasonal, podcast-only format.

"I didn't realize how bullied and constrained we were by the public radio clock—how much of our editorial energy was spent killing kittens," Tippett reveals in 2024. Already, the show was heralded as a ground-breaker for putting both "radio timed" and unedited versions of every interview up on its feed. But this newfound freedom meant that Tippett could "let each individual conversation determine how long it wants to be, edited for clarity and arc but not timed and tidied; where and whether the breaks, et cetera." Her voice changed, too, dropping its performative made-for-broadcast lilt in favor of a warmer, more natural whisper. That voice . . . it is enough to make you cry sometimes, weighted as it is with implications of kinship and compassion. Many guests do.

Religion &
Spirituality

Those with a healthy skepticism of any media that proselytizes, promotes faith-based connection, or purports to engage with that most challenging of topics—religion—may find the sound of all this a little bit scary. Fair enough: In podcasting especially, the abundance of pseudospiritualism and extremist evangelists masquerading as figures of balance and enlightenment has only bred distrust. Tippett, for what it's worth, experienced that firsthand. "I had to fight very hard to get this show taken seriously inside my own first organization (American Public Media; Minnesota Public Radio)," she told me. "My subject was suspect, as was I."

Be comforted, then, that *On Being* is, by design, the paradigmatic safe space for seekers of any inclination. In addition to leaders of religious and spiritual thought, the podcast also opens itself to the experiences of diverse creative characters in the hope that they, too, can offer guidance—like the musician Nick Cave, who mused on the grief of child loss with Tippett, and the activist-writer Rebecca Solnit, an expert on the consequences of natural disaster. Tippett says that in the wake of the pandemic, her team is "thinking hard about what our particular work is to do, what people turn to us for." That includes creating the Lab for the Art of Living, which mines the podcast's twenty-plus-year-spanning archive for tools that listeners can actively use in their lives, as well as moving toward more "convenings" meant to ignite generative conversations at a time when "the world is in such pain, and faces such vast audacious callings." Were it anyone else assigning themselves such a writ, it would all seem too significant to shoulder alone. But in Krista Tippett, my faith is unshakable.

HOSTED BY
Krista Tippett

GENRE
Religion and Spirituality

FIRST EPISODE
"Where Was God?" (September 22, 2001)

INFLUENCES
"Gaggy," Tippett's grandfather; Pema Chödrön; Rainer Maria Rilke

WHERE TO LISTEN
The On Being Project

SEAN'S PICK
"John Polkinghorne: Quarks and Creation" (January 13, 2011)

The Witch Wave

For Pam Grossman, creator and host of *The Witch Wave*, podcasting is a matter of life or death. While hers is, in format, primarily an interview show in the *NPR* style (Grossman has been called "the Terry Gross of witches"), at its heart is the more onerous project of educating listeners about the daily lived realities shared by countless numbers of people like her: modern practitioners of non-Abrahamic belief systems endangered by centuries of entrenched sexism, xenophobia, and misinformation.

As a curator and historian on the subject—as well as the author of *Waking the Witch*, a stunning autobiographical tome about her embrace of alternative spirituality as a young woman—Grossman is a walking repository for all things magick. This is key, because while cosmic spiritualism and the occult are experiencing what she calls a "current trendiness," those whose only knowledge of them comes from fairy tales, urban legends, and children's stories (more often than not written and promulgated by men to enforce patriarchal hierarchies) still use them to discriminate against the mystically sensitive.

Grossman's job is therefore not only to research, write, and narrate each week's episode with the utmost fluency and verisimilitude on her subject; it is also to create an environment of trust and safety so that other keepers of ritual and craft can share their ancient knowledge without needing to worry about what kind of shit will get thrown at them on social media afterward.

Grossman says that this has made speaking with "the pioneering elders" of contemporary magick for the podcast particularly urgent. She

Religion &
Spirituality

cites a 2020 interview with Rachel Pollack, "a tarot scholar and witchly writer" responsible for co-creating the first transgender superhero, Kate Godwin, a.k.a. Coagula, for the comic book *Doom Patrol*, as one such career highlight. "Rachel gave me my first-ever professional tarot reading many moons ago, when I was in my twenties and in need of guidance," the host recalls. She reconnected with Pollack at the Occult Humanities Conference at NYU in 2019, when Pollack was battling cancer, and invited her onto the podcast. Their interview—an overdue attempt, Grossman admits, to celebrate Pollack's lifetime of work on a global platform—was "a full-circle moment" for the host. It was also one of the guest's final interviews. Pollack died in April 2023.

Yet the fight goes on for Grossman, as she writes in the "afterwyrd" of *Waking the Witch*: "But let us also realize that this waxing age of the witch has come at great cost. The very fact that so many of us can now joyfully speak the witch's name aloud is a glorious thing. But we must remember the many thousands of people who have had their lives threatened or taken in her name as well." Listeners to *The Witch Wave* need never forget.

HOSTED BY
Pam Grossman

GENRE
Religion and Spirituality

FIRST EPISODE
"Bri Luna of The Hoodwitch"
(October 24, 2017)

INFLUENCES
"*Fresh Air* for the magically
inclined" (Grossman)

WHERE TO LISTEN
Patreon

SEAN'S PICK
"Tere Arcq, Remedios Varo
Aficionado" (November 17, 2021)

THE WITCH WAVE
WITH PAM GROSSMAN

You Made It Weird

How can someone guess if *You Made It Weird* will be for them? "If you can handle a filthy sex joke followed by an unpacking of Joseph Campbell's mythos followed by a sincere yearning for Christ consciousness followed by a twenty-minute conversation on wiping strategies after you poop," according to host Pete Holmes. Holmes would know: Across more than seven hundred episodes and tens of thousands of hours, he has discussed all these subjects and more with some of the world's most respected creatives, including musicians Quincy Jones and Mavis Staples, filmmakers James L. Brooks and Judd Apatow, and scientists Bill Nye and Brian Greene. Each shares with Holmes—and the "Weirdos" who follow his weekly show (literally) religiously—what he calls "a deep yearning for vulnerability and authenticity. And [they're] not easily offended."

You Made It Weird premiered on October 25, 2011, with guest Kumail Nanjiani, one of Holmes's peers from the world of stand-up. Raised in an evangelical family in Lexington, Massachusetts—a common landscape for his onstage work—Holmes had conceived of a podcast that merged "conversations with comedians and spirituality" after appearing on "dozens" of others' shows during the comedy podcast boom of the late aughties. Though the medium was still relatively nascent in retrospect, Holmes remembers that "it was still considered too late" to launch his own podcast; even his manager at the time ("and I'm not saying this to call out my manager!" he laughs nervously) said, "It seems like the window is closed. What would make this different?" But Holmes felt confident that despite an increasingly cluttered landscape, he had a proprietary, secret weapon up his sleeve: himself.

From the moment he and Nanjiani got on mic, his mission was as it is today: to conduct loosey-goosey, emotionally riveting conversations about the pain of existence and how laughter serves to help human beings reckon with it. The sole difference from the *You Made It Weird* of today was length. In that first episode, Holmes and Nanjiani talked for only a measly sixty-one minutes. By January 2012, when Marc Maron himself joined the show for the first time (primarily to hassle the host for his unbridled admiration—"He's like my older brother," Holmes says),

HOSTED BY
Pete Holmes

GENRE
Religion and Spirituality

FIRST EPISODE
"Kumail Nanjiani" (October 25, 2011)

INFLUENCES
WTF with Marc Maron,
Duncan Trussell Family Hour

WHERE TO LISTEN
Spotify

SEAN'S PICK
"Moshe Kasher" (November 16, 2011)

that had grown to 103 minutes. Three months later, Holmes broke the two-hour barrier for the first time with a rousing discussion about "getting kicked in the professional balls" with *The Simpsons* writer Dana Gould. After that, Holmes never looked back. "Something happens around the ninety-minute mark where everyone just sort of melts and merges into the experience," he says. "It's got to be around two hours or more. That's the sweet spot for me."

Holmes's addiction to long-form interviews, coupled with a natural—dare I even say God-given—ability to remain present throughout them lent him an intensity unlike any other. In response, *Paste, Vulture*, and *The Village Voice* published warring lists of the episodes that best balanced spiritual inquiry with ridiculous, obscene

tangents. As the podcast exploded, so did Holmes's comedy career. Over the next ten years, he co-created and starred in *Crashing*, a quasi-autobiographical series for HBO; released four stand-up specials; and published his first book of humor, the cheekily titled *Comedy Sex God*.

Thankfully, throughout it all he has remained committed to keeping *You Made It Weird* as "vibrant" and "real" for Weirdos as it was from the get-go. "Podcasting is a little bit like journaling or rings on a tree," he explains. It offers both a snapshot of where Holmes is on a given day and an opportunity to hear some of the greatest artists, authors, and thinkers play with their ideas for a rapt listening audience. For Holmes, it also represents the ultimate game: "Ideally, if we win, the success is a more vital and electric life."

Gilmore Guys

On September 17, 2014, comedian Kevin T. Porter waggishly tweeted "Wanna start a podcast where we go through every episode of Gilmore Girls called Gilmore Guys. Who wants to co-host / be a guest?" A week later, his bluff called, Porter enlisted Demi Adejuyigbe to record the first episode of *Gilmore Guys* in the office of an evangelical church. "I had worked there years before and still had a set of the keys and a good relationship with the staff," Porter explains. Unusually, the show eschewed a pilot, choosing instead to loose their first episode—an ambivalent, light discussion about the series premiere of Amy Sherman-Palladino's seven-season WB dramedy *Gilmore Girls*, which had that week begun streaming on Netflix—on the denizens of the internet with minimal fanfare.

Two hundred and nine episodes, three hundred and seventy–plus hours of audio, and tens of millions of downloads later, Porter and Adejuyigbe are now recognized for being far ahead of their times. While *Gilmore Guys* was neither the first nor the most famous so-called rewatch podcast—in which hosts reflect on the cultural impacts of old media with the benefits of hindsight—ever made, its hosts permanently distinguished themselves in the genre for the breezy intellectualism with which they approached their critiques.

Rather than pander to each other through constant agreement or to audiences by masquerading as unequivocal superfans, Porter and Adejuyigbe spent much of their two-year run debating the structural, aesthetic, and creative decisions made by the showrunner, cast, and network(s) behind the show. They initiated segments like "Pop Goes the Culture," a supercut compiling Sherman-Palladino's expansive references to pop culture; the "(Fa-Fa-Fa-Fa-Fa-Fa-Fa-Fa-Fa-Fa-Fa-) Fashion Report," a sometimes-brutal analysis of the questionable costuming forced upon Alexis Bledel, Lauren Graham, and their co-stars over the years; and "Where You Tweet, I Will Follow," a tongue-in-cheek promotional segment named for the Carole King song that served as *Gilmore Girls'* theme. They also brought on guests who shared in their diversity of opinions, such as Jason Mantzoukas, an avid keeper of *Gilmore* lore equally comfortable declaring his love for Sherman-Palladino as professing that lesser episodes should "go fuck themselves," and *Hacks* writer/producer Aisha Muharrar, who on one occasion argued with Adejuyigbe about a single line of dialogue for nearly half an hour.

The result was a corpus of critical thought on classic television as sophisticated as any ever broadcast. Adejuyigbe, who unlike Porter knew little about the original series before their collaboration, admits that, though making *Gilmore Guys* "was a blast," its inordinate success came with certain baggage: "Part of the stress of doing a podcast about a show is that the audience is usually big fans of the show and listening because of that show, so you feel this immense pressure and responsibility to be very detailed and correct." At its worst, that even meant killing an episode with guest Ben Schwartz that went so far off the rails—meaning, it failed to stay focused on the community of Stars Hollow, Connecticut—that Adejuyigbe "worried our audience would revolt." To this day, that episode has never been broadcast for fear of putting "a target" on Schwartz's back.

Not that there haven't been opportunities. Though the Guys finished their *Gilmore* rewatch in November 2016, Porter has kept the legacy alive with follow-ups centered on Sherman-Palladino's later series, including *Bunheads* and *The Marvelous Mrs. Maisel*, and *Gilmore Girls: A Year in the Life*. Still, he acknowledges, nothing can replace the early community of "Gillies" that made him and Adejuyigbe into podcast kings. "Group chats were started between friends discussing the episodes. One listener even proposed to his now wife at our live show in Dallas. I'll always be proud of the space we made for people."

HOSTED BY
Demi Adejuyigbe and Kevin T. Porter

GENRE
Rewatch

FIRST EPISODE
"101—Pilot" (October 1, 2014)

INFLUENCES
"Hanging out" (Adejuyigbe); "Paul F. Tompkins, *Filmspotting*, Wayne Brady" (Porter)

WHERE TO LISTEN
Headgum

SEAN'S PICK
"621—Driving Miss Gilmore (with Jason Mantzoukas)" (May 4, 2016)

Office Ladies

Office
Ladies

In her *New York Times* feature "The Magic of Your First Work Friends," journalist Emma Goldberg writes about the "electricity" that passes between people who connect with one another in the workplace: "It's the thrill of staying too late at drinks to keep giggling. It's the delight of darting to someone's desk and dragging her to the bathroom to gossip. It's the tenderness of showing up to work on a rough morning and realizing a co-worker will know instantly that something is wrong."

Those sensations are brought vividly to life on *Office Ladies*, the reigning dame of rewatch podcasts. The eponymous ladies are Jenna Fischer and Angela Kinsey, erstwhile stars of the goliath NBC sitcom *The Office* and, ever since meeting on that show, real-life best friends. Nearly every week, Fischer and Kinsey mosey through an episode of the series together and introduce each other to details they missed while in the trenches of actually making it.* Along the way, they dole out "Fast Facts" (Jenna Fischer™) and "Kinsey Tidbits" (Angela Kinsey™) about every aspect of production, including how certain shots were accomplished, which co-stars "broke" most easily, and inside jokes planted by creator Greg Daniels and his writing staff.

Here are some lesser-known Fast Facts about the podcast itself:

1. Fischer brings coffee and water to every recording, "but that's just because we record at 9:30 A.M. after the kids get dropped at school. That's my coffee time."
2. Kinsey always has "a cup of hot tea (my favorite is Darjeeling)," water, and "usually a cheese stick and some crackers" to snack on.
3. It took several years for them to uncover old production call sheets and scripts that helped guide them through the series, according to Fischer: "In our latest episodes, we've been

* Sometimes, they do interviews for podcast critics' books too. Big whoop!

able to track the story evolution a bit more and that's been really fun. Especially as we got to the episodes without Steve Carell. I think we were able to uncover a lot of details about that transition that weren't out there before."

Fischer hits on something key here. Though the pod was designated an instantaneous classic upon launching on Earwolf in 2019, earning a barrage of nominations for Podcast of the Year and Best Television and Film Podcast, it also challenged and redefined the boundaries of traditional "rewatch" podcasts. As Kinsey sees it, *Office Ladies* is "almost two shows in one: a recap of *The Office* and a podcast about friendship." Where many predecessors and imitators settle for glossy, low-lift nostalgia trips through their old work, Kinsey's conversations with Fischer often skip past the expected minutiae of, say, Phyllis Smith getting caught looking for house fences throughout production of season three or John Krasinski's tacit micro-impressions of writer Michael Schur in favor of more detailed and personal considerations about their all-consuming years portraying Pam and Angela. In addition to being possibly the most extensive artist-made commentary track about a TV show ever produced, it is often also the most philosophical.

"My hope is that we are creating a tiny historical record for every episode," Fischer says. She notes that the pod represents her and Kinsey's first time as the bosses of a project—both produce the series, which moved to Audacy in 2024. Clearly, they still share one mind decades after that first fateful pilot shoot: "I respect her work ethic and we are such a good creative team," Kinsey says. "Not only is she one of the funniest people I know, but there is also no one else whose mind for business I trust more," Fischer chimes back. As for the Ladies' next chapter together? I'll say what we're all thinking: medical show.

HOSTED BY
Jenna Fischer and
Angela Kinsey

GENRE
Rewatch

FIRST EPISODE
"The Pilot"
(October 16, 2019)

INFLUENCES
"Family, friendship, June Diane Raphael, Oliver Hudson, Anna Faris" (Fischer); "Family, friendship, Karen Kilgariff, Georgia Hardstark, *Serial*" (Kinsey)

WHERE TO LISTEN
Audacy

SEAN'S PICK
"Booze Cruise w/ Greg Daniels" (February 25, 2020)

Radiolab

Nothing sounds like *Radiolab*, so much so that to describe what it *does* sound like using human language is a struggle. Sure, there is banter and interviews and sound beds and music, the standard component parts of every audio documentary program. But there is also a charcuterie board of bleeps and blorps, robo-noises, Altmanesque overlapping dialogue, what sounds like some kind of fizzing (?), and plenty of nature's most mysterious emissions, whose origins I daren't guess. It is structurally deceptive too, often opening and closing an episode with a different version of the same clip, or using narration from one story in a later one, or batting the voices of two people who have never spoken back and forth to construct a simulacrum of a conversation. As with the aurora borealis, or whale song, the only true way to grasp *Radiolab* is to experience it.

Jad Abumrad, a Mozart figure in spoken audio, created the show in 2002 for WNYC. Trained as a musician and composer, Abumrad introduced a jagged avant-gardism that refuted the polished, geometric public radio methodologies so in vogue at the time. His approach was revolutionarily auteurist, demonstrating that *This American Life*–style multi-chapter storytelling could be effective even when it was chopped up and Frankensteined back together. Listen to an episode of any competing program that aired the same week as *Radiolab*'s debut, "Firsts," and it becomes clear how, to pull once again from Mary Shelley, *alive* its creator's approach was.

That said, it took two further steps for *Radiolab* to achieve global phenomenon status. First, Abumrad hooked up with veteran journalist Robert Krulwich and executive producer Ellen Horne, with whom slightly more streamlined, science-adjacent hours compiled from two or three thematically unified stories ("Sleep," "Memory and Forgetting," "Laughter") became the norm. Second, WNYC began distributing *Radiolab* as a podcast, wherein that very same format could be consciously fucked with. This was both so enticing and confusing to fans that, in February 2008, they released an explainer on their artistic approach called "Our Podcast Comes in All Shapes and Sizes." "Sometimes we podcast an entire hour-long episode. Sometimes we podcast a shorter piece that may only be eight minutes or so," the explainer said. "That's just how we roll."

During this period, Abumrad and Krulwich emerged as the most alchemically listenable duo in podcasting, as evidenced by the prestige of the accolades they received: a National Academies Communication Award in 2007, their (first) Peabody in 2010, Abumrad's MacArthur Fellowship in 2011 (for further proof, seek out "Jad and Robert: The Early Years").

This should not, however, be read as shade on Lulu Miller and Latif Nasser, who took over for Abumrad in 2022 (Krulwich retired in 2020). While the *Radiolab* of the early 2020s no longer centers its hosts' dynamic so strongly, it has expanded its thematic horizons to include, as executive editor Soren Wheeler describes them, "arcs and questions that can be social, or political, or legal." At first, Nasser says, "the show was Jad and Robert. Two guys talking, goofing around, debating. That became a bit of a podcast cliché, and also as our staff grew, so, too, did the number of personalities and voices." He and Miller take a more "clubhouse slash magazine slash vaudeville variety show" approach nowadays. Miller refers to this as *Radiolab*'s "growing up," a coming of age that has entailed moving "from loving to capture 'a good story' to trying to capture complexity itself." What has not changed, she clarifies, is its commitment to releasing "cinematic" and "wildly gripping"

podcasts: "This team really helps one another never settle on a simple answer; we're always striving to showcase the wrinkles and crinkles."

HOSTED BY
Jad Abumrad, Robert Krulwich, Lulu Miller, and Latif Nasser

GENRE
Science

FIRST EPISODE
"Firsts" (Radio: April 14, 2002); "Who Am I" (Podcast: February 4, 2005)

INFLUENCES
Kathleen Hanna, Wayne White, Alix Spiegel, Jonathan Goldstein, Annie Dillard, Spike Jonze, Ms. Frizzle (Miller); Kurt Vonnegut, George Carlin, Walter Murch, Carl Sagan, Stephen Jay Gould, Steven Strogatz (Wheeler)

WHERE TO LISTEN
WNYC

SEAN'S PICK
"The First Radiolab" (January 28, 2022)

Limetown

The central mystery of _Limetown_,
the Two-Up Productions sci-fi thriller
created by Zack Akers and Skip
Bronkie, is not what happened to more
than three hundred residents of Limetown, Tennessee (though it is certainly
a big question); it is how a pilot compelling enough to reach the top spot
on the download charts without any
famous cast members to promote it or
any further episodes produced ever got
made in the first place.

The answer, according to Bronkie,
is: stressfully.

"When the pilot was released, it was the only episode produced and
written, which is incredibly unusual for a scripted podcast," he says.
Bronkie and Akers had by then devoted the "nights and weekends" of
two years straight developing _Limetown_'s supernatural-adjacent world,
including conceiving of its appropriately intense conclusion. But once
they put the first installment out on July 29, 2015, they simply . . . waited.
Bronkie offers two reasons for why they held off so long before making a
follow-up. "One, the pilot was purely a passion project for us and we had
zero expectations for it," he says. "And two, being as bootstrapped as
we were, we needed to see if there was an audience for the show before
investing more funds into it."

They needn't have worried. Within two months, "What We Know"—
with its _This American Life_–style reporter character, Lia Haddock, embedded at a mysterious abandoned government facility—had become the
most popular podcast in the country.

Listeners were starving for more information about Oscar Totem
and the caves beneath the city. Lots of listeners. "The inbound interest
and pressure felt enormous: fans, press studios itching for the rights.

People wanted to know how it ended, but we hadn't even made the second episode yet." Within six weeks, the co-creators were forced to build a full-blown production operation capable of making what would ultimately become their entire six-episode first season. Episode two, which introduced the Ozian Man We Were All There For, did not arrive until September 6, 2015; the finale, with its horrifying and frankly depressing cliff-hanger ending, was released on December 14 of that year. Amid all of this, Akers was getting married: "I was literally setting up tables in our reception area when Skip started texting me that the show was number one," he says.

So, yeah—stressful. But history has shown that Akers and Bronkie's efforts were well worth the pain. In the years since, *Limetown* has become revered as the zenith in modern literary audio fiction for its invocation of works as distinct as Orson Welles's "War of the Worlds" broadcast, David Lynch and Mark Frost's *Twin Peaks*, and, of course, *The Wizard of Oz*. It also led to a cottage industry for Two-Up,

CREATED BY
Zack Akers and Skip Bronkie

GENRE
Science Fiction

FIRST EPISODE
"What We Know" (July 21, 2015)

INFLUENCES
"*This American Life*, *Radiolab*, old radio dramas my dad would listen to in the car when I was a kid (I think one was a James Bond radio drama? I have no idea if this exists or not, but that's what it was in my head), Oak Ridge (near where I grew up)" (Akers); "Los Alamos National Laboratory, Facebook's Menlo Park campus, *World War Z* and *The Great War* (great oral histories), Sherry Turkle's *Alone Together*" (Bronkie)

WHERE TO LISTEN
Two-Up Productions

SEAN'S PICK
"Napoleon" (October 12, 2015)

which later produced an acclaimed television series of the same name, a prequel novel for Simon & Schuster, and finally, in 2018, a second season just as intriguing and intelligent as its predecessor. Even so, warns Bronkie, fellow podcasters should not look to their wild production model for inspiration. In fact, he says, "I would very much advise against it!"

Marvel's Wolverine: The Long Night

Wolverine (you know, the claw guy) is Benjamin Percy's favorite character in the canon of comic books. So, as he tells it, when he learned he was "in a bake-off with several other writers" for a new Marvel gig set in the expansive world of the X-Men, "I went into berserker mode and attacked my keyboard, putting together a massive pitch." Inspired by podcasts like *Serial*, *S-Town*, and *Homecoming*—interrogative narratives that anchored their audiences in particular times and spaces without leaning on clumsy expository dialogue—Percy conceived of a ten-episode audio murder mystery set in the small fishing village of Burns, Alaska. Wolverine, or Logan, as he is mainly known, was to be one of the suspects, with the hunt for him told from the perspective of two federal agents harboring secrets of their own. The final pitch document Percy submitted to Marvel, he recalls, was "thirty single-spaced pages, the subtext of which was 'Give this to me, or else.'" He got the job.

The resulting series, Marvel's first-ever scripted podcast, *Marvel's Wolverine: The Long Night*, premiered in the spring of 2018. Produced by Daniel Fink and Jenny Radelet Mast for Stitcher, it boasts a state-of-the-art ambisonic soundscape shaped by director Brendan Baker and a cast of high-caliber character actors, including Bob Balaban, David Call, Zoe Chao, and Brian Stokes Mitchell. Yet while it taps into lore long familiar to fans of the original X-Men comics (Sentinels and Weapon X, anyone?), it also features an altogether more classical version of the adamantium-clawed mutant (made iconic on film by the actor Hugh Jackman) than had been heard from in decades. As voiced by Richard Armitage, the super-antihero of *The Long Night* isn't a strapping, lovable sourpuss with movie star charisma; he is a "squat, snarling animal of a man" and "a dangerous dude who's spilled enough blood to fill a reservoir."

For Percy, this Logan is personal: "As a hairy, grumpy, smelly, muscular, square-shaped, whiskey-swilling, cigar-chomping loner from the frozen north . . . writing *Wolverine* felt like writing thinly veiled autobiography."

But he recognized that deviating from the franchise's recent, highly popular mythology might meet with pushback from his corporate overlords, especially since it meant putting their prized character primarily in the shadows for the first nine episodes. When Fink and

Radelet Mast sent him a rough cut of the first episode during production, he "could feel [his] heart hammering in [his] chest," he says. To his relief, the result was a fine-tuned melding of personal vision, aesthetic talent, and established canon: "It was so gratifying to hear that dream come alive."

Audiences, it turned out, agreed with him. *The Long Night* was named one of the Best Podcasts of 2018 by Apple and ranked among its twenty-five most-downloaded shows of that year worldwide; Percy and Radelet Mast were invited to speak about making it at the prestigious South by Southwest; and it even birthed an acclaimed second season, *The Lost Trail*, set in the Louisiana bayou. To this day, it represents the high-water mark for sci-fi storytelling in audio (and, depending on who you ask, the wider Marvel mediaverse). Even so, Percy still hasn't quite shaken off the nerves from those early days pitching his intensely intimate story to the powers that be. "Funny enough, I think it was the price tag that convinced them," he jokes (or perhaps not). "Richard Armitage was expensive, so the fewer lines he had, the more affordable the podcast."

CREATED BY
Benjamin Percy

GENRE
Science Fiction

FIRST EPISODE
"Chapter 1: A Thousand Ways to Die in Alaska" (September 12, 2018)

INFLUENCES
True Detective, Denis Johnson, modern Westerns, *Prisoners* (Fink); *Love + Radio*, "the show where I first heard Brendan Baker's work and knew he was the right artist to bring *WTLN* to life" (Radelet Mast)

WHERE TO LISTEN
Simplecast

SEAN'S PICK
"Chapter 9: The Changing" (October 30, 2018)

The Mental Illness Happy Hour

THE

MENTAL ILLNESS

HAPPY HOUR

WITH PAUL GILMARTIN

A teenage heroin addict from the Isle of Man convinced that he carries the mark of Satan.

A new mother thrust into a psychotic break immediately after having her first baby.

A child actor quietly developing obsessive-compulsive disorder under the glare of global recognition.

These are but three of the many guests who have come to discuss their health struggles on *The Mental Illness Happy Hour* since comedian Paul Gilmartin launched it in 2011. Caught at the precise midpoint between talk therapy, celebrity interviewing, and stand-up, the podcast was an instant hit, gaining over a million downloads in its first year and an unshakable spot among iTunes' Top 100 Health and Fitness podcasts.

As Gilmartin remembers it, some of his peers worried at first that its subject was too hardcore to work as entertainment. "I bumped into a long-time stand-up acquaintance (with a brilliant comedic mind and a long list of impressive credits) in a grocery store. After some small talk, I asked him if he'd like to be a guest on my new podcast. He was intrigued and flattered and wanted to know if it was about a particular topic. I said, 'Well, it's called *The Mental Illness Happy Hour*.' His face dropped. He turned and walked away." Ultimately, Gilmartin got the last laugh. In addition to renewed interest in his work as the host of TBS's *Dinner and a Movie*, he has received breathless accolades from *The Atlantic*, *The New York Times*, and *Psychology Today* for his abundant humor and empathy-driven style.

Though anxiety, trauma, and depression (a condition that Gilmartin was diagnosed with in his mid-thirties) are common topics of discussion, his show is far from a miserabilist slog; instead, it remains staunchly committed to being compelling, heartfelt, and funny, a model inspired by Gilmartin's time in support groups.

"I wanted the podcast to not be a solution for people's problems," he explains, but "rather a place of comfort or inspiration during them." He took guidance in creating that energy from fellow podcaster (and *MIHH* guest) Marc Maron, who he says demonstrated a "willingness to let the conversation take dark turns" without losing its humor. That much is evident in dozens of episodes, both in Gilmartin's interviews with the likes of pedophile-ring survivor Anneke Lucas (episode 245) and NBA player Royce White (episode 307), and in the bookend sections, for which Gilmartin reads listeners' responses to mental health–targeted survey questions.

Gilmartin says the show is simply intended to move people "like a good story" does, rather than to mislead anyone into thinking of him as a self-proclaimed

HOSTED BY
Paul Gilmartin

GENRE
Self-Help

FIRST EPISODE
"Janet Varney" (March 26, 2011)

INFLUENCES
Personal support groups, *WTF with Marc Maron*, particularly "Episode 190— Todd Hanson"

WHERE TO LISTEN
Spotify

SEAN'S PICK
"Brody Stevens"
(February 8, 2013)

doctor. In fact, a disclaimer on the website makes this clear: "*The Mental Illness Happy Hour* is NOT a substitute for professional diagnosis or treatment." Still, it doesn't hurt that its host has spent more than a decade talking with people about the most vulnerable events and experiences of their lives. This point, at least, he acknowledges. "The image I had in my mind was a hand that people could hold in the therapist's or psychiatrist's waiting room," he says, "as well as someone occasionally leaning in to tell a super fucked-up joke."

Couples Therapy

Andy Beckerman and Naomi Ekperigin call their podcast, *Couples Therapy*, "a weekly respite for a weary world." The show is a long-running diary of the couple's relationship interrupted with color commentary from their fellow comics and writers. Often, it is hilarious (highlights include "Ryan O'Connell" from May 2019, "Kumail Nanjiani and Emily Gordon" from June 2020, and the unlocked "Paetch" [a.k.a. Patreon] episode "Between Ass-Eaters and Thieves" from January 2023), but it can also be enthrallingly intimate. When big life events happen, as in "Between Ass-Eaters," the "sex-negative/sex-neutral" couple go straight to the audience with their live read on the state of their relationship. After revealing the pains of Andy's experience with "Coco" (the novel coronavirus) and their need to take a little break the previous year, Beckerman and Ekperigin then offer listeners who have endured horrific dates advice in exchange for a nice review on Apple Podcast. Read them, or those of any other episode, and you'll see the same word used over and over: "compelling."

"As someone who was used to communicating with audiences primarily through live stand-up, when we started the podcast, I had no sense of what was landing or connecting with people, given that the listeners aren't in front of me when we're talking," Ekperigin writes me. In 2014, she and Beckerman launched *Couples Therapy* as a live comedy show in the back of a now-defunct indie rock club called HiFi Bar in New York's Lower East Side. It was a quick hit, despite the fact that its name was inconveniently common. (Once, recalls Beckerman, they were forced to retitle it to *In Stereo* rather than fight over sharing the name with another event in Brooklyn. On a separate occasion, they had to send a cease-and-desist letter to a fellow podcaster using the name with impunity. "Considering we are conflict-averse folks, each of these little skirmishes is like our souls having diarrhea," Beckerman says.)

Even so, his and Ekperigin's relationship made it through these crises and survived a move to Los Angeles, where in 2018 they launched the audio version. Like the live show, the first iteration of the podcast hybridized

Sex &
Relationships

198

interviews with romantic couples and professional partners with candid, sometimes achingly intense storytelling. That version, too, nearly experienced calamity when the pandemic struck. With the live aspect of their podcast no longer possible, the hosts were forced to turn their mics inward full-time—irrevocably changing their format for the better.

These days, Beckerman and Ekperigin have incorporated the job of interviewing just one comic an episode into the large project of maintaining their own harmonious, hilarious relationship. It seems to be working: Ekperigin and her "Jew Boo" married in March 2023. Still, Ekperigin says she finds it "unbelievable" how many people have stuck with

this version of the show, including one listener who even "designed and created all the stationery and paper goods for our wedding!" But she demands that, in closing this chapter, I set the record straight: "We paid her!!"

HOSTED BY
Andy Beckerman and Naomi Ekperigin

GENRE
Sex and Relationships

FIRST EPISODE
"Paula Pell and Janine Brito, Yassir Lester and Chelsea Devantez" (July 17, 2018)

INFLUENCES
"*Comedy Bang! Bang!*; Marc Maron; a pathological need to do creative work with the people I love, a tendency which I am examining in therapy" (Beckerman); "Dreams of being an accessible Oprah" (Ekperigin)

WHERE TO LISTEN
Patreon

SEAN'S PICK
"John Early and Kate Berlant, Amy Miller and Steve Hernandez" (February 12, 2019)

Guys We Fucked

A **LUMINARY** ORIGINAL

Guys We F****d

KRYSTYNA HUTCHINSON   CORINNE FISHER

"I guess the most interesting thing about 'the making of *Guys We Fucked*' is that there was no making of *Guys We Fucked*," Corinne Fisher, co-founder and co-host of the anti-slut-shaming podcast *Guys We Fucked*, declares. When Fisher met Krystyna Hutchinson at a talent management company in 2010, they were both still what the former calls "twentysomethings on a Warholian quest to fraternize with fame." Comedians working in New York, they quickly formed a two-woman team, hosting open mics, live events, and their own showcase at the Upright Citizens Brigade Theatre in an attempt to rectify the "injustice" of their mutual obscurity. It wasn't until three years later, however, that one of those self-generated projects finally bore fruit.

In the first episode of *GWF*, published online in December 2013, Fisher and Hutchinson boldly welcomed listeners "to a new revolution." On the podcast, they announced, they intended to conduct deeply personal, unapologetically detailed conversations about sex with the men they'd had or were currently having it with, regardless of how embarrassing that might be for the men. To achieve that meant spending countless minutes of their earliest episodes discussing jizzing, jerking, slurping, sucking, and squirting, as well as all manner of kinks, cunts, and cocks. And so they did, earning the show—which is often represented with its titular epithet asterisked—a reputation as both groundbreaking in its courage and, according to dark corners of the internet, unnecessarily outré.

It quickly became clear to listeners, however, that those dismissing Fisher and Hutchinson as simple provocateurs were missing their point entirely. Quietly at first, then more explicitly, the women began to engage directly with scholarship around gender politics, the daily pressures of sex work, and the philosophical tenets of feminism. In addition to their lovers, they also invited renowned guests—including the urologist and erectile dysfunction expert Dr. Yaniv Larish, veteran pornographer and production company founder Joanna Angel, and intimacy coach Michelle Renee—to come, as it were, on the program. Perhaps predictably in hindsight, the podcast's popularity began to surge. Between 2017 and 2019, Hutchinson and Fisher released a critically acclaimed spin-off book, *F*cked: Being Sexually Explorative and Self-Confident in a World That's Screwed*, and moved their distribution to the Luminary app. They also hosted a series of live shows to benefit sexual health nonprofits, raising thousands of dollars for issues impacting LGBTQIA+ and unhoused women. Finally, in 2022, they joined the ranks of elite podcasters commissioned to bring their talent to television, signing a deal with Fox Entertainment for a multi-camera comedy adaptation of the hit show.

Though its hosts' dreams of fame came true, *Guys We Fucked* has continued, week in and week out, to deliver on its premise: to tell hundreds of thousands of subscribers about the guys they fucked. It isn't that Hutchinson and Fisher ever ceased being confrontational (on the contrary, both hosts remain dangerously intelligent and

HOSTED BY
Corinne Fisher and Krystyna Hutchinson

GENRE
Sex and Relationships

FIRST EPISODE
"VINNIE: CAN I CHOKE YOU?"
(December 6, 2013)

INFLUENCES
"Our initial pitch was, verbatim, 'Howard Stern for girls.' Other mood board items include: John Cusack's journey in *High Fidelity* and getting dumped in Panera Bread" (Fisher)

WHERE TO LISTEN
Luminary

SEAN'S PICK
"HIS PUBES WERE HAUNTED?"
(July 8, 2016)

forthright conversationalists) so much as it's that they have committed to pushing buttons of an altogether different nature. Nevertheless, the haters still don't seem to get their real message, Fisher says. "These days, as the show has more and more weekly feminist realizations, I find that women, men, and nonbinary folks alike enjoy attempting to weaponize the podcast's title . . . as if that was not meticulously crafted to firstly trick you into listening to feminism under the guise of smut, and secondly, place us, the women, in the position of power. We aren't the object anymore; we fucked you."

Queery

Stand-up comic Cameron Esposito is something of a podcast lifer, having hosted or co-hosted three of them since 2013. Each of those ventures would have been at home in this book, so I deferred to the one that gets at my heart the most: Esposito's second at bat, *Queery*.

Consciously designed to concatenate the real-life experiences of self-identified members of the LGBTQIA+ community, each episode comprises an hour-long conversation between the comic and a fellow creative force exemplary in their field. Journalists (Jordan Crucchiola), musicians (G Flip), actors (Alan Cumming), restaurateurs (Kelly Fields), activists (Jeffrey Galaise), athletes (Adam Rippon)—all discuss the "queeroes" who inspired and guided them to the understanding that they are merely one entry in podcasting's most expansive oral history project.

Queery's journey into the hearts of listeners and the minds of scholars has not been without its bumps. Originally distributed by the now-defunct media network Feral Audio when the show launched in 2017, it soon jumped to Earwolf, and finally to Maximum Fun in June 2023 before ending in 2024. "I somehow didn't predict that folks were gonna get really good at translating podcasting to video, or that large media companies were gonna want to acquire podcast networks," Esposito says of those many transitions. Yet across each of its incarnations, *Queery* never dipped in quality, with the production team continuing to produce episodes that share a uniform sense of length, sound quality, and tone. In fact, drop into one of the first or final ten episodes and you'll hear the same introduction asking listeners to maintain an open mind. ("None of that would have been possible without my longtime producer, Sierra Katow," Esposito notes.)

Were there to follow from this book a history of touchstone podcasts that center queer identities, Esposito suggests, hers would occupy the second generation alongside contemporaries like *Keep It!*, *Pod Save America*, and *Las Culturistas*. She counts *Savage Lovecast* (see p. 16) and *Homophilia* amid key predecessors, and names *Getting Curious*, *Handsome*, and *We Can Do Hard Things* among newer landmarks expanding the global public's understanding of queer experiences. But comparing *Queery* to any of these is difficult, for while it, too, is recorded for broadcast on the internet and distributed among other such programs, its modus operandi shares more in common with the person-to-person story collecting of Arden Eversmeyer's Old Lesbian Oral Herstory Project and E. Patrick Johnson's *Sweet Tea*.

Esposito recognizes that managing such an expansive, multi-faceted project solely via audio had both its pros ("more control and more freedom") and cons ("more responsibility and fewer resources"). Nevertheless, she remains undeterred in what seems to be a lifelong journey to document the expanse of queer life around the planet. "Podcasting as I first did it is over," she confirms. But "as a medium, it's continuing to evolve."

HOSTED BY
Cameron Esposito

GENRE
Sex and Relationships

FIRST EPISODE
"Rhea Butcher"
(August 5, 2017)

INFLUENCES
This American Life,
Savage Lovecast, Fresh Air,
WTF with Marc Maron

WHERE TO LISTEN
Maximum Fun

SEAN'S PICK
"Margaret Cho"
(April 9, 2018)

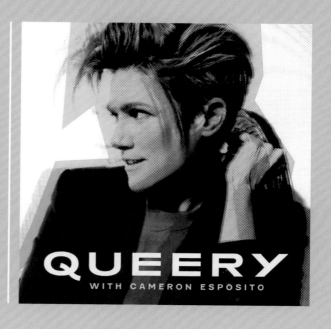

QUEERY
WITH CAMERON ESPOSITO

All My Relations

Indian Country, in its infinite vastness, contains more stories than any one podcast could ever hope to tell. Rather than giving the team behind *All My Relations* pause, this has only pushed them to construct an audio patchwork of ever-expanding style and color. Established in 2019 with author and scholar Adrienne Keene and photographer and filmmaker Matika Wilbur at the helm (sociologist Desi Small-Rodriguez joined in season three), the show spends seven-to-twelve-episode seasons in active dialogue with artists, activists, educators, and community leaders about what kinship and relationality between Indigenous folks look like in today's so-called United States. From gender politics and civil rights, to fashion and art, to precontact matriarchalism and family structures, these conversations take on permutations as variegated as the cultural practices of the First Nations, creating a changeable, always-involving spin on the modern talk show.

The model for the series emerged from Keene and Wilbur's private conversations "around contemporary Indigenous identity and critical thinking about issues that Indigenous people face," according to Wilbur, *AMR*'s director and the creator of *Project 562*, a documentary endeavor dedicated to showcasing citizens from every federally recognized tribal nation. They developed the first season in a kind of "podcast camp," building a set and recording in the Tacoma Art Museum. Increasingly, the series emerged as a sort of meeting place for thinkers to propose concepts for an "Indigenous Wakanda," a continent returned both literally and culturally to the knowledge, practices, and social structures of its true guardians.

Building on this effort, they brought in professional educators, like McGill professor Geraldine King, who spoke on the ecological erotics inherent in Anishinaabe communities ("All My Loving Relations"); Dr. Jamaica Heolimeleikalani Osorio, who offered strategies for protecting Mauna Kea in the wake of settler colonialism ("Hawaiian Resistance, Tourism & Abolition: For the Love of the Mauna, Part 3"); and genetic researcher Charlotte Logan, who debunked blood quantum theory, the racist proposition that a person's Native American status is defined by the fraction of Native American ancestry they possess ("Beyond Blood Quantum").

ALL MY
RELATIONS

HOSTED BY
Adrienne Keene,
Desi Small-Rodriguez,
and Matika Wilbur

GENRE
Society and Culture

FIRST EPISODE
"All My Relations & Indigenous
Feminism" (February 26, 2019)

INFLUENCES
Text Me Back!,
This American Life, *Radiolab*

WHERE TO LISTEN
Patreon

SEAN'S PICK
"Rematriate" (April 6, 2023)

Decolonizing Native minds was not their only purpose, however. Wilbur notes that the series also "aimed to entertain" by producing "compelling stories at the highest level," the likes of which are fewer and farther between than more strictly educational programming. ("There are a lot of Native podcasts, but a lot of them are missing the technical mark for how people would be listening," she acknowledges.) Episodes like "Native Women Are Funny" (featuring showrunner Sierra Teller Ornelas and star Jana Schmieding of *Rutherford Falls*) and "Rez Doggin' with Ryan RedCorn and Sterlin Harjo" (featuring filmmakers RedCorn and Harjo of *Reservation Dogs*) exemplify this approach: While both begin as sincere talks with Native groundbreakers in directing and performing for television, they eventually give way into fits of supportive, if uncontrollable, giggling. (Wilbur, a famously loud laugher, tells me she's been practicing tilting her head away from the microphone during recordings.)

With around three million listeners between the first and fourth seasons (around 60 percent of which are Native women, according to Wilbur), this balance of joyful connection and serious scholasticism has proved clearly productive. Critics have been equally kind, with two honoraria for

Diversity, Equity & Inclusion given to the *AMR* team at the 2020 and 2021 Webby Awards. And while Keene departed for new pastures before the fifth season launched, Wilbur, creative director Teo Shantz, and the production staff have stayed committed to "filling in the gaps where we need resources and coherent, literate conversations to shape the moral fabric of where Indian Country is going" through such projects as a brick-and-mortar podcast incubator and live events around the podcast's Seattle home base. "It is really amazing, the impact that can have," Wilbur says, exuding hopefulness. "Really high-quality storytelling is what we need."

Ear Hustle

"The first podcast created and produced in prison, featuring stories of the daily realities of life inside California's San Quentin State Prison, shared by those living it," is the doozy of a description for *Ear Hustle*, a finalist for the 2020 Pulitzer Prize in Audio Reporting and the recipient of many other august awards. For the kind of podcast afficionado who prefers easy comforts on their morning commute, such a pedigree can sound intimidating, as if listening might be more challenge than pleasure. But any such impression is false, for in addition to being as resonant, intelligent, and intense—and yes, as important and as powerful—as its accolades imply, the series is also a work of beauty, joy, and warmth as satisfying and digestible as a sunset. And also just like a sunset, it is a gift for many who encounter it.

HOSTED BY
Nigel Poor and
Earlonne Woods

GENRE
Society and Culture

FIRST EPISODE
"Cellies" (June 14, 2017)

INFLUENCES
"This American Life" (Poor);
"Nigel Poor" (Woods)

WHERE TO LISTEN
Radiotopia

SEAN'S PICK
"Inside Music"
(August 1, 2019)

The podcast is the brainchild of Earlonne Woods and Antwan "Banks" Williams, who co-created it while incarcerated at San Quentin with Nigel Poor, a visual artist who taught the history of photography at the prison's media lab. Together, the trio pitched the concept—named after prison slang for gossiping—to the inaugural Podquest (a Radiotopia-launched contest seeking "story-driven podcast ideas") and won, beating more than fifteen hundred other submissions in 2016. Episode one, a look at the dynamics between "cellies" in San Quentin, premiered a year later. The podcast has been downloaded more than eighty million times since.

"I've always liked some type of creativity or creative storytelling," says Woods, who received a sentence of thirty-one years to life in 1999 for attempted second-degree robbery. Prior to his incarceration, he dreamed of becoming a filmmaker and screenwriter. "I remember when I was in prison the first time, when I was a youngster, I sat back and actually wrote my life story in a movie light," he remembers. Like her partner, Poor was also a podcasting novice when the idea for the project emerged. The biggest hurdle she faced wasn't transitioning from visual to audio art making, as one might expect; it was, she says, "learning how to listen and be responsive and respectful of other people's ideas, and that you can't do this all alone."

When Poor adds that "doing a podcast is very collaborative," it is clear what she means. Each episode of *Ear Hustle* is gloriously polyphonic, a collage of voices, music, and sounds collected and sutured together from many sources (at first by Williams and later by Woods). In addition to sharing their own banter—the lightness and humor of which would stack up against that of any comedy podcast—Woods and Poor, as well as producers such as Rahsaan "New York" Thomas, have also interviewed vast numbers of imprisoned people; their lovers and partners, friends and family members; correctional officers; formerly incarcerated folks in transitional housing; and policymakers directly engaged with the carceral system. Many episodes feature singing and concerts, stand-up performances and basketball games, animals and weather. Woods notes that he often hears from lawyers about just how expansive the show's canvas is when it comes to representing incarcerated life. "They always say something like, 'Y'all make my job easy,'" he says. "Meaning that when it's time for them to explain prison or to explain something to their client, 'Go listen to *Ear Hustle*.'"

Ear Hustle co-creators Earlonne Woods, left, and Nigel Poor.

Beyond its aesthetic merits, few other podcasts have created more significant real-world changes than *Ear Hustle*. Today, it is available in all of California's prisons via tablets, as well as in about four hundred other prisons around the United States, one hundred and fourteen prisons in the United Kingdom, and several prisons in Ireland and Australia. California governor Jerry Brown commuted Woods's sentence in 2018 for his work on the show, allowing him to continue to produce and co-host it full-time on the outside. Even Kim Kardashian has supported the show by recording a content advisory for the third episode of season twelve in 2023. But Woods insists that the process of making the show the best and most honest it can be is the only reward he really seeks. "People are listening. They like what we do. That's what does it for me—is just say, 'Hey, you're doing something right.'"

Gender Reveal

What the hell is gender? It's a question that Tuck Woodstock—the creator, voice, and "resident gender detective" of *Gender Reveal*—has spent much of his career investigating. Through interviews with trans and nonbinary "activists, authors, artists, academics, and actors" like Meredith Talusan, Salimatu Amabebe, and Jane Schoenbrun, Woodstock and senior producer Ozzy Llinas Goodman have established a vast oral archive that engages gender and its infinite permutations head-on. The project also includes grant programs that have provided over $100,000 in snacks (particularly on Trans Day of Having a Nice Snack, a holiday Woodstock established in 2021) and general mutual aid to trans folks.

Woodstock appreciates knowing "that we are doing some kind of tangible good out in the world by organizing mutual aid efforts and grant programs, so I don't have the existential question of 'Is my work helping anyone???' cloud every episode of the show." Yet he also makes clear that such work is a pressure release for the production, not an extension of some weighted responsibility. "I also think that many people (cis and trans but especially cis) tend to add this extra gravitas to any story about trans people, as if to imbue every moment of trans life with Pain and Struggle and Bravery and whatever," he says. "But trans life can also be silly and petty and fun and weird and playful and hot, and I think it's important to capture those elements in the podcast as well."

In that regard, Woodstock and Goodman are unequivocally effective. Since the podcast's launch in January 2018, the conversations they've conducted have centered glee, compassion, and pleasure in counterpoint to the ceaselessly tragic and often violent slant of mainstream media reporting on transness. One aspect of this delightfulness is its elegance: Episodes are blessedly and (almost) uniformly simple sandwiches surrounded by Breakmaster Cylinder's earwormy theme. In one representatively direct interview for the season five premiere, Woodstock and author Cyrus Grace Dunham speak with infectious enthusiasm about the role colonialism plays in top surgery, the delusion of cisness ("I tend not to trust people who don't feel doubt," Dunham says), and the "big Libra energy" inflecting the Aquarian memoirist's *A Year Without a Name*. When it concludes, as each interview does, with Woodstock asking what Dunham considers to be the future of gender (Dunham's answer: an end to racialized economic oppression and the police state), fifty-five exceedingly listenable minutes have flashed by.

The pod also features several recurring segments, including a "Theymail" section for listener inquiries and "This Week in Gender." The latter, Woodstock says, originally "started as a news segment, but I've adopted a loose McElroy-style 'No Bummers' rule for that segment, because trans people don't need to hear a five-minute spiel on the latest anti-trans laws. We know how bad it is out there!" In addition to lightening his personal workload, Woodstock notes, adjusting the segment allowed it to feature more collaborations with trans writers, such as "Niko Stratis writing about gender tracking apps, Dakota Hommes's explanation of how her (former) union won trans-inclusive health-care coverage, and Krys Malcolm Belc's review of Caitlyn Jenner's memoir."

This kaleidoscopic creativity makes for mighty entertainment, certainly. But it also offers a useful opportunity for anyone looking to deepen their engagement with, or support for, a community still subjected to expressions of ignorance or hate. "It's not optional to know how to talk about trans and nonbinary folks with respect," Woodstock reminds listeners in the episode "Gender 202." "It is just a basic part of being a human being on this earth."

HOSTED BY
Tuck Woodstock

GENRE
Society and Culture

FIRST EPISODE
"Gender 101" (January 8, 2018)

INFLUENCES
"*Bitch* magazine, early transition
naivety" (Woodstock)

WHERE TO LISTEN
Patreon

SEAN'S PICK
"Cyrus Dunham" (January 27, 2020)

Sklarbro Country

There are two eras of *Sklarbro Country***:** Before and After. Before, it was among the very earliest sports podcasts to earn global recognition. After, it was among the very earliest to answer the raging call of COVID-19. In between, it made the most daring turn in podcasting history, a feat that would not have been possible without a once-in-a-lifetime cocktail of talent, flexibility, and timing. Or, rather, twice-in-a-lifetime.

Sklarbro is the creation of identical twin stand-ups Jason and Randy Sklar. Best known for hosting ESPN Classic's *Cheap Seats*, the duo had by the mid-aughties earned a reputation for making even the most analytic sports commentary breezy and understandable. Around 2009, they were coming off a successful run of guest appearances doing precisely that on *Jim Rome Is Burning* when they performed at one of Scott Aukerman's *Comedy Death-Ray* shows at UCB Franklin. "We were backstage with Chris Hardwick, Greg Fitzsimmons, and Doug Benson," Jason recalls, "and they were all talking about podcasting as a new form of creativity, comedy, revenue. Reaching an audience and building it . . . They talked about it in a way that we didn't understand."

Not long after, Aukerman rang them: Would the Sklars be interested in turning the sporty material they'd developed for Rome's show into a sister vehicle for *Death-Ray* (soon to be renamed *Comedy Bang! Bang!*; see p. 36) on his and Jeff Ullrich's fledgling network, Earwolf? The twins were excited by the prospect but concerned about its crossover appeal, thinking that "the podcast version would have to make sports understandable for comedy fans. We had to find a way to bridge between those two worlds." To do so, they condensed the three hours' worth of radio programming they had been producing into a tighter weekly version consisting of two "Takes" on the week's most interesting sports stories, an interview segment, three "Quick Hits" of shoptalk, and a brief sketch with a comedy character (typically comedian Chris Cox impersonating stars like Tiger Woods and Dennis Rodman) to seal the deal.

Sklarbro Country launched in 2010 and immediately became a hit. Celebrity guests like Amy Poehler, Glenn Howerton, and Patton Oswalt

HOSTED BY
Jason and Randy Sklar

GENRE
Sports

FIRST EPISODE
"Welcome to Sklarbro Country"
(August 1, 2010)

INFLUENCES
Greg Fitzsimmons, Doug Benson,
Chris Hardwick, Jim Rome

WHERE TO LISTEN
YouTube

SEAN'S PICK
"A Tale of Two Richards"
(August 10, 2012)

lent it early street cred, and it went viral over and over again for interviews with a weepy "Rowdy" Roddy Piper and a strangely maniacal Richard Simmons. One of the twins' personal high points is an appearance by fellow Missourian Jon Hamm. "We had all this shared history about the Cardinals," Randy reminisces. "That became a very nostalgic episode about St. Louis, growing up in the '80s, the blues."

Nevertheless, in 2017, the Sklars moved to Feral Audio, just months before that network shut down entirely, taking the podcast with it. While they continued to perform with longtime partner Daniel Van Kirk on their other podcast, *Dumb People Town*, the dream of revamping *Country* never died. That opportunity finally presented itself when their adoptive home state, California, went into quarantine in March 2020. Less than a week after Governor Gavin Newsom issued a stay-at-home order, the first episode of *Sklarbro Country: Virus Edition* premiered.

Yet the "pandy pod" was nothing like its predecessor. Sports popped up occasionally, sure, but the reanimated version was more of an ongoing poll: Could Jason and Randy workshop material funny enough to distract their fans from existential terror? "Thirty minutes in which you can just turn it all off" was their promise, and they soon began delivering enough jokes to meet it. (Here's one: "It's getting pretty rough out there. I just read that Snow White refuses to go to work until Sneezy gets tested.") In lesser hands, such a sharp pivot might have alienated fans of the original and killed its legacy for good, a concern the brothers shared. "Nothing would make us happier than for us to look like fools for doing this," they admit. But now that it's over, there's no one I would have rather Sklarantined with.

The Fantasy Footballers

In most cases, a healthy curiosity about American football seems like a hard prerequisite for enjoying podcasts dedicated to the sport. But Andy Holloway, Jason Moore, and Mike Wright have spent more than a decade disproving this theory on *The Fantasy Footballers*, their humor podcast about male friendship wrapped inside a tough leather shell.

The Ballers, as they're known, founded the podcast in 2014 after "working" together (a.k.a. making trades in the breakroom) at a video game company in Arizona. "In the very earliest days of the show, the three of us decided to hop in full force, quit our day jobs, and focus entirely full-time on [the podcast]," Moore says. "The problem was we each had three kids, a wife, and a mortgage, and now had no revenue to support ourselves." Moore and Holloway both told me they remembered early attempts to turn a profit that nearly cost them their independence: a sale to a bigger competitor, a painfully bad advertising deal. Thankfully, it all failed to launch—until it didn't.

Borrowing as much from comedians like Jim Carrey and Norm Macdonald as from sportscasters like Dan Patrick and Rich Eisen, the Ballers' goofiness-driven approach attracted an unusual amount of attention. They began addressing hardcore fans as "the Foot Clan," a millennial reference to the vengeful sewer ninjas of *Teenage Mutant Ninja Turtles*. Amid games of "Rookie Roulette" and "Studs and Duds," Moore would break out into a Gandalf impression or one of his signature "Boom Boom Kicker of the Week" soliloquies. And it didn't hurt that the hosts' suggestions for when to tilt, pivot, or invest your fab were all remarkably accurate (all three are nationally ranked experts, according to Fantasy Pros).

Predictably, by 2018, *The Fantasy Footballers* had become the most popular independent sports podcast on the planet, regularly hitting number one on Apple Podcasts and drawings tens of millions of downloads each month. A live tour that year—then considered an extraordinary risk for an indie podcast—was so packed that meet-and-greets took an hour.

According to Wright, that had all been part of the plan since the days when he and his pals "would scratch and claw for any improvement or edge over our competition." One impactful early decision was to adopt a holistic perspective on the NFL, turning the Ballers into all-seeing league cartographers rather than just another group of bored-at-work fanboys. Another tactic was to produce their show for podcast fans as much as for football aficionados. For his part, Moore fought to shrink each episode's file size down without impacting the original file's "vastly superior" sound quality. The move paid massive dividends with listeners, he says: "We took great pride in our audio sounding professional and believe it was (and continues to be) a part of our success."

In subsequent years, and despite the Ballers' expansion into a company with thirty-plus employees and multi-million-dollar revenues, the podcast has honored its commitment to reaching both football know-it-alls and know-nothings, a prospect that might have become impossible had they not remained independent. While Holloway, Moore, and Wright continue to dispense worldly wisdom on weekly draft picks, *TFF* remains primarily an excuse to hear it offered in the kind of lingua franca that can only be developed by those who have recorded an hour of audio together nearly every day for years. Even for the sports ignoramuses, it typically only takes a few episodes to get just how sincerely Holloway means it when he yells "Welcome in!" Unfortunately, if you still haven't locked in after hearing that, you might get Megala-shown the Wheel of Shame.

HOSTED BY
Andy Holloway, Jason Moore, and Mike Wright

GENRE
Sports

FIRST EPISODE
"Fantasy Football Podcast and Live Draft" (September 2, 2014)

INFLUENCES
Dan Patrick, Jim Carrey, Rich Eisen, Norm Macdonald, Conan O'Brien

WHERE TO LISTEN
Spotify

SEAN'S PICK
The most recent episode

THE FANTASY FOOTBALLERS

The Pivot Podcast

Tom Brady, Shaquille O'Neal, Floyd Mayweather Jr., Ken Griffey Jr.: world champions, national heroes, and *The Pivot Podcast* guests, all. Their shared caliber is a feature, not a bug, in the system that has with lightning speed propelled this still-growing whipper-snapper to a position of reverence in sports media. The main attraction for stars of their stature is the opportunity to be interviewed by three of the most unpredictable hosts in the game: Ryan Clark, Channing Crowder Jr., and Fred Taylor. In exchange for their unflinching openness, guests gain access to "about three million viewers" an episode, according to the sports apparel company and promotional partner Fanatics.

The Pivot sprouted out of the acrimonious departures of Crowder and Taylor, both ex–NFL players, from a separate popular sports podcast, *I AM ATHLETE*, in 2022. Together with executive producer Alicia Zubikowski, they approached Clark, a Super Bowl XLIII winner with the Pittsburgh Steelers and an Emmy Award–winning analyst, about creating something anchored by what writer Isaiah De Anda Delgado calls "locker-room camaraderie"—that is, talk programming made for, with, and by athletes of world-class distinction. "Anybody can podcast," says Taylor, a legendary Jacksonville Jaguars running back, "but not everybody can pivot."

With Clark appointed moderator and ex–Miami Dolphins linebacker Crowder in situ as the resident contrarian ("Let me retort!" he demands of Clark in the pilot), *The Pivot* lives and dies by its guests' ability to endure conversational whiplash. Unlike some of its more robotic counterparts, the podcast—which airs episodes concurrently on YouTube—often makes radical jumps in tone, "pivoting" midstream, as it were, from the boilerplate talking points of most sports analysis programs to subjects far grittier or more personal.

An emblematic interview with Dwayne Johnson, for instance, begins with a breezy ramble through his early years in Nashville, only for Taylor to sharply turn the talk to the suicide attempt of Johnson's mother, Ata. To his credit, Johnson never flinches, confiding that his parenthood to three daughters has helped in his own lifelong struggle with depression before praising Taylor and company for "making all the guests feel comfortable" enough to go deep. On another occasion, a solemn soliloquy for those lost to COVID-19 spirals out of control when Crowder randomly mentions battling with pubic lice. "We need guidance, we need somebody to ask questions to, we need to know where the hell the topic is going!" Clark cries, shaking his head in resignation. "But this is knowledge for the people," Crowder retorts, "the crabs community!"

Through Zubikowski, Clark tells me that being part of an enterprise so far afield from the dominant sports show paradigm has been "beyond what I ever imagined." "After Drew Robinson told his story on our show, I received a message from a fan who was contemplating suicide. He told me that episode saved his life," he says. But "hitting a home run so fast you can't get back to home plate," as Taylor puts it, has its costs.

"People always say, 'Y'all are everywhere,' and we really are," Crowder says. "Always working. Everybody sees our baby, but they don't know about the labor." On the other hand, that labor has earned *The Pivot* over 150 million views and more than 900,000 YouTube subscribers as of July 2024, not even three years since the pilot dropped. Now, the next pivot is up to the hosts. "If they lean left, we're going right," Taylor says. "If they lean right, we're going left."

HOSTED BY
Ryan Clark, Channing Crowder Jr., and Fred Taylor

GENRE
Sports (*Content Warning: Suicide*)

FIRST EPISODE
"The Truth" (January 4, 2022)

INFLUENCES
"Sitting on the back porch with country dudes having raw conversations, speaking their truth" (Crowder)

WHERE TO LISTEN
YouTube

SEAN'S PICK
"Athing Mu World's Fastest Young Female in Track & Field History, 2x Gold Medalist at 20" (March 17, 2023)

The Dan Le Batard Show with Stugotz

Conductor, director, coach—all feel more apt than calling Dan Le Batard a sports podcaster, just as it sounds wrong to call Jon "Stugotz" Weiner merely his co-host. Maybe "general" and "lieutenant" are too militaristic, but the enterprise that is their talk show, *The Dan Le Batard Show with Stugotz* (a.k.a. *DLS*), is as megalithic as a small nation. Consider the facts: twenty-plus years of sports analysis and news coverage across radio, television, and podcasting formats; uncountable interviews with the world's most famous athletes, including Alex Rodriguez, Deion Sanders, and Saúl "Canelo" Álvarez; and, depending on the day, the top spot on the world's sports podcast charts.

Who else can claim this level of cultural domination if not a commander in chief and his loyal veep? It takes a gut of iron and a well of charisma to convince an audience to stick with the same program for decades. Le Batard learned this the hard way as a sports columnist for the *Miami Herald*. "Writing sharpened everything for me," he shares. "Most people reading this, I'm guessing, don't think it sounds like much of a job to write four columns a week. But the act of doing that, of having to be unrelenting in finding untraveled paths, shaped me like little else in this industry."

"Unrelenting" is an apt description for Le Batard's brand. At the turn of this century, he began pursuing a career "away from the general loneliness of writing," appearing on camera for ESPN programs like *College GameDay* and *The Sports Reporters* with increasing frequency and controversy. By 2004, he and Stugotz had started *DLS* on South Miami's WAXY AM radio station, where they developed a reputation for bombastic, often confrontational takes. ("Do you get annoyed every time Dan Le Batard pontificates about the sports media industry? Well, too bad, motherfuckers!") That same industry couldn't get enough; Le Batard even remembers an occasion when producers for *Pardon the Interruption* attempted to spin *DLS* into its own TV show, only to be dissuaded when Stugotz asked legendary fullback Jim Brown about his God-given endowments.

Nevertheless, after moving full-time to ESPN in 2013 and later to Le Batard's venture with John Skipper, Meadowlark Media, the pod erupted with volcanic intensity. Le Batard attributes this to a complete lack of reverence for his predecessors, saying he "learned what *not* to do by listening to the way sports radio was done all my life in Miami." Indeed, his rotating crew of producers and color commentators (Mike Ryan, JuJu Gotti, Chris Cote, and too many others to name here) often mocks the hands that feed it. One recent move included intentionally mispronouncing "DraftKings Network," which carries the podcast in video form, as "DraftKrings" and "Giraffe Kings"; in another, Le Batard accused analytics expert Kirk Goldsberry of single-handedly ruining basketball forever by pushing the NBA toward data-mindedness.

Le Batard also attributes the podcast's singularity to its running time: "Talking for television, in thirty-second cubes, or for documentaries isn't the same as three hours. Three hours allows the wandering and space to create real intimacy with your audience." One particularly thrilling recording from April 2024 tackled the following: 76ers center Joel Embiid's Bell's palsy diagnosis; Taylor Vippolis's twenty-eight-hour train ride to see a Knicks game; Greg Cote's unprecedented record of "Super Zagacto" draft picks; and Weiner's new book ("I wrote a bick," came the classically insipid Stugotzian refrain). So much knowledge being spouted in one day

HOSTED BY
Dan Le Batard

GENRE
Sports

FIRST EPISODE
Untitled (Radio: September 1, 2004;
Podcast: September 30, 2013)

INFLUENCES
Mitch Albom, Dan Patrick, Tony
Kornheiser, Michael Wilbon

WHERE TO LISTEN
World of Suey

SEAN'S PICK
"Hour 2: I Would Never Shoot a
Dog" (April 30, 2024)

might have overwhelmed another show, but Le Batard's team solved the issue by offering it in chopped-up downloadables propped up by interstitial parody songs about Jalen Brunson and Mike Pouncey.

That formula has turned *DLS* into a 24/7 content machine for casual and dedicated sports fanatics alike, which explains why it shows no sign of losing steam in the foreseeable future. Inarguably, no one is more grateful for that than Le Batard, who credits his listeners' loyalties with "giving meaning" to the weird "arrested development" of being a professional podcaster: "It's legitimately overwhelming to consider what I do [to be] that kind of helpful salve."

Dead Eyes

Imagine you're an actor in the early stage of your career. You go to audition after audition hoping to land the big opportunity that could change the course of your life. One day, you hear about a role in a major network miniseries produced by one of the most powerful people in Hollywood. You decide to toss your hat into the ring for it. Not only do you nail the audition; you actually book the job. You call your agent, your friends, your parents. A life of paid-on-time rent and complimentary water bottles at general meetings with bigwigs flashes before your eyes. But just as quickly as you start celebrating, word gets back to you that there's been a little, uh, confusion. It turns out that you didn't get the job at all—in fact, even though you never actually shot a frame of footage, you've already been fired. And that big-time Hollywood power player? Well, he's actually the person who wanted you gone.

HOSTED BY
Connor Ratliff

GENRE
Storytelling

FIRST EPISODE
"01—He's Having Second Thoughts" (January 23, 2020)

INFLUENCES
Serial, David Letterman's "Oprah Log"

WHERE TO LISTEN
Headgum

SEAN'S PICK
"09—Neighbors & Pals" (June 25, 2020)

This is the foundational incident behind *Dead Eyes*, the painfully human and ultimately cathartic masterpiece created, written, and hosted by actor Connor Ratliff. In real life, Ratliff booked, then lost, a gig on HBO's *Band of Brothers*, all because—as he was later told by a representative—the show's producer, two-time Academy Award winner Tom Hanks, said he had "dead eyes." It was a savage blow for a man trying his hardest to become a working actor, and, as you might imagine, Ratliff spent years reeling from it. But after cobbling together a not-too-shabby career from smaller parts in hit shows like *The Marvelous Mrs. Maisel*, *Search Party*, and *Orange Is the New Black*, Ratliff began to wonder if he had perhaps been done a little dirty by David S. Pumpkins himself. Clearly, he was talented enough to have pulled off the role, so why hadn't they even given him the chance to try? And could Hanks—a movie star known for his rare kindness—have really said something like *that*?

So in early 2020, barely two months before the COVID-19 pandemic reached American shores, Ratliff launched *Dead Eyes*. "I knew I wanted to use the form of a prestige investigative podcast for my own lower-stakes comedic version," he says. While crafting the heart-wrenching ten-episode first season (which involved interviews with actor friends like D'Arcy Carden and Jon Hamm as well as *Band of Brothers* stars Ron Livingston and Stephen McCole, to try to figure out what went wrong with Hanks), he looked to true-crime podcasts like *Serial*. Ratliff also (somewhat unwittingly, he now admits) borrowed from David Letterman, who for eighty-two consecutive episodes of *Late Night* publicly campaigned to appear on *The Oprah Winfrey Show* after a decade-long pseudo-feud with Winfrey. The resulting podcast, a tonal mishmash of earnest curiosity, wounded misery, and goofiness, baffled some listeners, Ratliff acknowledges. "'Is it a spoof?' No, it's nonfiction. 'Wait, so is it real, or is it comedy?'"

Still, thanks in part to the global lockdown and reverent word of mouth, *Dead Eyes* picked up steam, earning Ratliff two more seasons and hordes of devoted listeners. Then, in what now seems an inevitable turn of events but at the time felt like a miracle, he received an email from Hanks himself asking if they could talk on the air. The resulting episode, "31—Tom," remains among the most rewarding listens in podcast history, with Hanks and Ratliff discussing the *Band of Brothers* role that might have been in obsessive, fiercely honest detail.

Dead Eyes host Connor Ratliff, right, with his "white whale," two-time Academy Award winner Tom Hanks.

While he didn't directly intend to follow in Letterman's footsteps, Ratliff likens the saga to the talk show host's "Oprah Log" bit in one key way: Both served as distractions from terrible moments in history. "Letterman started doing it in November 2001, at pretty much the exact moment that viewers really needed something silly and low stakes," he says. "It gave me the confidence to know that a thing like this does not require you to achieve the end goal in order for it to work—even though we both eventually got what we wanted."

RISK!

Kevin Allison had been doing his storytelling show, *RISK!*, for around a year when the emails started. "One of the first was from this guy who said his eighteen-year-old son had been addicted to heroin for a few years, and he had tried everything he could possibly think of to help the kid stop," Allison recalls. The man invited his son to join him in working on the car in his garage, where he played him "Life After," a seminal *RISK!* story by comic Blaine Kneece about Kneece's sister's death from cocaine addiction. That, the man told Allison, was it: "His son heard that story and broke down and finally agreed to go to rehab."

For more than a decade now, Allison has been on a dogged quest for true tales, like the one mentioned above, that the teller might otherwise never share with the public. A writer and performer for the surrealist comedy troupe The State, he was long accustomed to eliciting simultaneous gasps and laughs from audiences when he launched *RISK!* in 2009. Much like his work with The State, the podcast immediately distinguished itself from contemporaries like *The Moth* and *This American Life* with outré subject matter and a streak of dark, caustic humor unlikely to be heard on FCC-regulated airwaves. Racism, sexual abuse, scatology, death—no topic was off-limits for those brave enough to share.

Allison also worked to prove early on that *RISK!* was "not just your run-of-the-mill storytelling podcast" when it came to its format. Inspired by the mixed media work of Laurie Anderson and Jon Nelson's sound collage show of the early aughties, *Some Assembly Required*, he featured stories recorded both live in front of audiences and in private studios; used extant songs as well as original ones as bumpers between segments; and inserted sound collages, poems, and comedy sketches into random episodes, creating a program known for its unprecedented variety. At first, confused by such aesthetically diverse and challenging material, some particularly prickly listeners wrote in to complain: " 'I came here for stories. What are some of these other things I'm hearing?! Is that really necessary?' " Allison wisely ignored them. The result was immense and immediate popularity: According to *The Wall Street*

Journal, by 2018, the series was receiving an average of a million downloads per month.

In the years since, *RISK!* has expanded into a veritable empire that includes its own storytelling training center, the Story Studio; several international live tours; and even a book adaptation, *RISK!: True Stories People Never Thought They'd Dare to Share*, from Hachette. Allison, however, is clear that his motivation is simply to help people who have experienced grief, loneliness, shame, terror, and everything else find connection in our sometimes lonely, often isolating world. "Even though I had foreseen how powerful the show could be right from the start, it wasn't until the listeners and the storytellers started sharing with me how much the show meant to them that I realized, 'Wow. I have got to keep this going,'" he says. "This may not be a moneymaker. This may not stay in the Top 100 podcasts out there. But this show really helps people. That's invaluable."

HOSTED BY
Kevin Allison

GENRE
Storytelling (*Content Warning: Overdose, Sexual Abuse*)

FIRST EPISODE
"Strange Sex" (October 6, 2009)

INFLUENCES
Joe Frank, *Some Assembly Required*, Spalding Gray, Laurie Anderson

WHERE TO LISTEN
Audacy

SEAN'S PICK
"Blush" (August 10, 2012)

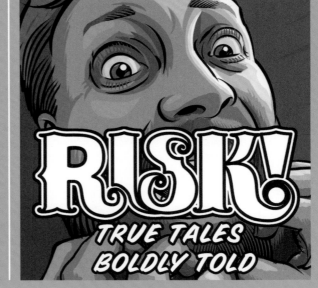

Snap Judgment

On the evening of November 10, 2014, Glynn Washington was getting ready for the performance of a lifetime. "I'm showering backstage at the Kennedy Center," he begins telling me, "about to do a big storytelling show with my artistic heroes whom I've never met: Questlove and Black Thought from the Roots. I'm super nervous, know I gotta look good, so I'm shaving as I rehearse lines in the shower." Though few are as well prepared for the stage as Washington, who since 2010 has hosted the Public Radio Exchange's *Snap Judgment* and its many, many subsequent live events, the excitement still proved too much. "My hand wobbles, and I shave the back of my scalp off. A crimson fountain spurts from my head, blood geysers everywhere. Panicked, I run naked into the hallway, hollering for assistance, barely covered with bloody towels. I look up and see cultural icons Questlove and Black Thought peering back at me. 'Hey fellas, nice to meet you . . .'"

Such a tale would be right at home on *Snap Judgment*, a spicy, rhythmic showcase for stories of wounded and rebellious humanity, the chaos of existence, and tasty, tasty irony. Released weekly and seasonally, each episode brings strangers together to throw down on an existential theme: artificial intelligence (July 2017), isolation (May 2020), youth culture (January 2024). Some feature four or five orators roped into one thirty-minute assemblage ("A Wives' Tale"); others offer space for only one primary speaker ("On the Mat").

Originally trained as a nonprofit administrator, Washington has spent the best part of two decades helixing it all together, adding off-kilter intonations and immutable rizz to a format famous at one time for its sterility. In 2013, *The Atlantic*'s Mark Oppenheimer dubbed him "NPR's Great Black Hope" for kick-starting a campaign to increase the then-wanting diversity of public radio, as well as for his refusal to play by the industry's increasingly outdated rules of style. That entailed infusing anecdotes about petty grudges ("Nemesis," from November 2012), playing basketball for warlords ("Bloodsport," from June 2019), and Washington's own childhood in an apocalyptic cult ("The World Tomorrow from Love & Radio," from March 2022) with original hip-hop-inflected scores and the staccato bounce of slam poetry. As Oppenheimer wrote, it was made clear at the end of every recording that "while there has long been minority talent on public radio—a realm that includes National Public Radio and other producers of noncommercial radio, like American Public Media and Public Radio International—Washington is the first African American host to swing a big cultural stick."

While "Snappas" in North America can catch Washington regularly on more than four hundred radio stations, per his website, it is his and co-creator Mark Ristich's podcast that brings the most ears to his work. *Snap Judgment* is a regular honoree at multiple annual podcasting awards, including for its magnificent COVID-themed series, "Letters from Lockdown," in 2021. Additionally, according to the *East Bay Express*—which, like the show, is produced in Oakland, California—downloads reach "about two million" per month, a startling statistic when one considers that the same team also produces *Spooked*, the chart-topping supernatural storytelling spin-off. Where, one wonders, do these guys find the time?

HOSTED BY
Glynn Washington

GENRE
Storytelling

FIRST EPISODE
"Warning Signs" (July 3, 2010)

INFLUENCES
"*The Muppet Show*, Michael Jackson (BEFORE the bad stuff!), *Soul Train*, *Star Trek*, Slick Rick's *The Art of Storytelling*, David Blaine, growing up in a crazy apocalyptic cult, *The Wiz*" (Washington)

WHERE TO LISTEN
Pocket Casts

SEAN'S PICK
"The Cannonball Run" (March 21, 2024)

The Moth

The Moth is much more than a New York–based nonprofit; it is a sacred temple dedicated to the ancient art of oratory. Since novelist George Dawes Green founded it in 1997, the most imaginative and compelling speakers of multiple generations have flocked to tell true-to-life stories at its events, which are today staged in every US state as well as in dozens of other countries. It was as predictable as the seasons that such an iconic enterprise would excel in the world of podcasting, which it did starting in 2008. But it also begot something of a chicken-or-the-egg paradox: Of course it is true that the Moth's twin flagship shows, *The Moth Radio Hour* and *The Moth Podcast*, could never have been made if not for innovations in live sound recording and file distribution in the late aughties—but would podcasting, a medium engineered to connect people through sound and narrative, even exist as a concept without Green?

One feed, two programs: This is how, on Tuesdays and Fridays, over a million people hear the Moth's *Radio Hour* and podcast each week. Jay Allison, producer of the former, explains the arrangement like this: "The Moth had a podcast before the radio show, and it was posted on the Public Exchange. The Moth and PRX and I decided to start producing *The Moth Radio Hour*. We began with a special series of five shows under a grant from the Corporation for Public Broadcasting. Bit by bit, we worked our way up to a weekly hour as we gathered more and more stations to carry us.* Like other public radio shows in the early days of podcasting, we also put up the radio show as a podcast, plus other stories, some of which were too racy for radio."

In Allison's opinion, the shows differ in key ways that make both essential for Moth superfans. For a start, *The Moth Radio Hour* is a collage, often weaving five or more stories together around a shared theme, such as "the things we hold dear" ("Object of Desire"), "fraternal bonds and sibling pranks" ("Oh, Brother"), and "seemingly interminable moments" ("When Time Slows Down"). *The Moth Podcast*, on the other hand, runs half as

Storytelling

* Editor's note: As of April 2024, the hour is carried on over 575 public radio stations .

HOSTED BY
Various

GENRE
Storytelling

FIRST EPISODE
"I Am Paid to Write Love Notes to Phil Collins"
(March 6, 2008)

INFLUENCES
"The feeling of sultry summer evenings in Georgia,
when moths were attracted to the light on the
porch . . ." (Green); "Documentary films" (Bowles)

WHERE TO LISTEN
iHeart

SEAN'S PICK
"All-Stars, Veterans, and Boxers" (July 10, 2013)

long and more often centers on only one ("Opening the Page") or two ("Take Me Out to the Ballgame") tales. The latter also includes follow-up studio interviews with its live performers to discuss how sharing stories with the public reshaped those stories in retrospect. One common factor is reach: According to its website, the podcast is downloaded a staggering one hundred million times a year. Host Kate Tellers recalls when she first sensed the impact of that ubiquity on those involved in it: "Shortly after the podcast launched, the audience poured into the hall for our Mainstage in Milwaukee, saying, 'This is exactly how I pictured it,' and we realized the power that the podcast had to lift us beyond reaching audiences at our shows, to audiences all over the world. We'd started eyes to ears, and now we were ears to eyes."

In lofty terms, the Moth's two-headed feed is a shoo-in for the pantheon because it represents the most expansive archive of rhetoric recorded in the twenty-first century. But the larger remit, writes senior director Meg Bowles, remains more straightforward: "We have always tried to find stories that entertain but also stories that allow listeners to meet and hear from people we might never have a chance to sit down with in real life. We also try to find stories that will start conversations rather than those that are merely reacting to events." By that standard, hers is a job *exceedingly* well done.

This American Life

It is no accident that this book contains more references to *This American Life* than to any other program. Its creators, Ira Glass and Torey Malatia, are regularly described as contenders for the designation of "Podfather," a.k.a. key figureheads in early podcast history. Glass, who also hosts, executive produces, and owns the show, may be the most recognizable voice in audio. But try to impress upon the breadth of all this influence, and Glass demurs: "Wow. That's really nice. We were early adopters."

It isn't that he and Malatia were simply ahead of the curve when they launched *TAL* on WBEZ in 1995; they *were* the curve. The show pulled from theater, film, and literature to create something altogether unique on the radio, an hour-long nonfiction storytelling program centered around themes of shared experience in the Western world. (Consider these decks: "Bad neighbors: What can you do about them?" "People caught in limbo, using ingenuity and guile to try to get themselves out.") Each episode was collapsed into acts, which in turn were constructed by a small team of producers and editors from a wide range of sources: investigative reporting, documentary footage, first-person monologues, book excerpts. Every theme required a distinct editorial approach, making the production polyphonous, multi-faceted, and unpredictable. It was groundbreaking from moment one.

"We really felt like this weird idea for a show seemed kind of like an indie movie: There will be people who like it, and we don't know if it's going to be a lot of people. But the feeling was that there would be enough people who liked it that it could sustain an audience," Glass says. That feeling was, to understate it, accurate. Glass runs through a slew of defining early successes: getting picked up for national distribution after six months; signing with Public Radio International (PRI) to go out wider ("within two months, they doubled our carriage; they were magnificent at selling the show"); and performing onstage with David Sedaris, an early contributor, at the Public Radio Conference to buoy interest. Within a year, *This American Life* had received its first national accolade, a Peabody Award. Four years later, it began reaching one million listeners a week.

When it became a podcast is a source of some debate. In June 2000, prior to the coining of the term "podcast," the spoken-word audio provider Audible began offering forty *TAL* episodes "delivered to listeners' PCs automatically" via paid subscriptions. But in a 2020 interview for *The Guardian*, one of *TAL*'s first producers, Nancy Updike, pinpointed the decision to release a specifically podcasted version to 2006, when it was proposed by then-new production manager Seth Lind. Whatever the truth, one thing is certain: Their choice was a wise one. The podcast version is believed to be the most statistically popular on the planet today, with many hundreds of millions of downloads across more than eight hundred episodes. None is more widely lauded, or creatively imitated.

When Glass and I meet for the first time, I ask if being in that position impacted the work he and his staff (which has grown from four people to dozens) still produce each week. His response is firm: "I don't feel the weight of that. My experience with the success of the show is that we are still making the show." Even after thirty years, he notes, "you still have the panic of 'What the hell are we gonna put on the air this week? And when can it be ready?! And we've got to write this by when?!?'" That *TAL* has shepherded the likes of *Serial*, *S-Town*, *The Retrievals*, and myriad more to blockbuster status serves only to prove that they should keep going, Glass says. "It sort of feels like, 'Oh, we were right.'"

HOSTED BY
Ira Glass

GENRE
Storytelling

FIRST EPISODE
"New Beginnings"
(Radio: November 17, 1995;
Podcast: June 27, 2000)

INFLUENCES
"Old-school NPR voices, first among them Alex Chadwick, Robert Krulwich, Noah Adams, Keith Talbot, and Joe Frank" (Glass)

WHERE TO LISTEN
WBEZ

SEAN'S PICK
"The Problem We All Live With—Parts One and Two" (July 31, 2015)

Darknet Diaries

Jack Rhysider was at a hacker conference in Las Vegas when he felt a tap on his shoulder. "There's three guys standing there, and one asks me, 'Hey, want a story from the NSA?'" Rhysider was intrigued, if skeptical: A trained expert in cybercrime and a digital security veteran who had once worked in a security operations center for a Fortune 500 company, he was under the impression that "the NSA doesn't talk, ever." But the tapper, it turned out, was "a commander in some operations that the NSA conducted" who wanted to share his experiences on what was quickly becoming *the* touchstone podcast about the internet: Rhysider's *Darknet Diaries*. Even though his "DMs and inbox are full of everything you can imagine," the podcaster concedes, offers to interview staff from the notoriously tight-lipped government agency were beyond rare, as they required permission from high-level muckety-mucks.

Apparently, *Darknet Diaries* merited just such an exception: A leader at NSA approved the interview, and the mission commander for a 2016 combat mission team at USCYBERCOM appeared on episode fifty, "Operation Glowing Symphony." "Sorry; in this one, I can't say our guest's name," Rhysider notes in the introduction. Then, just as he starts to dig into how his high-ranking subject develops and utilizes "cyber bullets" against the "terrorist apparatus" of groups like the Taliban and ISIL, the commander interrupts. "This is kind of a fanboy moment for myself, to be honest," he tells Rhysider.

Fans of *Darknet Diaries*—and they are legion, with the show receiving 27.6 million downloads in 2022 alone—will instantly understand why the NSA might prohibit its agents from speaking on the podcast, only to then, according to Rhysider, turn around and use it to train new recruits. Since its launch in 2017, the series has told "tales from the dark side of the internet" with unparalleled intensity and a dedication to "principles of truthfulness, accuracy, objectivity, impartiality, fairness, and public accountability." Its aesthetic is singular: spartan, hyperreal, a smart nonfiction thriller in cyberpunk dress. Its closest counterparts are not other podcasts, but films like *The Matrix* and *Blackhat*.

Then there is Rhysider. Though he keeps an intentionally low profile, representing himself online with his signature red, white, and black avatar, his qualities as a host and producer are utterly distinctive. Whether he is investigating cyber warfare between India and Pakistan, the rise and fall of Kim Dotcom, or Greek Watergate, Rhysider is perpetually guided into his subjects' depths by untrammeled curiosity, as well as by a rare humility that he expresses whenever he knows he's a noob on the subject at hand. This has gained him access to guests and fans far beyond the NSA, he says, from "police officers and law enforcement telling me stories of criminals they've caught," to "victims reaching out in a cold panic asking what they should do after they've been hacked," to "cyber criminals showing me screenshots of their devious lick where they stole thousands of dollars and then swiftly gambled it away."

With all this attention, it's no surprise that *Darknet Diaries* has retooled itself over the years. In 2019, Rhysider—who had previously served as a one-man production, marketing, and hosting band—hired a staff of additional writers, researchers, editors, and graphic designers to contribute to episodes, and switched from dropping them biweekly to monthly in 2023. But the spirit of inquiry and expertise that informed his first few broadcasts persists, as demonstrated by recent masterworks on topics such as an online child sexual abuse material ring in South Korea and the antics of notorious hackers like D3f4ult and Gollumfun. I strongly advise you to take a trip down this rabbit hole.

HOSTED BY
Jack Rhysider

GENRE
Technology

FIRST EPISODE
"The Phreaky World of PBX Hacking"
(September 1, 2017)

INFLUENCES
Radiolab, *This American Life*, *Criminal*,
Snap Judgment, *Love + Radio*, *Heavyweight*,
Revisionist History, Rod Serling, Paul Harvey

WHERE TO LISTEN
DarknetDiaries.com

SEAN'S PICK
"The Indo-Pak Conflict" (November 12, 2019)

Afterword

Over the years that I wrote this book, the lives of many of the podcasters in it changed drastically. The audio landscape oscillated wildly from inviting to rejecting, with thousands of dedicated engineers, producers, writers, reporters, editors, designers, talent bookers, publicists, graphic artists, and performers chewed up and spat out by budget cuts, buyouts, mergers, and other such corporate bullshit for months on end. Even the most immortal of the icons in the pantheon were not immune: *Keith and the Girl, Normal Gossip,* and *All My Relations*, for instance, faced key changes to their hosting lineups; *Death, Sex & Money* and *Bad with Money* moved networks. Many of the interviews I conducted concluded on a forlorn note: "You're going to be okay," I assured countless people, knowing that was far from certain.

Yet as one chapter in the history of this fine form came to a close, another began to show its petals. In a rare and expansive Zoom conducted toward the end of the writing process, Adam Sachs—SiriusXM's SVP Podcast Content and a former executive at Midroll Media and Team Conan, among others—expresses the kind of optimism about the direction of this young, beautiful form that can come only from a seasoned veteran. "More stuff is getting greenlit today than was getting greenlit nine months ago. And I take that as a good sign," he explains enthusiastically. "Maybe there is a little less crazy money getting thrown around, but I don't necessarily see that as a bad thing. I see it as a more deliberate way to build a healthy, sustainable, long-term business."

Looking forward a couple years, Sachs instructs me to expect another wave of massive investment in the on-demand audio space as global media companies seek ever-more avenues to hawk their wares and as more and more countries grow hip to the power and popularity of podcasts. "The industry will be significantly bigger than it is today," he declares. "We are in growth mode; it's just, again, careful growth mode."

Ira Glass also argues forcefully when we talk that the Golden Age of Podcasting supposedly ushered in by the one-two punch of *WTF* and *Serial* is actually just beginning, as demonstrated by a slew of shows he admires at the time, including *Tooth and Claw*, *Hacks on Tap*, *The Blindboy Podcast*, and *Appearances*. "When I look at my phone, at all the weird shit I've been listening to—a lot of these shows are just so interesting and inventing something and doing a really fucking amazing job!" he says. "People can still do stuff that's original and groundbreaking. I don't think everything that can be done in audio has been done."

Given the breadth of his and Sachs's expertise, I have no real choice but to agree. As I type this, thousands of new shows are in production that are sure to expand and challenge the current pantheon with their innovativeness, beauty, and cultural impact. Of course, what the next twenty years hold for podcasters and their fans is something that not even Nostradamus could predict. But I promise to keep my ear to the ground for you in the meantime.

Acknowledgments

Like all creative endeavors, *The Podcast Pantheon* exists solely thanks to the dedication and support of a network I'm lucky to be included in.

Thank you first and foremost to Joy Tutela and the team at the David Black Literary Agency, who fought to make these pages come to life and made me feel at all times like I had a coterie of Burgess Merediths in my corner.

Thank you also to my incisive editor, Olivia Roberts, brilliant designers Neil Egan and Liam Flanagan, and the folks at Chronicle Books, whose vision for this book inspired it and me to heights I could not have foreseen.

Furthermore, thank you to those who helped make this project possible through the generosity of their time, particularly Colin Anderson, Brett Boham, Marika Brownlee, Ben Fishel, Ron Gaskill, Katy Hanson, Emily Hessel, Jennifer Houlihan Roussel, Chet Mehta, Rachel Nelson, and Adam Sachs. This goes double for all the publicists, agents, and managers who connected me with their clients without complaint or demand, particularly Connie Tavel and Adrianne Sandoval.

A quick word, too, for the educators who reminded me time and again that my way of thinking about this subject had worth when I was certain of the opposite. Gratitude especially to Tom Schatz, whose excitement over this particular idea was utterly contagious; Geoffrey Green, who blew gently on the first embers of this project without even knowing it; Shanti Kumar, who—and I'm paraphrasing here—suggested I could do anything I wanted; Caroline Frick, who guided me through my first attempt at serious writing; and the late, missed Jennifer Hammett. Thanks also to Jeffrey Skoller, Sue Joseph, Sarah Attfield, Barton Smith, David Russell, Eric Morgenstern, Donna Kornhaber, Munira Lokhandwala, my sister Molly Malin, and the saintly caregivers at Camp Alonim and American Jewish University who showed me patience and nurtured my creativity even when I didn't much deserve it. All made such a difference here.

Megh Wright, Bill McDonald, LeAnn Wilcox, Charanna K. Alexander, Farley Elliott, Mekado Murphy, Jeremy Egner, Stephanie Goodman, Matthew Kang, Kevin Robinson, Carol Eisner, Tania Ketenjian, Ben Stein (not that one), Robert Faires, and Josh Kupecki gave me the kinds of opportunities and guidance that any writer should be lucky to have once, much less over and over again.

Katie Grillo held me together with salmon rice and *Columbo* reruns. Fanks, KTG.

The Podcast Pantheon was written on unceded Tongva, Tataviam, Serrano, Kizh, Chumash, Coahuiltecan, Tonkawa, Comanche, and Lipan Apache lands. Read more about the movement to return the lands of North America back to Indigenous sovereignty at Landback.org.

And most importantly, thank you, thank you again, and thank you once more to the podcasters who gave so graciously of their expertise and time to this project. I annoyed some of you to high hell trying to get this book over the line, I know, but I hope I did you and your work right in the end.

Art Credits

P. 9: Marc Maron and Jon Hamm from episode #215 of *WTF*. Courtesy of *WTF with Marc Maron*. **P. 17**: *Savage Lovecast* cover art. Credit: Nancy Hartunian and Dan Savage. **P. 19**: *Why Won't You Date Me?* cover art. Credit: Carly Jean Andrews. **P. 20**: *Love + Radio* cover art. Courtesy of Nick van der Kolk. **P. 25**: *Nocturne* cover art. Credit: Magdalena Metrycka. **P. 27**: *Bad with Money* cover art. Courtesy of Gabe Dunn. **P. 28**: *Freakonomics Radio* cover art. Credit: Lorissa Shepstone (Being Wicked). **P. 31**: *Holly Randall Unfiltered* cover art. Courtesy of Holly Randall. **P. 36**: *Comedy Bang! Bang!* cover art. Courtesy of Earwolf. **P. 38**: *Conan O'Brien Needs a Friend* cover art. Courtesy of SiriusXM and Team Coco. **P. 41**: *Hey, We're Back!* cover art. Courtesy of Dana Friedman. **P. 42**: *Hollywood Handbook* cover art. Courtesy of Kevin Bartelt. **P. 43**: Hayes Davenport, left, and Sean Clements of *Hollywood Handbook*. Credit: Kevin Bartelt & Headgum. **P. 44**: *How Was Your Week?* cover art. Credit: Mindy Tucker. **P. 47**: *Keith and the Girl* cover art. Courtesy of Chemda Khalili and Keith Malley. **P. 48**: *Never Not Funny* cover art. Courtesy of Jimmy Pardo. **P. 51**: *Normal Gossip* cover art. Credit: Tara Jacoby. **P. 53**: *This Is Branchburg* cover art. Credit: Abso Lutely Productions and Adult Swim. **P. 54**: Episode art for *Criminal* #84, "Masterpiece." Credit: Julienne Alexander. **P. 55**: *Criminal* cover art. Courtesy of Criminal. **P. 59**: *My Favorite Murder* cover art. Courtesy of Exactly Right. **P. 60**: *Small Town Murder* cover art. Courtesy of *Small Town Murder*. **P. 61**: *Small Town Murder*'s Jimmie Whisman, left, and James Pietragallo. Credit: Jim McCambridge and Cobb's Comedy Club. **P. 63**: *Twenty Thousand Hertz* cover art. Credit: George Butler. **P. 65**: *Moonface* cover art. Credit: Chava Sanchez. **P. 67**: Illustrated *Lecture Hall* artwork. Credit: Devin Bostick. **P. 68**: *Stuff You Should Know* cover art. Courtesy of iHeartPodcasts. **P. 71**: *The Red Nation Podcast* cover art. Credit: Designed by members of the Red Nation, digitized by Marcus Trujillo with Haatzee Designs. **P. 73**: *Hello from the Magic Tavern* cover art. Credit: Allard Laban. **P. 74**: *Add to Cart* cover art. Courtesy of Lemonada Media. **P. 77**: *Throwing Fits* cover art. Courtesy of James Harris and Lawrence Schlossman. **P. 78**: *The Thrilling Adventure Hour* cover art. Courtesy of Ben Acker and Ben Blacker. **P. 81**: *Black Men Can't Jump [in Hollywood]* cover art. Credit: JPNT17. **P. 83**: *How Did This Get Made?* cover art. Courtesy of Earwolf. **P. 84**: *On Cinema at the Cinema* cover art. Courtesy of Tim Heidecker. **P. 86**: *The Flop House* cover art. Credit: Tony Ochre, courtesy of Housecat Productions. **P. 87**: (top left) Elliott Kalan of the Peaches, right, with comedian Hallie Haglund. Courtesy of Housecat Productions. **P. 87**: (top right) Stuart Wellington, left, and Dan McCoy. Courtesy of Housecat Productions. **P. 88**: Karina Longworth. Credit: Lee Jameson. **P. 89**: *You Must Remember This* cover art. Credit: Teddy Blanks. **P. 91**: *Doughboys* cover art. Credit: Chris VanArtsdalen. **P. 93**: *Gastropod* cover art. Credit: Kathi Bahr. **P. 94**: *The Sporkful*'s Dan Pashman. Credit: Christopher Appoldt. **P. 95**: *The Sporkful* cover art. Courtesy of *The Sporkful*. **P. 97**: *The Splendid Table* cover art. Courtesy of American Public Media. **P. 99**: (1) Chemda Khalili and Keith Malley. Courtesy of Keith and the Girl. (2) Keith Malley, Chemda Khalili, and Adam Conover. Credit: Anne Whitman. **P. 100**: (3) Episode art for *Criminal* #154, "The Max Headroom Incident." Credit: Julienne Alexander. (4) Episode art for *Criminal* #260, "The Dial Painters." Credit: Julienne Alexander. (5) Jerah Milligan, James III, and Jonathan Braylock. Credit: Viktor Erik Emanuel / Kings Place. **P. 101**: (6) Brendan O'Hare and Cory Snearowski. Credit: Cory Snearowski. (7) Dan Pashman and Chef Pietro Lonigro. Courtesy of Dan Pashman. (8) Paul Gilmartin. Credit: Johnny Olsen. **P. 102**: (9) The Ballers. Credit: Engaging Media LLC. (10) Episode art for *Nocturne*'s "3-2-1!" Credit: Magdalena Metrycka. (11) Episode art for *Nocturne*'s "Into, Under, Through." Credit: Magdalena Metrycka. (12) Episode art for *Nocturne*'s "Rest for Them." Credit: Magdalena Metrycka. (13) M. Mack. Credit: Marlo Mack. **P. 103**: (14) *Hello from the Magic Tavern*'s Usidore the Blue. Credit: Kyle Telechan. (15) *Hello from the Magic Tavern*'s Noah Paine and Chunt. Credit: Kyle Telechan. (16) *Uhh Yeah Dude* skateboard. Credit: Joe Frontel. (17) SuChin Pak, Kulap Vilaysack, and Jason Mantzoukas. Credit: Dennis Kwan. **P. 104**: (18, with backwards hats) Jimmie Whisman and James Pietragallo. Credit: Andy Argyrakis / Auditorium Chicago. (18, in costume) Jimmie Whisman and James Pietragallo. Credit: Sarah Hunt. (19, Mac Attack) *Doughboys* "Munch Madness." Credit Chris VanArtsdalen. (19, Pie Noon) *Doughboys* "Munch Madness." Credit Chris VanArtsdalen. (19, Lebowski) *Doughboys* "Munch Madness." Credit: Chris VanArtsdalen. (19, Halloween) *Doughboys* "Shockdoughbooerdeath." Credit: Chris VanArtsdalen. **P. 105**: (20) The Boys of *Hollywood Handbook* with Jake Johnson. Credit: Kevin Bartelt & Headgum. (21) *Freakonomics Radio*'s Stephen J. Dubner. Credit: Audrey

Bernstein. (22) The Peaches. Courtesy of Housecat Productions. (23) *Couples Therapy* Wedding Photo. Credit: Mandee Johnson. **P. 106:** (24) Marc Maron and Barack Obama from episode #613 of *WTF*. Credit: Pete Souza. (25) Marc Maron and Robin Williams from episode #67 of *WTF*. Courtesy of *WTF with Marc Maron*. (26) *The Witch Wave* artwork. Credit: "Portrait of Pam Grossman," Cat Willett, copyright © 2024. From Prosperity Mantras by Destiny. (27) Krista Tippett in dialogue with Bishop Desmond Tutu. Credit: Trent Gilliss. **P. 107:** (28) *Welcome to Night Vale* Bad Snowman artwork. Credit: Jessica Hayworth. (29) *Welcome to Night Vale* Glow Cloud artwork. Credit: Jessica Hayworth. (30) *Welcome to Night Vale* Lost and Found artwork. Credit: Jessica Hayworth. (31) *The Fantasy Footballers* "The People's Fantasy Tour" poster. Credit: Engaging Media LLC. (32) Dan Taberski and Henry Molofsky. Credit: Henry Molofsky. **P. 108:** (33) Joe Pera, Carmen Christopher, and Ryan Dann. Credit: Ellen Qbertplaya. (34) Joe Pera and Ryan Dann. Credit: Ellen Qbertplaya. (35) Dallas Taylor. Credit: Phillip Slaughter. (36) *Twenty Thousand Hertz* synth artwork. Credit: Daniel Špaček. **P. 109:** (37, basement) *Darknet Diaries* artwork. Credit: odibagas. (37, spy) *Darknet Diaries* artwork. Credit: odibagas. (38) Marc Maron with Bruce Springsteen from episode #773 of *WTF*. Courtesy of *WTF with Marc Maron*. (39) *In Stereo* poster. Credit: David Saracino. (40) Naomi Ekperigin and Andrew Beckerman. Credit: Mindy Tucker. **P. 113:** *Happier with Gretchen Rubin* cover art. Courtesy of Gretchen Rubin Media. **P. 114:** *The Accessible Stall* cover art. Credit: MK Ultra. **P. 115:** Kyle Khachadurian and Emily Ladau. Courtesy of Kyle Khachadurian and Emily Ladau. **P. 117:** *Behind the Bastards* cover art. Credit: Allen Lee (iHeartPodcasts). **P. 119:** *Citations Needed* cover art. Credit: Jack Phelps. **P. 121:** *Slow Burn* season 1 cover art. Credit: Teddy Blanks. **P. 123:** *Lore* cover art. Courtesy of Aaron Mahnke. **P. 125:** *Welcome to Night Vale* cover art. Courtesy of Night Vale Productions. **P. 126:** *Bullseye with Jesse Thorn* cover art. Courtesy of Maximum Fun. **P. 128:** *Fresh Air* cover art. Courtesy of WHYY. **P. 131:** *Here's the Thing with Alec Baldwin* cover art. Courtesy of iHeartPodcasts. **P. 133:** *WTF with Marc Maron* cover art. Courtesy of *WTF with Marc Maron*. **P. 137:** *Headlong: Missing Richard Simmons* cover art. Courtesy of Stitcher. **P. 146:** *How to Be a Girl* cover art. Courtesy of Marlo Mack. **P. 147:** A collage by M. of *How to Be a Girl*. Credit: M. Mack. **P. 147:** An illustration by M. of *How to Be a Girl*. Credit: M. Mack **P. 148:** *Story Pirates* cover art. Courtesy of Lee Overtree. **P. 151:** *Death, Sex & Money* cover art. Courtesy of WNYC Studios. **P. 153:** *Drifting Off with Joe Pera* cover art. Credit: Nicole Duennebier. **P. 155:** *Analyze Phish*

cover art. Credit: Earwolf. **P. 156:** *Cocaine & Rhinestones* cover art. Credit: Coe Operation. **P. 158:** *Punch Up the Jam* cover art. Courtesy of Headgum. **P. 159:** Demi Adejuyigbe's unreleased punch-up of "Do They Know It's Christmas?". Credit: Demi Adejuyigbe. **P. 161:** *Song Exploder* cover art. Credit: Hrishikesh Hirway. **P. 163:** *The Best Show* cover art. Courtesy of Tom Scharpling. **P. 164:** *The Take* cover art. Courtesy of Al Jazeera. **P. 166:** *Chapo Trap House* cover art. Courtesy of *Chapo Trap House*. **P. 169:** *Fake the Nation* cover art. Courtesy of Headgum. **P. 171:** *The Majority Report with Sam Seder* cover art. Credit: Nichole Sokoloff. **P. 173:** *Another Round* cover art. Courtesy of Tracy Clayton. **P. 174:** *Uhh Yeah Dude* cover art. Courtesy of Seth Romatelli. **P. 177:** *Asian Not Asian* cover art. Credit: Chris Cheney. **P. 179:** *Yo, Is This Racist?* cover art. Courtesy of Sub-Optimal Podcasts. **P. 180:** Krista Tippett. Credit: Bethany Birnie. **P. 181:** *On Being* cover art. Courtesy of The On Being Project. **P. 182:** "Primum Ens Melissae (Pam Grossman)." Credit: Carrie Ann Baade. **P. 183:** *The Witch Wave* cover art. Credit: Thunderwing. **P. 185:** *You Made It Weird* cover art. Courtesy of Pete Holmes. **P. 187:** *Gilmore Guys* cover art. Credit: Taylor Nicole Hotter. **P. 188:** *Office Ladies* cover art. Courtesy of Audacy Podcasts. **P. 191:** *Radiolab* cover art. Courtesy of WNYC Studios. **P. 192:** *Limetown* cover art. Courtesy of Two-Up Productions. **P. 195:** *Marvel's Wolverine: The Long Night* cover art. Courtesy of Marvel. **P. 196:** *The Mental Illness Happy Hour* cover art. Courtesy of Paul Gilmartin. **P. 199:** *Couples Therapy* cover art. Courtesy of Andrew Beckerman and Naomi Ekperigin. **P. 200:** *Guys We Fucked* cover art. Credit: Marcus Russell Price. **P. 203:** *Queery* cover art. Courtesy of Cameron Esposito and Maximum Fun. **P. 205:** *All My Relations* cover art. Courtesy of *All My Relations*. **P. 207:** *Ear Hustle* cover art. Courtesy of Radiotopia. **P. 209:** Earlonne Woods and Nigel Poor. Credit: Eddie Herena. **P. 211:** *Gender Reveal* cover art. Credit: Ira M. Leigh. **P. 213:** *Sklarbro Country* cover art. Courtesy of Jason Sklar and Randy Sklar. **P. 215:** *The Fantasy Footballers* cover art. Credit: Engaging Media LLC. **P. 216:** *The Pivot Podcast* cover art. Courtesy of Alicia Zubikowski. **P. 219:** *The Dan Le Batard Show with Stugotz* cover art. Courtesy of Meadowlark Media. **P. 221:** *Dead Eyes* cover art. Credit: Tom Mike Hill. **P. 223:** Tom Hanks and Connor Ratliff. Credit: Todd Schulman. **P. 225:** *RISK!* cover art. Courtesy of Kevin Allison. **P. 227:** *Snap Judgment* cover art. Courtesy of Snap Judgment Studios. **P. 229:** *The Moth* cover art. Credit: Stephen Doyle / Doyle Partners. **P. 230:** *This American Life* cover art. Credit: Erik Jarlsson. **P. 233:** *Darknet Diaries* cover art. Courtesy of Jack Rhysider.

Library of Congress Cataloging-in-Publication Data

Names: Malin, Sean, author.
Title: The podcast pantheon : 101 podcasts that changed how we listen / by
  Sean Malin.
Description: San Francisco : Chronicle Books, 2025.
Identifiers: LCCN 2024048378 | ISBN 9781797232249 (hardcover)
Subjects: LCSH: Podcasts--United States--Reviews.
Classification: LCC PN1992.9233.U6 M35 2025 | DDC
  791.46/7--dc23/eng/20241202
LC record available at https://lccn.loc.gov/2024048378

Manufactured in China.

MIX
Paper | Supporting
responsible forestry
FSC
www.fsc.org   FSC® C008047

Design by Liam Flanagan.
Cover design by MacFadden & Thorpe.
Jacket illustrations by Johnny Sampson.

10 9 8 7 6 5 4 3 2 1

Chronicle books and gifts are available at special quantity discounts to
corporations, professional associations, literacy programs, and other organizations.
For details and discount information, please contact our premiums department at
corporategifts@chroniclebooks.com or at 1-800-759-0190.

Chronicle Books LLC
680 Second Street
San Francisco, California 94107
www.chroniclebooks.com